Dear Helen and Greg,

Since you have beautiful plants and flowers in your yard and you both are interested in nature, I thought you might enjoy this book. Happy planting!

Love Michelle

The Calgary Gardener, Volume Two

BEYOND the BASICS

Praise for Volume One of *The Calgary Gardener*

"Well written in a very easy-to-read style, *The Calgary Gardener* is packed from cover to cover with invaluable information recorded by people who have been home gardening in Calgary for many years ... if anyone moves to the area and tries to garden without first reading this book, it will be a grave mistake."

–David Tarrant

"This book explains gardening in Calgary as it should be explained, by those who have tackled the challenges head-on and found the way to success."

–Ken Eadie, Curator of Botanical Collections, Calgary Zoo, Botanical Gardens and Prehistoric Park

"Gardening in Chinook country requires patience, knowledge, and a certain amount of faith ... This [book] will provide gardeners with some inspiration for their gardens and continue Calgary's horticultural tradition."

–Kenn Knights, Manager, Parks Division, Calgary Parks and Recreation

"*The Calgary Gardener* is a well-illustrated and organized guide to the planting and care of gardens in this city. The illustrations and photographs throughout are of excellent quality. The Calgary Horticultural Society should be proud of this book."

–Byron Veilleux, geologist and novice gardener

Also Available, Volume One of *The Calgary Gardener*

The Calgary Gardener *includes:*

— *to-do lists for each season*

— *garden planning ideas*

— *recommended plants*

— *advice on watering, pruning, fertilizing, composting, mulching, lawn care*

— *tricks for extending your growing season*

— *resource list for the Calgary area*

— *illustrations and colour photographs*

— *seed and bloom charts*

The Calgary Gardener, Volume Two

BEYOND the BASICS

Liesbeth Leatherbarrow and Lesley Reynolds
with The Calgary Horticultural Society

FIFTH
HOUSE
PUBLISHERS

Front cover image courtesy of Maureen Ireton
Line drawings by Grace Buzik
Back cover image courtesy of Liesbeth Leatherbarrow
Cover and interior design by Brian Smith/Articulate Eye

The publisher gratefully acknowledges the support of the Department of Canadian Heritage.

Printed in Canada
99 00 01 02 / 5 4 3 2

Canadian Cataloguing in Publication Data

The Calgary Gardener

   Includes bibliographical references and index.
   Contents: Vol. 1, The essential guide to gardening in Alberta
      chinook country; v.2, Beyond the basics.
   ISBN 1-895618-67-3 (v. 1) — ISBN 1-894004-00-0 (v. 2)

   1. Gardening—Alberta—Handbooks, manuals, etc.
   2. Horticulture—Alberta—Handbooks, manuals, etc.
   I. Calgary Horticultural Society

SB453.3.C2C34 1996   635'097123   C95-920081-9

Fifth House Ltd.
#9-6125 11th Street S.E.
Calgary, AB, Canada
T2H 2L6

Contents

Charts

Acknowledgements

It would be difficult to find a more generous group than gardeners when it comes to sharing knowledge, experience, and encouragement. We wish to thank the Calgary Horticultural Society for making this project possible and for providing friendly support and education for all Calgary gardeners.

The following helpful individuals were consulted for *The Calgary Gardener, Volume Two* and contributed invaluable ideas and expertise: Elizabeth Beaubien (Devonian Botanic Garden), James Borrow (Grounds Maintenance Supervisor, Calgary Zoo, Botanical Garden, and Prehistoric Park), Adam Gibb, Robert Giles, Robert Graham (Heritage Planner, City of Calgary), Colin Hergert (Vegetation Control Technician, City of Calgary), Jeffry De Jong, Mark Lalonde (Head Groundskeeper, Heritage Park), Duncan McKillop, Pamela Reid (Water Efficiency Specialist, City of Calgary), Sharon Rempel, Ruth Staal, Edzard Teubert, and Kathy Wood.

The Calgary Horticultural Society's newsletter, *Calgary Gardening*, is an outstanding resource for local gardeners, and we wish to express our appreciation to those CHS members who allowed us to draw from their articles: Rosalie Cooksley, Judith Doyle, Angela du Toit, Barbara Kam, Henri Lefebvre, Kevin Lee, Clancy Patton, and Ruth Staal.

Our expert readers provided welcome advice and guidance: Ken Girard (Greenhouse Manager, Department of Biological Sciences, University of Calgary), Duncan Himmelman (Olds College), and Calgary Horticultural Society members Barbara McKillop, Barbara Preston, and Marilyn Wood— avid gardeners all.

We would like, particularly, to acknowledge the Calgarians whose gardens were photographed for this book and who have given us such inspiration. Katherine Pederson and her crew of Calgary Horticultural Society volunteer photographers took many of the photographs, and Grace Buzik created the line drawings. Much appreciation is due them for their talent and hard work. Thanks to Michael Kelly and Bob McLarty of Lee Valley Tools. We also acknowledge the Glenbow Archives for providing prints of the historic photos in this book.

Once again, Fifth House Publishers has been a wonderful partner. Thanks to Charlene Dobmeier (managing editor), Jane Billinghurst (editor), and Geri Rowlatt (copy editor) for their understanding, insights, and suggestions during the preparation of this book.

Finally, our love and gratitude to Bob, Vic, Kate, and Camille for their support and patience throughout the past year.

Preface

About the Calgary Horticultural Society

In 1905, the year Alberta became a province, Calgary was a thriving frontier community of almost 12,000 people, located at the confluence of the Bow and Elbow Rivers and surrounded by rolling grassland as far as the eye could see. Citizens recently arrived from eastern Canada and Europe found the prairie landscape to have a stark, forbidding beauty. They also quickly learned about the realities of a short growing season, alkaline soils, drying winds, and deep-freeze temperatures, and wondered wistfully if they would be able to grow anything more than the essentials for survival. The possibilities of ever again enjoying the lush beauty of a perennial border, the subtle fragrance of a bower of roses, or the exquisite taste of a freshly picked apple seemed remote.

Fortunately, many of the early settlers came from countries with strong horticultural traditions and were eager to re-create the charm and splendour of gardens left behind but not forgotten. Four such enthusiasts were Fred Mayhew, Harry Burrows, William Reader, and Mr. Lambert, who together founded the Calgary Horticultural Society (CHS) and named the first board

The 1918 Calgary Horticultural Society flower show was a grand event, featuring magnificent floral displays and quality entertainment. Courtesy Glenbow Archives

of directors in 1908. The directors stated as their objectives "the encouragement of horticulture, arboriculture, agriculture, and the arts related thereto, and aiding in the beautifying and improving of the City of Calgary, and the horticultural conditions therein."[1] They anticipated accomplishing these goals by holding regular meetings and exhibitions, carrying out experiments, and offering prizes for horticultural essays.

From the day the original board of directors assumed their responsibilities under the direction of H. W. White, there has been no turning back for the Society. The board immediately focussed its energies on organizing the first annual flower show, which was held in 1908 and was by every account a great success. Flower shows in all their magnificence have been held every year since, most often in a pavilion at Calgary Stampede Park, but also in venues as diverse as the Hudson's Bay store, the downtown post office, the Glencoe Club, and most recently in historic Lougheed House.

In 1910, in an effort to educate the public, members of the CHS wrote and published a series of articles in the *Calgary Daily Herald*. By the early 1930s, due largely to the combined efforts of the CHS and the *Calgary Daily Herald*, Calgary had developed the reputation of being the garden city of the West.[2] The Society did not limit its efforts to the beautification of private homes; businesses, apartment buildings, and gas stations were also targeted for improvement, with special classes being introduced into the garden competition for incentive. In 1916, the president reported that upwards of 10,000 trees were planted in Calgary on May 12 through the direct efforts of the CHS, and that another 10,000 were planted by the city parks department and private citizens.[3] For many years the Society also provided continuous support to the Calgary Vacant Lots Garden Club (formed in 1914), which, as its name suggests, undertook to cultivate vacant city lots to improve their appearance and to provide bountiful produce for winter use by local residents.

From its earliest days, the CHS was held in high esteem by the citizens of Calgary and their leaders. The list of patrons and honorary presidents reads like a Who's Who of western Canadian VIPs and includes the likes of W. R. Hull; Senators Patrick Burns, Sir James Lougheed, and Harry Hayes; Premiers William Aberhart and Peter Lougheed; Lieutenant Governor Grant MacEwan; Dr. Mary Dover, O.B.E.; and for many years the Right Honourable R. B. Bennett, the prime minister of Canada. When Bennett retired in 1939 to his estate in Surrey, England, the CHS presented him with a Canadian spruce tree to thank him for the considerable support he had shown to the Society over the years. The commemorative spruce was planted for Bennett by William Reader during a trip Reader made to Great Britain that same year.[4]

Mary Dover—daughter of A. E. Cross, one of the original Big Four underwriters of the Calgary Stampede, and granddaughter of Colonel J. F. Macleod, founder of Calgary—was a patron, life member, and active supporter of the CHS. In 1973, she and her siblings donated the historic family home at 1240 - 8th Ave SE to the city to provide space for horticultural activities. For the next 14 years, the CHS shared the Cross House premises with the City of Calgary horticulturist and other local garden interest groups. It was a most appropriate setting for the CHS, considering that Mrs. A. E. Cross was a participant and winner in the first flower show organized by the CHS.[5]

The history of the CHS has been rich in rewarding relationships with affiliated horticultural societies, a tradition that continues to this day. The Calgary Dahlia and Gladiolus Societies were early partners, as were the Calgary Rose Society, the Calgary Garden Club and Junior Gardeners, and the Garden Club of the Junior League.

Over the years groups of volunteers have contributed to special projects that have benefited the Calgary community at large. One such undertaking was the development of the entry gardens at Heritage Park. From 1987 to 1988, a group of dedicated CHS volunteers raised over $40,000 for the purchase of an underground irrigation system, topsoil, and hundreds of trees, shrubs, and perennials to beautify the approach to the Heritage Park gates. This same group then took hundreds of hours out from tending their own gardens to install the sprinklers, spread and level the soil, and settle all the plants in their new homes. The results were impressive and are enjoyed by all who visit the park today.

Another significant project in which the Society participated was a collaboration with the City of Calgary in 1989 to select an official flower for the city. Representatives from both organizations met to determine the selection criteria. It was decided that an official flower for Calgary should be red (a City of Calgary colour), easily grown in Calgary, and readily available for purchase. Nominations were solicited from Society members and citizens at large. The official nomination list was narrowed down to include the pasqueflower, blanket flower, bee balm, potentilla, and nasturtium. A large advertisement in the *Calgary Herald* invited citizens to vote for one of the flowers on the list, and the response was excellent. There was also no doubt about the winner: the pasqueflower in its red form, *Pulsatilla vulgaris rubra*, won by a margin of 4 to 1. You can help promote Calgary's official flower by planting a cluster of red pasqueflowers in your yard for the springtime enjoyment of all who view them.

The last 20 years have seen the CHS establish a number of new traditions to blend with the old, all designed to contribute to the knowledge of local gardeners. Educational meetings, once held on a sporadic basis, have evolved into monthly meetings with guest lecturers making beautifully illustrated presentations about all aspects of gardening in Calgary and the vicinity. A formal program of workshops first made its appearance in 1976, giving CHS members and nonmembers alike an opportunity to learn about more detailed local gardening topics in a friendly, informal setting.[6] The Society newsletter was first published in 1983 with an infusion of funds from The Alberta Horticultural Association. Although it was issued only intermittently in the beginning, it has appeared non-stop, eight times a year since 1987.[7] It has also become much more than a newsletter for announcing events. Now called *Calgary Gardening*, it is a mini-magazine filled with informative articles on gardening in Calgary, and it is enjoyed by gardeners of all levels.

Even today the CHS views its primary role as one of educating both members and the community at large about the joys and unique challenges of gardening in the Calgary area.[8] The regular guest lecture and workshop series continue to be primary venues for sharing horticultural information; however, as interest in gardening grows, so too does the number of ways the Society reaches out to Calgarians. An important step has been to develop a vibrant outreach program whose prime function is to promote and encourage awareness in the community about the Society and the myriad opportunities it offers. The establishment of a speakers' bureau has given the Society the means to respond to the many requests received annually from local groups for information about gardening in Calgary. Researching and writing the comprehensive gardening book *The Calgary Gardener* (to which this is a companion volume) was a labour of love. This team effort resulted in the sharing of years of accumulated wisdom about the Calgary gardening scene. Finally, it is well known that a great way to learn about what works in local gardens is to view them firsthand. Every year CHS members generously open their private gardens to fellow members for their viewing pleasure. This aspect of gardening education is deemed to be so important that the Society is now developing a display garden of its own. It is a work in progress, but what garden isn't?

Membership in the CHS has fluctuated considerably over the years, with numbers ranging from a few dozen to more than 3600 members in 1997, making the Society one of the largest of its kind in North America. The indomitable spirit and the will to succeed in creating beautiful gardens, so characteristic of the first settlers in the area, continue in the modern-day gardener, who is always challenging the odds by pushing the limits of what will grow successfully in Calgary. It is truly remarkable to think how far Calgarians have come since those first tentative days of the existence of the Calgary Horticultural Society!

Introduction

About This Book

As the love for gardening grows among Calgarians, so too does the desire for knowledge about how to meet the challenge of gardening in Alberta's Chinook zone. *The Calgary Gardener,* published in 1996, was written by members of the Calgary Horticultural Society to help local gardeners achieve beautiful gardens in this difficult climate. It provides practical design, cultivation tips, and plant lists tailored to the Calgary area.

The Calgary Gardener, Volume Two was written in direct response to a genuine enthusiasm expressed by local gardeners for more information on successful garden design, planting, and maintenance. This "next step" is full of gardening tips, historical anecdotes, and useful plant lists. It will appeal to gardeners of all skill levels, whether a new gardener landscaping a first house or a veteran seeking fresh ideas to rejuvenate an older garden. Volume One of *The Calgary Gardener* provides you with the basics; this book expands on those concepts and takes you into some new gardening territory.

Ideas for designing and planting gardens that evoke the senses, excite the imagination, and are beautiful and practical extensions of a home's living space are presented in this second volume. The book emphasizes the pleasures of gardening as a creative pastime, and you will find within it ideas to dream over on long winter nights, such as design refinements and those delightful extra touches that elevate a garden above the ordinary. Featured colour photographs of diverse Calgary gardens will enchant, educate, and, most important, inspire gardeners to discover the potential of Chinook zone gardening.

A successful garden is not only the fruit of inspiration, but also the result of thoughtful and informed planning, careful plant selection, and proper maintenance. *The Calgary Gardener, Volume Two* has, for instance, planning and planting ideas for urban gardeners with limited space, including tips for choosing and purchasing suitable plants. There are useful suggestions on how to establish preventive maintenance routines to ensure a beautiful and healthy

A fine collection of colourful perennials hugs the terraced slope reflected in a quiet rocky pool. MAUREEN IRETON

garden throughout the growing season and, at the same time, respect the environment.

This book combines traditional gardening wisdom and pursuits, such as companion planting and seed-collecting, with the observations and experiences of today's adventuresome Calgary gardeners. Indeed, we are growing a greater diversity of plants in Calgary and area than was ever thought possible even a few years ago. The best methods of garden record-keeping and photography—essential tools in the development of a garden and the education of a gardener—are outlined as well.

For your convenience, subjects discussed in both volumes are highlighted with an asterisk in the index of this book.

Growing Conditions in Calgary

The inhabitants of the Chinook zone of southern Alberta face some of the toughest gardening challenges in Canada due to climatic conditions unique to this area. Never predictable, Calgary weather shows little respect for the seasons, and it is rare that a year will pass without several memorable weather events for Calgary gardeners to commiserate over.

Calgary is often classified on Canadian plant hardiness zone maps as Zone 3A. These maps use a scale of 0 to 10 to classify areas according to minimum winter temperature, but also take into account the maximum summer temperature, length of the frost-free period, precipitation amounts, and wind velocities. Calgary can have winter temperatures below -30° C (-22° F), alternating with Chinooks when the thermometer rises well above freezing. Summer temperatures may rise above 30° C (86° F), but nights are cool and, as the days grow shorter in late August, frost is always a threat. Moisture is often scarce, both in terms of precipitation and atmospheric humidity, and is usually sucked away by a wind that seems to blow incessantly, winter or summer. As well, the growing season is short—an average of 112 days.

Another environmental factor Calgarians must take into consideration is the naturally alkaline soil and water. This is a limiting factor for acid-loving plants, some of which, like blueberries or the coveted Himalayan blue poppies, require specially prepared beds and water from a source other than Calgary taps.

Calgary winters create particularly challenging conditions for growing trees and shrubs. These plants reach the full extent of their season's growth by mid-August, and as the days become shorter they harden off, making changes to prepare for winter. Water moves out of the plant cells into the spaces between, where it can freeze without damaging the plant.

Some water is retained by the cells, but in hardy plants it is in a form that generally will not freeze. The temperature at which cellular fluid freezes varies from plant to plant; many trees and shrubs are not hardy in Calgary because this freezing point is regularly exceeded, or because they require a longer growing season to mature and complete the hardening-off process before winter.

Since there were hundreds of species of native plants growing and thriving in this area before gardeners arrived, there are obviously botanical strategies to deal with this erratic climate.

Many herbaceous plants, which die back to the ground every year, have roots able to withstand the bitter cold as well as the scorching heat and dryness of the exposed prairies. Some, like the prairie crocus, bloom in the spring when moisture is available and then go dormant during the hottest weeks of summer, enabling them to survive with little water.

Native plants often survive by growing in the most advantageous sites available. A drive through the prairies will reveal trees and shrubs congregating in coulees, companionably sheltering from prevailing winds and hot temperatures. The slopes and bottoms of river valleys also have diverse plant populations, many of which thrive in these comparatively protected microclimates but not in less hospitable locations.

The Calgary area also has its microclimates. Low-lying locations such as river valley bottoms may be sheltered from wind, but they experience shorter frost-free periods and, therefore, shorter growing seasons. Cool air sinks to these low sites, making them susceptible to unseasonable frosts; higher altitudes can be subject to unrelenting drying winds. In some neighbourhoods many years may pass without damaging hail, whereas others suffer almost every year. Older Calgary neighbourhoods generally enjoy a milder climate than new subdivisions due to the protection afforded by mature trees.

Small-scale microclimates can also be found within the confines of individual gardens. Calgarians can mimic nature by planting in sheltered locations and by designing their gardens to create desirable microclimates. Every garden can be modified to make it more hospitable to a wider variety of plants, whether this is done by erecting protective structures; planting a hedge, trees, and shrubs; using mulches; or painting a fence white to reflect more light to plants. You need not restrict your planting to tough prairie survivors, although many Calgary gardeners cultivate these hardy plants with pleasure. Be adventuresome, take the occasional risk, and try your hand at pushing the limits; you never know what unexpected pleasures await.

Reader's professional credits over the course of his career were impressive: president of the International Association of Parks Executives of the Pacific Coast; director of the American Institute of Parks Executives; Fellow of the Royal Horticultural Society; member of the British American Alpine Garden Society; and director of the British Garden Association. He was also a contributor to magazines such as *Gardener's Chronicle, American Parks,* and the *Bulletin of the Ontario Parks Association.* Reader's reputation spread far afield: he was commissioned to plan the grounds of the Prince of Wales's E. P. Ranch and was reputedly sought out by Viscountess Byng, wife of the governor general of Canada, to take charge of her English estate. COURTESY GLENBOW ARCHIVES

Tulips are hardy survivors of the late-spring blizzards familiar to Calgary gardeners. GARY STEFKO

Something to Strive For

Every day thousands of Calgarians drive or ride the C-train past a largely forgotten garden that, in its prime, was a horticultural showpiece of international repute and a destination of royalty. The Reader Rock Garden is of great historical and botanical significance to Calgary as the crowning achievement of the remarkable William Reader, a man whose vision and years of dedicated work were largely responsible for transforming a dusty prairie town into a city of tree-lined streets and green sanctuaries.

William Reader was born in London in 1875. The son of a gardener, he spent his childhood in Kent, where at an early age he demonstrated a love of nature and plants. Reader began his professional career as a teacher, but it was not long before he succumbed to his passion for horticulture, and when he arrived in Calgary in 1908 he established himself as a landscape designer. During his first few years in Calgary, Reader worked on various landscaping commissions, including the gardens of Senator Patrick Burns, was involved with the newly established Calgary Horticultural Society, and published a series of gardening articles in the *Calgary Daily Herald.*

Reader became parks superintendent in April 1913, and during his 29-year tenure in this position many of the parks that grace Calgary today were planned and established. Often struggling to manage with inadequate funds, Reader was responsible for parks and parks planning, cemeteries, civic nurseries, and the maintenance of civic and hospital grounds in the growing city. In addition to these considerable duties, Reader found time to work closely with civic groups, encouraging citizen involvement in planning and civic beautification, and was president of the Calgary Horticultural Society in 1915.

Reader was a strong proponent of civic improvement and was involved in national and international civic beautification associations. An early priority was tree planting in parks and along boulevards. By 1917, three civic tree nurseries were in operation: in Union Cemetery, Victoria Park, and St. Patrick's Island. By 1931, Reader had supervised the planting of 105 km (65 mi) of boulevards with 21,495 trees, including those planted on Memorial Drive to commemorate soldiers killed in World War I.

As a horticulturist keenly interested in plant propagation, Reader was closely involved with the administration of the civic nurseries at Union Cemetery. The site was a 24-ha (60-ac) parcel of land adjacent to Macleod Trail, purchased in 1890. A mortuary chapel, still standing at the cemetery, was built in 1908, and in 1909, land was reserved at the site

William Reader introduced Calgarians to a unique and extensive plant collection displayed in his world-renowned garden. Courtesy Glenbow Archives

for a tree nursery. In 1912, the sandstone entrance arch was built, along with a residence for the parks superintendent, a parks and cemetery office, and a greenhouse. In 1913, 40,000 bedding-out plants were produced; in 1917, in addition to the plants produced for city parks, cemeteries, and hospitals, over 2500 plants from the nurseries were sold to florists and 5500 to individual citizens. In 1928, greenhouse manager William Stark arranged to run the greenhouse on a private basis, which he did until 1951.

The Union Cemetery nursery was the site of many horticultural experiments. Hotbeds were constructed for raising herbaceous perennials, and different varieties of trees, shrubs, and annuals were tested. Around 1914, Reader reported that the following numbers of varieties could grow successfully in Calgary: "28 species of trees, 37 shrubs, 14 vines, 132 herbaceous perennials, 51 annuals (by raising under glass), 42 annuals (by sowing in the open). Of these 121 species have been introduced by the parks department and many are now being grown by citizens."[9]

Despite his many accomplishments in parks planning and implementation, the plantsman William Reader was probably most at home in the public gardens he created, literally in his own backyard, between 1913 and 1942. When Reader moved into the parks superintendent's residence at the top of the hill at Union Cemetery in 1913, the site was barren and sandy, an exposed west-facing hillside subject to all the challenging extremes of temperature and wind that the Calgary climate can deliver. Between 1922 and 1929, Reader brought in thousands of tons of rock, including huge boulders, from places such as Banff, Drumheller, and Cochrane to create a beautiful alpine rock garden amid the prairie desolation.

The Reader Rock Garden was originally entered from the west through the sandstone arch, which has since been relocated to accommodate the C-train tracks. To the north of the entrance, in the lowest level of the garden, was a colourful area of formal annual beds. The road leading up the hill was constructed of cobbles with stone drainage gutters. One branch led to the mortuary chapel and cemetery to the south-east; another curved upwards to the superintendent's residence to the northeast. Along the road and up the hillside were spruce and plantings of other coniferous and deciduous trees, shrubs, and perennials. Rock retaining walls lined the upper part of the road to the house, forming rockeries, which were filled with hundreds of varieties of alpine plants. Steps built into the rockeries led to other paths along wooded trails.

Reader collected plants and corresponded with botanists from around the world in his quest for new species. His garden included not only plants he had collected in the Rockies, as well as others of North American origin, but

⤳ Abbreviated Reader Rock Garden Plant List ⤳

William Reader's impressive list of plants in the garden as of November 1936 includes, among many other species, 30 varieties of alliums, 59 campanulas, 49 dianthus, 34 gentians, 151 iris, 47 lilies, 30 peonies, 43 primulas, and 46 sedum. The following list is extracted from a much longer alphabetical catalogue of plants; while the genera will be familiar, many of these species are not commonly grown in Calgary gardens and some names have changed over the years.

Anemone (*Anemone patens, A. parviflora*)
Aster (*Aster paniculatus*)
Bee balm, bergamot (*Monarda ramaleyi,* also *M. fistulosa*)
Beardtongue (*Penstemon acuminatus, P. utahensis*)
Bellflower (*Campanula fragilis*)
Campion (*Silene nutans*)
Catchfly, campion (*Lychnis alpina*)
Catmint (*Nepeta ucranica*)
Clematis (*Clematis columbiana*)
Columbine (*Aquilegia longissima*)
Coral bell (*Heuchera glabra*)
Corydalis (*Corydalis sempervirens*)
Cranesbill (*Geranium argenteum, G. lancastrense*)
Gentian (*Gentiana tibetica*)
Globeflower (*Trollius pumilus*)
Grape hyacinth (*Muscari botryoides*)
Hen and chicks (*Sempervivum calcareum, S. tectorum*)
Johnny jump-up, viola (*Viola pedatifida*)
Lady's mantle (*Alchemilla micans,* also *A. gracilis*)
Lily (*Lilium hansonii*)
Meadow rue (*Thalictrum elegans*)
Monkshood (*Aconitum pyramidale*)
Ornamental onion (*Allium japonicum, A. zebdanense*)
Phlox (*Phlox diffusa*)
Pincushion flower (*Scabiosa graminifolia*)
Pinks, dianthus (*Dianthus glacialis, D. petraeus*)
Primrose (*Primula minima, P. uralensis,* also *P. veris* subsp. *macrocalyx*)
Rockfoil (*Saxifraga juniperina,* also *S. juniperifolia, S. trifurcata*)
Shooting star (*Dodecatheon latifolium,* also *D. hendersonii*)
Speedwell (*Veronica saxatilis,* also *V. fruticans*)
Stonecrop (*Sedum hispanicum, S. rhodiola,* also *S. rosea*)
Thyme (*Thymus nummularius*)
Virginia bluebells (*Mertensia lanceolata*)
Yarrow (*Achillea ageratifolia*)

Source: William Reader, *Alphabetical List of Plants in Rockery [Reader Rock Garden] as at November 1936,* Local History Collection, Calgary Public Library

Dainty shooting stars were part of
Reader's original plant collection.

also species from places as distant as Britain, France, Switzerland, New
Zealand, India, and China. Reader's successor as superintendent, Alex
Munro, recalled collecting as many as 850 varieties of seeds from Reader's
garden,[10] some of which were sent to such prestigious institutions as
London's Kew Gardens, the Royal Botanical Garden in Edinburgh, and the
New York Botanical Gardens.

Reader's house at the top of the hill was circled by a driveway and surrounded by an open space of lawn, which was enjoyed as a site for tennis
and croquet games. The home is described as having the effect of "a cosy
English cottage,"[11] softened by vines, including clematis, and sheltered from
the north winds by trees and shrubs. Near the house and the crest of the hill,
Reader built a gazebo from which visitors could view the surrounding gardens. A stream ran beneath the gazebo, through a series of ponds and waterfalls, and under a bridge. There was a marsh garden and many shady
wooded areas through which meandered flagstone and mown-grass paths.
In harmony with the rustic environment, twig benches were placed
throughout the garden.

Gardeners will find it easy to imagine the sensual pleasures of an
early summer stroll through Reader's garden from this description,
written in 1939.

> June brings perhaps the most glorious phase to this lovely garden.
> Through the trees, myosotis and columbines make a mist of blue.

Shaded stone steps invite visitors to explore the rockeries and glades of the Reader Rock Garden. LIESBETH LEATHERBARROW

Iris reflect their deep purple in the limpid pools. A trailing genista lies languidly golden across a warm rock like a dainty maiden bathing in the sun. The marsh is aglow with kingcups, with cowslips and primroses on its fringe. Everywhere saxifrages and moss campion grow out of the weathered rocks or wink at you with smiling faces as you walk the flagstone paths.

In cooler dells the little stream threads its way through as varied a collection of ferns as British Columbia's forests can furnish. Orchids are here, rising through the deep moss; great beds of lily-of-the-valley perfume the air with the scent of their silvery bells.

There is music too. The water trickles soothingly among the moss-greened stones or falls with tinkling melody into pools where brown trout lurk. But above all, the birds who find sanctuary here fill the air with their lilting love songs.[12]

While Alex Munro believed that Reader looked upon the rock garden as "his private domain,"[13] it was also the means by which he could teach the citizens of Calgary what was possible in this often inhospitable climate. His plant collection was carefully tagged and identified for all to see, and he encouraged Calgarians to grow new and unusual plants, to push the limits and discover what could be accomplished in their own gardens. Reader was responsible for introducing many hardy plants to Calgary with his experiments in propagating perennials.

Many of Reader's ideas for horticultural design, drawn from the British tradition of herbaceous borders, are widely practised today. He believed plantings should have a natural appearance, stressing "the advantage from an artistic standpoint of having the borders sweep out into the lawn in flowering promontories and recede into little bays in contrast to the straight lines that are so characteristic of many western cities."[14] Reader also advised that when planting perennials or other plants the gardener should not "scatter them all over the border" as this practice would result in "a confused mass of foliage and color,"[15] but rather plant in groups for a bold effect. Although Reader planned perennial borders to achieve harmonious colour schemes, using blocks of colour separated by green foliage plants where necessary, he also constantly experimented for startling effects, admitting that he found this aspect of the planning and planting of mixed borders fascinating.[16] He also advocated that, when planting, gardeners consider the bloom periods of various perennials so as to achieve continuous blossom.

In 1943, on his way home from a lecture to the Cosmopolitan Club with his collection of lantern slides and his favourite dog by his side, William Reader suffered a stroke and died. He had been retired for less than a month. Reader was eulogized by W. Ingwersen in the *English Gardener's Chronicle* as a "quiet unassuming man, whose knowledge was . . . profound. His love for the native flora of his adopted country was as great as his affection for the many plants and trees he introduced to Calgary."[17] Another tribute from the *Canadian Alpine Journal* noted that "no flower was too small nor too common to attract his notice."[18]

William Reader's influential and far-sighted planning for the City of Calgary lives today in the rich legacy of the parks he designed. The historic importance of this legacy has been recognized by Calgary Parks and Recreation, which is planning to undertake the huge task of reconstructing the Reader Rock Garden to its former glory. But something of Reader's pioneering spirit also survives in the thousands of dedicated Calgary gardeners who battle the same capricious climate and learn the same lessons as he did, gardeners who seek the unusual, beautiful, and hardy and who, like Reader, rejoice in creating an oasis in their own backyards.

ONE

The Creative Gardener

More and more, Calgarians are retreating to the serenity of their gardens, either for respite from the busy lives they lead or for filling the days and weeks of leisure that have been deservedly earned after a lifetime spent working at one job or another. Whether it is the process of gardening that attracts them or the finished landscape itself that appeals, many view their outdoor gardens as extensions of their indoor living spaces. One outcome of this trend has been the introduction of the garden room into the landscape. Gardeners are increasingly applying the design techniques favoured by interior designers to the outdoors by giving thought to the arrangement of garden floors, walls, overhead canopies, and transition zones from the house to the garden. They also strive for harmonious colour, form, and texture in both soft and hard landscaping features for the successful realization of their garden dreams.

Garden Rooms

Envision the sun-splashed brightness of a Mediterranean courtyard, or the soft romantic pastels of a walled English flower and herb garden. Enclosing gardens for privacy has long fulfilled the human need for sanctuaries from the outside world. Conceiving of and designing your garden as one or a series of rooms provides many benefits in addition to privacy, including cohesive design, the illusion of space, and variety in both form and function.

Garden rooms heighten the sense of mystery and anticipation when exploring a garden. If an entire garden is visible at one glance, there is nothing to entice you along a path to see what lies beyond a hedge, wall, trellis, or strategically planted screen of shrubs or trees. Well-placed partitions create a sense of intimacy, and the discovery of concealed spaces brings back the childhood desire for secret hideaways open only to the initiated. Garden rooms are also ideal for isolating colour schemes or garden styles that may not fit with the rest of the garden. If you've always wanted a perennial bed of carnival reds, yellows, and oranges, creating a separate space within your garden to accommodate this riot of colour may be the solution. Alternatively, a secluded corner might be the perfect place to tuck away a small Japanese-style courtyard screened off by a bamboo fence.

When deciding how to apply the garden room concept to your garden, consider your requirements for outdoor living space. A sheltered space for outdoor dining with easy access to the kitchen may be a priority for entertaining or casual family meals. Do you need a play area for children? If you are an avid plant collector, you will want plenty of space for your acquisitions. Whether you indulge in roses, alpines, vegetables, herbs, or any other specialties, you will wish to choose planting sites carefully to take advantage of suitable microclimates. A pond or small water feature could be essential to your idea of the perfect garden, as might a

A secret garden room among luxuriant ferns is the perfect retreat for afternoon tea. WINSTON GORETSKY

∾ Patios and Decks as Garden Rooms ∾

Extensions of your house such as decks or patios provide a transitional space between indoor and outdoor living areas and are good places to begin your garden room plan. These areas are already well defined and may require only furnishing and decorating to become attractive outdoor living spaces. Once your furniture for relaxing or dining is in place, add containers of salad vegetables, herbs, and flowers for a handy kitchen garden. Mount half-baskets overflowing with annual flowers on available wall spaces. Trellises for annual vines planted in containers may be against walls or free-standing, according to the space available. These vertical plantings will impart a sense of enclosure, as will trailing hanging plants. If your deck is large, consider enclosing a corner to make a small gazebo that can be provided with awnings if desired. Do not forget to make the most of the space under an elevated deck by screening it with containers of flowers or potted shrubs for a cool hideaway in the heat of the day.

While planting on decks is necessarily limited to containers, varying textures and designs may be added to patio floors with stone or brick interplanted with thyme, moss, or other crevice-loving ground creepers. These spaces will also inevitably be colonized by delightful volunteers such as Johnny jump-ups. Patios may also be enclosed with trellises or roofed as pergolas with overhanging beams upon which perennial vines such as Virginia creeper, climbing honeysuckle, or hops may be trained, creating a bower of dappled shade.

small gazebo or a shaded bench for quiet moments with a good book. You may wish to plan more than one seating area, choosing spots near favourite plants. This will allow you to follow the sun or shade, as you prefer, as well as to appreciate that spring primula bed or those summer roses at their peak.

Garden rooms may be completely or partly enclosed, well defined and separated, or linked and flowing naturally into each other. To demarcate the rooms, a transitional point from one to

Partially enclosed by vine-clad trellises, an appealing wooden deck unites house and garden into an attractive outdoor living space. LIESBETH LEATHERBARROW

another is helpful, such as a trellis, vine-draped arch, gate, or even a narrow pathway between screening shrubs or overhanging trees.

Garden rooms do not have to be large, structured, or expensive to create. In many gardens, these spaces already exist and need only to be enhanced by a strategically placed screen here or a path there. The very small garden (under 4 m²/5 yd²) is best treated as a single room with only one decorating theme. Larger areas may be divided into a number of rooms, thus creating several gardens within a garden, each with its own distinctive mood or purpose. Whether you garden on an acreage, an urban lot, or a postage-stamp-sized patio, the garden is your chosen summer abode, and you will be well rewarded by designing it as a place you can live in, as well as admire from afar.

❖ Variations on a Theme ❖

Creating a Courtyard

If you have a very small yard, consider turning the complete yard into a courtyard rather than trying to include both a patio or deck area and a patch of lawn bordered by flower beds. Use hanging pots and baskets and vertical plantings to make the most of courtyard space, clothing the walls with roses or perennial vines such as clematis, climbing honeysuckle, Virginia creeper, cinnamon yam, and hops. For a sunny courtyard, choose annual vines with colourful blossoms. Try morning glory, cup-and-saucer vine, sweet peas, canarybird vine, and black-eyed Susan. Courtyard gardens are the perfect place to indulge a passion for containers, including herb and vegetable plantings. Around the perimeter of your courtyard, plant small columnar varieties of trees. These will impart a sense of privacy without occupying a great deal of space, as well as adding the soothing sounds of leaves rustling in the wind.

Garden Floors

Floors and their coverings are essential to the successful execution of garden room design. Not only do floors define and reinforce the design, they also create ambiance in the garden as a whole. Whereas an unbroken sweep of hardwood or carpet looks wonderful inside, a similarly uniform expanse of stone or grass looks flat and dull outdoors. The key to a successful garden floor is a mix of materials, both hard and soft. Hard features include stone, brick, and wood; soft features comprise plants in all their shapes, colours, and textures. Remember that some variety in garden floor covering is indispensable in the creation of a perfect garden retreat, but don't overdo it.

Lawns. The majority of garden designs, both old and new, revolve around the establishment of a traditional lawn. The lush green, perfectly appointed lawn with nary a weed in sight is indeed a wonder to behold. It is a compelling invitation for walking barefoot, for lingering and revelling in its coolness, its softness, and, yes, even in its luxuriant emerald hues. It also makes you wonder what it takes to create such a masterpiece, often the envy of the neighbourhood, knowing full well that keeping up with the dandelions and the routine watering and mowing from week to week is already more than the average gardener really cares to undertake. As you might suspect, these elaborate showcases of green finery evolve at great cost to the owners; they take time, effort, and money—lots of each. The quintessential lawn can also be a bottomless pit for horticultural chemicals—fertilizers, herbicides, and pesticides—that eventually percolate into local groundwater. So why the almost universal aspiration in North America to grow a flawless lawn?

A peek at the past provides a few clues. Although the early presence of lawns has been recorded elsewhere in the world, it is likely that North Americans take their cue from the British gardening tradition. One theory has it that lawns, which were simply expanses of cleared land reverted to natural grasses, were created as protection zones between castles and the adjacent forests. This afforded the castle's occupants an excellent view of the surrounding areas, thereby preventing the enemy from arriving unobserved. Long after the military need for lawns had disappeared, nobles continued the tradition of establishing low-cut, grassy expanses for recreation, which were maintained by ranks of labourers endlessly swinging their scythes; nobles did not require every square metre of available land for subsistence farming as did the peasants. As such, lawns evolved into status symbols, affordable only by the rich. However, with the invention of the lawnmower in 1830, even middle-class and common folk could reasonably participate in establishing and maintaining much-desired lawns.[19]

Lawns might not have caught on in such a big way in North America if it hadn't been for the landscaping ideals described by the American landscape architect Frank J. Scott in his book *The Art of Beautifying Suburban Home Grounds,* published in 1870. So influential was he in his promotion of lawns as a reflection of social status, and so willing were the public to accept his views, that there has been no looking back since.[20] Most new home-owners, even today, don't question that the perfect home landscape design includes, by definition, lawn in both the front and back yards.

There is no doubt that turf carpeting the garden floor is a durable groundcover and a comfortable surface to walk and play on. A well-thought-out garden, however, offers excellent opportunities for gardeners to reduce the area devoted to traditional lawns by introducing other interesting floor coverings in their designs. It is even within the realm of the possible in the average urban lot to eliminate lawns and lawn mowing forever. Do not feel obliged to keep that square of lawn just because it is there; if you love the feel of grass beneath your feet, you can always restrict it to paths that can be easily mowed with an old-fashioned push mower.

∾ Removing Unwanted Lawn ∾

To remove unwanted lawn, use one of the following methods.

❦ Dig up sod by hand using a sharp, flat shovel or rent a sod cutter, a machine that slices lawn horizontally about 6 cm (2.5 in.) below the surface. Turf cut with a sod cutter can be rolled and reused elsewhere in the garden.

❦ Cultivate, either by hand or using a rototiller, at regular intervals throughout the growing season. Timing is critical; if you wait too long between cultivation sessions, the plants you are trying to destroy may have time to re-establish.

❦ Smother grassy areas using a combination of newspaper (12–20 sheets thick) covered with 15–20 cm (6–8 in.) of organic mulch such as wood chips, grass clippings, or leaves for at least a month. The grass and roots will eventually decompose and be incorporated into the soil. You may wish to pre-treat stubborn patches of quack or brome grass with Roundup before starting a regime of smothering; these grasses can persist long after regular turf has been integrated into the top layer of soil.

Introducing Natural Areas

Manicured lawns are still very much a part of our vision of formal landscape design. Here are some ideas for introducing natural plantings into your garden in which the presence of a conventional lawn would not be missed or, indeed, in some cases would even be inappropriate.

A Prairie Meadow. A meadow of wildflowers, usually a pleasant combination of native grasses and plants, is an excellent alternative to a traditional lawn, although creating a natural look is not without its responsibilities and challenges. What is one person's wildflower can be another person's weed; as a wildflower gardener you must be vigilant and prevent restricted plants, as determined by the Province of Alberta, from establishing themselves in your wildflower patch. There is also a fine line between a look that is natural and a look of neglect.

Limit your initial efforts at wildflower gardening to a space defined by boundaries. This gives you the opportunity to determine which combination of wildflowers and natural grasses work best in your soil conditions, and which to avoid; some native plants grow aggressively and will take over a patch in short order, to the exclusion of all else. A gradual move from pristine lawn to wildflower meadow will also give the neighbours an idea of what you are trying to achieve and time to get used to the notion.

Choose attractive, hardy, and drought-tolerant perennials such as blanket flower, prairie crocus, wild bergamot, yarrow, and prairie coneflower. Although not native, ornamental grasses are also striking. Good low-growing shrubs for your prairie theme include sage, potentilla, and russet buffaloberry. In addition, kinnikinnick is an excellent groundcover that thrives in dappled shade; for sunny areas choose horizontal junipers. As space permits, add taller shrubs such as dogwood, Saskatoon, or wolf willow.

A Woodland Garden. As communities mature, so do the trees that enhance their appearance. Gardens once exposed to full sun give over to the dappled shade cast by a deciduous canopy, and sun-worshipping plants eventually deteriorate, showing the

Alberta's blue skies enhance the vibrant colours of campanulas, sweet peas, veronica, cosmos, and heliopsis in this joyful prairie garden. RENATA WICHMANN

The arching branches of an old 'Thunderchild' crabapple tree cast dappled shade over this restful woodland garden. LIESBETH LEATHERBARROW

effects of lower light levels. When light conditions are so low that lawns become difficult to grow and maintain, you might want to consider replacing them with a natural woodland garden.

Take as your model the aspen groves of the prairie parkland or other deciduous/mixed deciduous coniferous forests. Their soils are rich in organic matter, and you can duplicate this at home by stripping the sod from your old lawn and amending the underlying soil with plenty of compost and leaf mould. Then, draw up a planting scheme to represent what you would expect to find populating the woodland understorey: low-growing, native plants that are sufficiently widely spaced that they don't compete for the available light. Colourful blooms, although definitely part of the picture, are usually displayed in small groups rather than in large clusters; they play a secondary role to the rich variety of foliage shapes, colours, and textures that is the essence of a woodland garden. Add to these the occasional stump, fallen log, or small rock pile, curved wood-chip paths, and a rustic wooden or stone bench, and your woodland garden will be complete.

An ever-growing number of native plants can be purchased at local nurseries or from merchants dealing exclusively in native plants. Make sure to ask for species and varieties that will tolerate the shade conditions in your garden. These may include baneberry, bunchberry, climbing nightshade, fairy bells, false Solomon's seal, ferns and mosses, lady's slipper, larkspur, mayapple, meadow rue, tall lungwort, trilliums, twinflower, twining honeysuckle, western Canada violet, and the wild white geranium. By limiting yourself to selections from this list, you will be able to create a completely natural native look without even trying. However, if that isn't your goal, you can supplement these choices with other favourite shade-loving plants such as astilbes, hepaticas, hostas, and primulas.

Naturalized Bulbs. If you have an area where the grass can grow long, at least in the spring months, consider devoting a section of your lawn to a mixed area of grass and spring-flowering bulbs. Planting bulbs in colonies to grow and multiply naturally, called natural-

Naturalized spring bulbs fashion an iridescent carpet before the leaves emerge on deciduous trees.
CHARL DU TOIT

A multicoloured blend of annuals and perennials makes this informal, mixed border a delight to behold. JOHN BUYSSCHAERT

This well-designed, sweeping perennial border is accented by large drifts of colour and pleasing variations in plant size and texture. LIESBETH LEATHERBARROW

izing, is a magnificent and colourful way to carpet the garden floor in the spring. It also makes sense when you realize that many of the bulbs used formally in our gardens today originated in grasslands, woodlands, and meadows from around the world. Plant drifts of species tulips, crocus, blue squill, glory-of-the-snow, and striped squill in the lawn or among woodland groundcovers under the canopy of a deciduous tree that leafs out after the bulbs have bloomed. Daffodils also work well in a woodland setting.

When planting bulbs directly into the lawn, choose an area that can be left unmowed until bulb foliage has ripened, usually late May. Select only the earliest flowering varieties, since you will have to wait for the bulbs to finish blooming and their foliage to wither naturally before you can cut them back. If you don't have the patience for that, it would be better to naturalize bulbs so they emerge from luxuriant groundcover or mingle with other plants that can help disguise unsightly foliage. Choose from lady's mantle, foamflower, hardy geraniums, and self-sowing annuals, including pot marigolds and poppies.

To naturalize bulbs, select only those that will multiply and spread readily, such as grape hyacinths, Siberian squill, crocuses, species tulips, striped squill, and glory-of-the-snow. Also choose large healthy bulbs so they can compete with grass and tree roots. Once they have finished blooming, give them a light application of fertilizer with a high proportion of phosphorus and potassium (second and third numbers). Do not use high-nitrogen (first number) lawn fertilizer around bulbs until after their foliage has turned brown.

For natural-looking groupings of bulbs, toss them by the handful onto the ground and plant them where they land. Use a trowel or bulb planter to remove plugs of sod and soil; mix some bone meal in the hole bottom; plant bulbs at a depth equal to three times their diameter; cover the bulbs with soil; and replace the plug. For larger areas, lift the sod with a sod cutter, plant the bulbs as described above, and then replace the sod.

Flower Bed Design. For most of us the word "garden" conjures up visions of flower beds in all their glory; some would say they are a fundamental element in most garden designs, although gardens without them still have a beauty all their own. Even though simple flower beds have been referred to in Greek, Persian, and Roman literature and art since the first century B.C., modern flower bed concepts were developed in early nineteenth-century England. Plant collections from around the world, and especially from North America, were the vogue in England at this time. As many of the acquired plants were more colourful than previously available plants, the desire to plant them where they could be seen and admired by all was intense. Initially, shrubberies were developed to house hardy woody ornamental plants from the Americas. These were soon followed by the development of beds for hardy flowering plants (perennials), and not long thereafter the idea of planting tender flowering plants on an annual basis was born. Both the shrubberies and flower beds were marked departures from earlier popular landscape designs that had focussed on pleasing combinations of trees, lawn, and water with a few flowering plants tucked away out of sight.

In a formal setting where symmetry, repetition, and proportion produce graceful, peaceful, and relaxing vistas, flower beds and adjacent lawns are usually geometric in shape and enclosed by traditional rolling lawns and bold pathways. Squares, rectangles, triangles, circles, and ovals all have their place in the formal garden, either as perennial or mixed borders echoing the shape of the perimeter of the property or often paired as island beds. Planting schemes within the beds should be restful to the eye and consist of a relatively small number of plant varieties.

In an informal garden, flower beds have curved rather than linear edges and are arranged in an asymmetric fashion around the lawn. They are relaxed in their approach but dynamic in their look. The lack of rigid repetition in informal beds brings a feeling of change or movement, leading the eyes and feet ever onward, though at an easy pace. In the absence of lawns or pathways, informal flower beds will have no rigid boundaries; woodland gardens under a deciduous canopy are an excellent example of abundant plants smothering the garden floor with no restraint.

Formal or informal, flower beds can take on a number of different forms, depending on the lay of the land. Raised beds add an extra dimension to the landscape and can be very attractive when carefully planned and successfully constructed. Terraces and less formal rock gardens are also good landscaping choices, especially on properties situated on a natural incline.

❖ Variations on a Theme ❖

Flower Bed Options

Many options are available to Calgarians who seek a change from the usual rectangular, curved, or island flower beds that are the strength of the modern garden. Alternatives include the very traditional and formal knot garden, which hails from Renaissance England and France, and the decidedly informal alpine rock garden that transports a slice of the mountains right into your own backyard. A look favoured by many is that of the English cottage garden in which flower beds abound, often to the exclusion of all else.

Knot Gardens. Formal, intricately designed knot gardens were popularized in sixteenth-century Renaissance England and France. The elaborate and symmet-

rical knots were traced out with low-growing, evergreen herbal hedges, planted to weave together in sophisticated patterns and usually set in a square framework. Herbs of differing foliage colour were selected for each band of the knot to create contrast and highlight the woven nature of the patterns. Lavender, thyme, rosemary, lavender cotton, and, less frequently, boxwood were all popular hedge materials; their shrubby forms lent them to the clipping that enhanced their formal design. The enclosed spaces within the knot were usually filled with a variety of herbs, flowering plants, or inert coloured materials such as sand or pebbles. Not only did the clipped hedges add beauty to the landscape, but they likely also served a more practical purpose as a

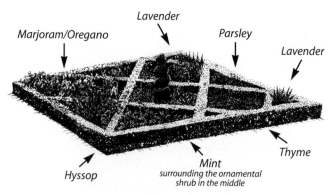

Marjoram/Oregano

Lavender

Parsley

Lavender

Hyssop

Mint
*surrounding the ornamental
shrub in the middle*

Thyme

Popular during the Renaissance, a formal knot garden can be designed with prairie-hardy herbs to suit Calgary growing conditions. GRACE BUZIK

place to dry laundry where the clothes would absorb the fragrance of the underlying herbs.

In Calgary, it is possible to outline a simple knot garden in hedges of lavender, thyme, hyssop, and cliffgreen. These are all relatively slow-growing perennial (though not necessarily evergreen), shrubby plants that will survive Calgary winters with some tender loving care. All manner of herbs and flowers may be chosen to fill the interior segments of the design. Plant them randomly or in carefully orchestrated colour patterns to heighten the air of formality. If you don't have the energy to nurture a perennial herbal hedge, consider outlining a knot with quick-growing broad-leaved annual herbs such as basil or parsley. Use contrasting herbs such as oregano, marjoram, and mint, or carpet bedding plants such as sweet alyssum, marigolds, or lobelia to fill the gaps and complete the picture.

Cottage Gardens. A gardening style enjoyed by many Calgary gardeners is the joyful exuberance of an English cottage garden. Most true cottage gardens consist of a friendly confusion of flowers, herbs, and sometimes even vegetables sheltered by stone walls or picket fences, crisscrossed with inviting pathways, enhanced with the occasional traditional wooden garden bench, and—no lawn! If your garden design already incorporates elements of the cottage garden style—old-fashioned plants creating a profusion of colour in deep flower beds overflowing their boundaries—then consider going all the way and replacing the entire lawn.

Even if you are starting from scratch to create an English cottage garden room in your landscape, the transition to a look of unrestrained gay abandon is an easy one to make. Start with a sunny yard and surround it with clematis-clad fences. Then add mixed traditional flowers such as delphiniums, peonies, cottage pinks, heliotrope, daisies, phlox, and hollyhocks.

The charm of a cottage garden is evoked through the use of dense informal plantings and clinging vines. JOHN BUYSSCHAERT

This rock garden is home to a collection of diminutive alpine plants; *Townsendia parryi,* blue-eyed grass, alpine veronica, encrusted saxifrage, *Erinus alpinus,* and dianthus thrive in the gravelly scree. WINSTON GORETSKY

Intersperse vegetables, and herbs such as lavender or thyme among the flowers or grow them spilling out of their own containers, planting generously to give a look of abundance. Keep woody ornamentals to a minimum to let the sunshine in; choose only those varieties that are naturally small, columnar, or have an open growth habit to minimize the amount of shade in the garden. Ornamental crabapples, hawthorns, and hydrangeas are all suitable for a cottage garden. Remember to develop enough paths to give you access to flowers and shrubs for easy maintenance. For a finishing touch, add a slightly meandering path leading to a sundial, stone or wooden bench, or a simple arch upon which is trained a 'John Cabot' rose.

Alpine Rock Gardens. For a completely different look in a small garden, consider replacing a portion of your lawn with an alpine rock garden. Miniature alpine plants have an exquisite beauty of their own and show to advantage on a background of the gritty soil that is their preference. Many of them are early blooming to accommodate the short growing season characteristic of their native habitat. For the Calgary gardener this is a bonus, with alpines creating vibrant splashes of colour in an otherwise beige landscape that is just beginning to emerge from winter's sleep.

Alpine plants are well suited to Calgary's dry summers and cool night temperatures, as long as they are adequately protected from the winter wind and sun. Their preferred growing medium is one that approximates the natural environment in the mountains: lean soil in sharply drained, gravelly meadows, and scree and talus slopes. To duplicate these conditions in the garden, provide plants with a general-purpose alpine mix of one-third screened and washed rock grit, one-third playbox sand, and one-third peat moss or compost. Before planting, sculpt and contour this mixture to create a bed of uneven terrain that is visually appealing. A top dressing of up to 2.5 cm (1 in.) of rock, grit, or sand helps keep roots cool and moist,

Raised flower beds are attractive and easy to maintain. Mary Nichols

and completes the vision of gravelly alpine scenery.

Starting an alpine rock garden is a plant collector's dream. Ground-hugging compact and dwarf forms of plants such as hen and chicks, saxifrages, dianthus, phlox, rock jasmine, silene, and sandwort lay the foundation for a successful garden. Yellow mountain avens and a variety of drabas are also welcome, low-growing additions. For contrast, add the delicate but beautiful lewisias, townsendias, and alpine forget-me-nots. To introduce some height into the landscape, try alpine and dwarf harebells, dwarf larkspurs, three-flowered avens, and a variety of dwarf columbines and poppies. Penstemons are a mainstay of the alpine garden, so make sure to include a few of these in your collection. Browse local garden centres for new ideas on what to grow or join a local alpine plant society to learn more about the endless variety of dainty yet striking plants available for beginner and avid alpine gardeners alike.

Groundcovers. The most obvious alternative garden floor to traditional lawns and flower beds is a dense mat of herbaceous groundcover. There are two types of groundcovers, neither of which withstand foot traffic very well. The first type colonizes naturally, and sometimes rampantly, spreading by stolons or underground rhizomes. Included in this category are lily-of-the-valley, ajuga, creeping Jenny, periwinkle, and goutweed, all of which are effective, and also a bit unruly from time to time. The second type forms clumps that, when densely planted, are equally effective at filling in empty spaces, albeit in a more orderly and predictable fashion. In other words, these plants are groundcovers because we choose them to be. To qualify further as desirable groundcovers, plants in the latter group must be relatively maintenance free; be efficient at keeping weeds out and moisture in; show no centre die-back; and be of visual interest over a long season. Bergenia, ornamental grasses, daylilies, pinks, hostas, thrift, and artemisias are just a few of the many clump-forming plants that are popular and well loved as groundcovers.

Herbaceous groundcovers can be used anywhere and everywhere. They are especially beautiful in combination with spring-flowering bulbs naturalized in their midst. They are also excellent for filling in tricky spaces where grass is difficult to grow or maintain. A steep grassy slope that is awkward or dangerous to mow is easier to look after when clothed in a combination of low-spreading junipers, ornamental grasses, daylilies, Virginia creeper, and periwinkle. A dry, sunny side garden takes on a new look when filled with an attractive pathway bordered by the likes of hen and chicks, sedums, artemisias, thymes, and kinnikinnick. Moist shady gardens under a woodland canopy are appealing when underplanted with ferns, mosses, bunchberries, wild ginger, sweet woodruff, golden corydalis, and creeping phlox. Even the average collection of suburban shrubs and trees takes on an appearance of glamour when connected by curved beds profusely planted with two or three favourite groundcovers.

When designing with herbaceous groundcovers, start out with an expanse of well-prepared soil that is as weed free as possible; it can be a nuisance to battle entrenched weeds among groundcovers. Then, create a tapestry effect by planting groundcovers densely in blocks or drifts, allowing adjacent types with contrasting textures to intermingle at their common boundaries. Once groundcovers are established, it pays to do a bit of annual maintenance, cutting plants back to encourage bushiness and trimming them, especially where exuberant growers have a tendency to encroach on garden paths. Finally, show some consideration to your neighbours when planting beautiful but invasive groundcovers such as goutweed or mint. One innocent Calgarian who was in the middle of a serious goutweed eradication program in her own garden gave a clump to a grateful neighbour who had a problem spot that would be perfectly served by the indomitable creeper—right next to said Calgarian's fence. You guessed it—she now has two or three new goutweed colonies on which to focus her icy stare!

∿ Containing Invasive Plants ∿

Plants that spread rapidly through underground rhizomes are useful as groundcovers, resulting in almost instant coverage of bare ground. They definitely have their place in the suburban landscape, but care must be taken to contain them, especially when they have the potential for invading neighbours' gardens as well as overrunning your own.

- On your own property, plant wisely by taking advantage of pre-existing barriers (for example, contain invasives between a driveway or sidewalk and the house foundation).
- In flower beds, submerge invasive plants in large pots. As long as the pots have adequate drainage, you do not need to remove the bottoms. Make sure the rims stand 5 cm (2 in.) above the soil level.
- On the property line, make sure you install a barrier that reaches a depth of at least 45 cm (18 in.) to prevent roots from taking hold at the neighbours', where they might not be welcome; rigid plastic or metal sheeting works well.

❖ Variations on a Theme ❖

Combining Hard and Soft Groundcovers

The flowing lines of herbaceous or soft groundcovers contrast effectively with the rigid, angular lines of patio stones, decks, brick paths, and other hard groundcovers. Soft and hard groundcovers can be combined in many eye-catching ways. One engaging look can be achieved by covering all or part of your garden floor with alternating squares of patio stones and planting spaces to create a delightful checkerboard effect. The end result can be as enchanting as a patchwork quilt, with the patio stones cutting a zigzag path through regularly spaced blocks of groundcovers, annuals, and perennials. Such a design would also work well as a transition zone between a formal stone or poured concrete patio and the lawn beyond.

One common garden feature that inevitably leads to the juxtaposition of hard and soft groundcovers is the garden path. Formal plantings rigidly contained along path borders accentuate the straight lines of cut stone, terracotta brick, or poured concrete and aggregate, favourite materials for path construction. Informal plantings left to ramble over straight path boundaries greatly moderate their angular and sometimes abrupt effect.

Planting between bricks, natural stone, and cobbles creates an impact that appeals to many people. The textures of foliage and blossom soften the otherwise rigid boundaries of paving materials and make a natural transition from the path to adjacent flower beds. Keep in mind that these plants do not withstand heavy foot traffic and do best when planted along

An appealing low stone wall adds a vertical dimension to this garden and shelters potted annuals from the wind. VAL PRITCHARD

A bird house perches atop a wooden lath fence, a delightful backdrop for roses, violas, and yellow sedum. VAL PRITCHARD

Goutweed, an attractive groundcover for lighting up a shady corner, must be kept in check by physical barriers. VAL PRITCHARD

path perimeters. Here are some ideas for filling in the gaps; make sure you choose plants that are appropriate to the soil and light conditions of your path or patio.

For sunny locations

Arctic phlox *(Phlox subulata)*

Cheddar pink *(Dianthus gratianopolitanus)*

Creeping speedwell *(Veronica prostrata)*

Dwarf lady's mantle *(Alchemilla erythropoda)*

Dwarf sedum *(Sedum* spp.*)*

Harebell *(Campanula rotundifolia)*

Periwinkle *(Vinca minor)*

Purple rock cress *(Aubrieta deltoidea)*

Rock soapwort *(Saponaria ocymoides)*

Snow-in-summer *(Cerastium tomentosum)*

Sweet alyssum *(Lobularia maritima)*

Thyme *(Thymus* spp.*)*

For shady locations

Bugleweed *(Ajuga reptans)*

Bunchberry *(Cornus canadensis)*

Dwarf lady's mantle *(Alchemilla erythropoda)*

Foamflower *(Tiarella* spp.*)*

Johnny jump-up *(Viola tricolor)*

Stoloniferous phlox *(Phlox stolonifera)*

Wintergreen *(Gaultheria procumbens)*

Partitions

Walls, fences, and hedges serve both practical and aesthetic purposes, demarcating transitions between garden rooms and creating microclimates of shelter and shade.

Walls. Enclosing small garden rooms partly or completely with low stone or brick walls helps to shelter plants from the year-round damaging effects of the wind. Walls can also help mitigate the effects of cool evenings by providing suntraps for heat-loving flowers, herbs, and vegetables. Tuck fast-growing trailing annuals into soil pockets in dry stone walls, or plant climbers at the base to create a colourful wall garden. Crevice-loving perennials, such as Arctic

Fragrant thyme softens the edges of angular Rundle rock steps.
LIESBETH LEATHERBARROW

phlox, saxifrages, and many other alpine species, will probably not survive the wildly fluctuating temperatures of a Chinook-zone winter unprotected, but they may be planted in the wall for the summer and dug into a bed and mulched in the fall.

Fences. Low fences within a garden define areas without obstructing views, and an open design is an irresistible invitation to explore further. A rustic look can be achieved with low crossed poles or a scaled-down split-rail fence. Painted picket fences create the mood of an English country garden. Iron railings with classic lines or fanciful Victorian filigree better suit formal gardens.

Internal fences do not need to be as sturdy as those about the perimeter of the garden, but there should be a sense of unity in the materials chosen for all visible fencing. Your garden will appear larger if boundary fencing is screened by plantings, or painted or stained an unobtrusive brown or grey, so the limits are not immediately apparent. Utilitarian chain link fence may be painted brown and interwoven with willow or other twiggy branches. If you enjoy the sense of enclosure a fence provides, paint it white to set off the colours of the flowers against it.

Hedges. Many gardeners prefer green, living enclosures to those of wood, brick, or stone. While requiring a certain amount of maintenance, deciduous or evergreen hedges are attractive screens to either divide areas of your property or hide or replace an unsightly fence. Evergreen hedges require pruning only once a year but, as they can eventually occupy a great deal of space, are probably best used for large properties. Good choices for the Calgary area are native spruce, Colorado spruce, Swiss stone pine, mugho pine, and Rocky Mountain juniper. Cedar is a popular choice for creating formal hedges in the Maritimes, Ontario, and British Columbia. Although there are several cultivars that are hardy on the prairies, they are costly and difficult to establish, with even the most hardy being susceptible to the severe drying effects of winter winds. Drying results in unsightly brown patches from which the cedars may or may not recover.

Deciduous hedges can be chosen to provide bark or foliage colour, blossoms, or fruit. Flowering hedges must be selectively pruned by hand, but plants such as bush honeysuckle, spirea, potentilla, and some hardy roses make excellent hedges that produce a profusion of blooms when properly trimmed. Densely twiggy hedge plants that tolerate frequent shearing include sweetberry honeysuckle, hedge cotoneaster, three-lobe spirea, and Turkestan burning bush. Choices for tall screening hedges include Siberian elm, lilac, and Amur maple.

∾ Deciduous Hedges for Calgary Gardens ∾

T or S after the plant indicates whether it is most suitable for tall (over 1.5 m/5 ft) or short (under 1.5 m/5 ft) hedges. BC indicates bark colour; F indicates attractive flowers; Fr indicates fruit; FC indicates fall colour.

Altai rose *(Rosa spinosissima altaica)* **T F**
Amur maple *(Acer ginnala)* **T BC FC**
'Arnold Red' honeysuckle *(Lonicera tatarica* 'Arnold Red'*)* **T F Fr**
Golden willow *(Salix alba vitellina)* **T BC**
Golden-flowering currant *(Ribes aureum)* **S F Fr FC**
Hedge cotoneaster *(Cotoneaster lucidus, C. acutifolia)* **T Fr FC**
Lilac *(Syringa* spp.*)* **T F**
Potentilla *(Potentilla fruticosa* cultivars*)* **S F**
Redstem willow *(Salix alba chermesina)* **T BC**
Siberian coral dogwood *(Cornus alba* 'Sibirica'*)* **T BC Fr**
Siberian elm *(Ulmus pumila)* **T FC**
Sweetberry honeysuckle *(Lonicera caerulea edulis)* **T F Fr**
Three-lobe spirea *(Spirea trilobata)* **S F**
Turkestan burning bush *(Euonymus nanus* 'Turkestanicus'*)* **S F Fr FC**

Pathways

Pathways are among the most important design features in a garden, sharing almost equally with the surrounding scenery in establishing a welcoming mood and favourable first impression for visitors. To this end, gardeners are well advised to take as much care in the planning and installation of pathways as they take in fashioning other landscape features. Paths that work well simultaneously define and link elements of a garden to produce a coherent, visually satisfying appearance. Paths that fail in this regard look awkward and out of place, and detract from what might otherwise be a harmonious design.

Not only do paths provide the practical means for coming and going, for keeping people's feet clean and dry, and for easy yard maintenance, they also serve as a transition between house and property and as a unifying force throughout the garden. Well-planned paths are dynamic, extending invitations to passers-by, beckoning them in. They create a sense of antici-pation, guiding visitors' eyes and feet to promised destinations that are either readily visible or mysteriously hidden. Paths also determine how people move through gardens; this may be at a brisk pace with a sense of purpose on a straight path, or at a more leisurely pace with many opportu-nities to linger on a meandering path.

Throughout history, garden path designs have been formal, laid out in straight lines defining symmetrical spaces. Early Egyptian and Persian gar-dens, medieval European gardens, the Renaissance gardens of Italy and Holland, even the great European gardens of the eighteenth century were all traversed by straight paths. This is not surprising when you consider that many cultures of the past survived in communities with walls for protection and irrigation canals for water; both these features imposed geometric lines on their surroundings that were echoed in all other aspects of design. Precise straight lines were also likely a reflection of people's needs to tame and exert control over what were often harsh environments.

There occurred, however, one exception to this trend. In China, informal winding paths were part of the Chinese effort to re-create the soft, flowing lines of nature in their gardens. The Koreans and Japanese were quick to adopt the concept of informal path design, but it wasn't until the eighteenth century that British landscapers started to incorporate wandering, curved paths into parkland settings as part of the romanticized, return-to-nature movement that rejected the controlled, classical approach.

Today, the choice of whether to construct a straight, formal path or a curved, informal one is dictated as much by house style as by personal taste. No matter what the size of your property, both styles will work, as long as the one you choose complements the appearance and spirit of the building

A potentilla hedge gives a cheerful display of colour all summer long. Ruth Staal

architecture. Some people are even successful at incorporating elements of both formal and informal styles into one coherent landscape.

Formal Paths. If your house has a formal appearance, then straight paths are called for in your garden plan. Use them to define and separate symmetric flower beds with pleasing geometric shapes and at the same time to lead your eyes and feet to a dramatic focal point—perhaps a statue, fountain, garden bench, or decorative urn elevated on a pedestal. By playing with perspective you can also use straight paths to create illusions. For example, a path that narrows slightly along its length creates the impression that your garden is deeper than it actually is. Also, because the routes presented by straight paths are direct and unobstructed, you will not be inclined to linger over individual plants and features; rather, your inclination will be to take in the whole garden in a series of glances, to appreciate it as the sum of its components, and to leave with a lasting, overall impression.

Paving materials with hard, straight edges are excellent choices for constructing formal paths. True, they are expensive and require skill to install,

A curved, informal slate path invites you to meander through this enchanting garden.
John Buysschaert

but on the upside, they are attractive, durable, and relatively maintenance free. Cut stone, bricks, concrete pavers, even poured concrete or frost-proof terracotta tiles make appropriate, comfortable walking surfaces. If your house is made of brick, it makes sense to create unity in the landscape by building complementary brick paths. Similarly, a cut stone path greatly enhances the appearance of a house with stone facing. Poured concrete, although plain by itself, has great visual appeal when

This wide formal path leads directly to a trellis-enclosed courtyard. Calgary Horticultural Society

stamped with one of the many patterns currently available or embedded with textured aggregate. Contrasting paving materials can be used in the same garden, especially to break up the monotony of large expanses of pavement; however, using too many different types can make the final result look busy.

Individual units of these paving materials require careful installation; they are usually secured in concrete on top of a well-prepared base, designed to prevent frost heaving during cold northern winters, and, as such, are permanent features. The exceptions are concrete pavers that are loosely laid on top of a base of gravel and sand, and then backfilled with sand. This gives them a degree of flexibility that other formal pavings don't have; a path made out of these pavers can be shifted or rearranged should the need arise.

Informal Paths. Homes of a less formal architectural style are well served by gently curving pathways. Although more difficult to design, in the long run they are also more adaptable. Curved paths mimic and are in harmony with the flowing, irregularly shaped flower beds of an informal garden. They encourage you to explore at a relaxed pace, to take your time, and to pause and enjoy the details and minutiae of a garden's design. At the same time the mystery of what lies waiting to be seen around the next bend prevents you from stopping dead in your tracks—it lures you on to explore further and discover the pleasures that await you.

Curved paths need a reason for curving, so must go around something substantial, such as a collection of shrubs or tall perennials, an interesting tree, or an arrangement of containers. Paths that meander for no apparent reason leave you wondering about their purpose. Also, to be effective, curved paths must proceed in broad sweeps, not in short wobbles; there is nothing beautiful, serene, or relaxing about a path that wiggles willy-nilly across the landscape.

The formal hard-edged paving materials described as suitable for straight paths can also be adapted for constructing informal walkways. Brick and concrete pavers lend themselves especially well to fitting into curved shapes, although their bold, straight lines must be softened by plants spilling over the path's margins for the informal look to be complete. Uncut natural flagstones, cobblestones, or stepping stones that are at least 30 cm (12 in.) across and mulches such as gravel, wood chips, leaves, and pine needles are also appropriate for informal paths. They are all easy to work with and relatively inexpensive to install. However, they do not define a path's edges very clearly, allowing bordering plants to encroach and become established within its boundaries, which is a look some like, but others do not. Also, mulch coverings, unobtrusive and natural looking as they are, break down quickly and therefore require constant replacement and considerable maintenance. The use of stepping stones should be restricted to secondary paths, since their

∾ Designing Steps ∾

It may be necessary to include steps in your path design to accommodate variable terrain on your property. Steps usually mark a transition and should be planned with comfort and safety in mind. To determine the ideal proportions of your steps, remember this rule of thumb: (2 x riser height) + depth of tread = 66 cm (26 in.).

The normal range in riser heights is from 10–18 cm (4–7 in.), and the depth of tread should be at least 30 cm (12 in.). The maximum number of steps in an unbroken flight ranges from 12 to 14. For more steps than this, break up the flight with a landing and possibly a change of direction.

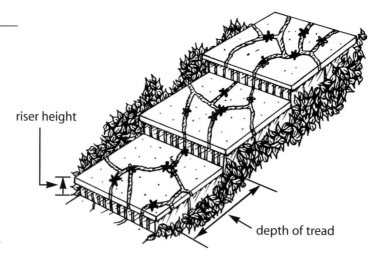

riser height

depth of tread

Steps to link varying garden elevations should be designed for comfort and safety. Grace Buzik

uneven surfaces force you to slow down and pay attention to your footing as well as the surrounding landscape.

Basic Path Design. Whatever the style, a pathway leading to the entrance of your home should be grand. It should be at least 1.5 m (5 ft) wide, the minimum width that will allow two people to approach walking side by side. All other primary paths that are vital to the flow of movement through your garden should be the same width. Less important secondary paths should be a minimum of 0.75 m (2.5 ft) wide, a comfortable width for walking single file. Make sure that every path has a purpose or a destination; avoid dead ends. In this regard, the best shape for a path would be a loop, conducting visitors through the garden and out again in a fluid motion. When this is not practical or possible, a path should, at the very least, lead you to an object or a special plant that gives you reason to linger before turning around to retrace your steps. Avoid building paths directly beside house or garage walls; they can be awkward for the pedestrian. Also, from a design point of view, foundation plantings make a smooth transition from house to garden.

Designing and installing the perfect system of paths in your garden may seem like a daunting task, as there are many details to be considered and decisions to make. However, it is well worth the effort; take the time to do it right. The coherence, unity, and visual satisfaction imparted by a well-conceived path definitely exert a positive influence on how your garden presents itself, to you and to the world around you.

Structures

A peek over the fences of most Calgary gardens would reveal few architectural structures apart from sheds or garages, those practical outbuildings for lawnmower and vehicle storage. How far we have come from the days when ornamental architecture was the height of garden fashion! Some of this tradition survives in the vocabulary of garden structures—belvedere, pavilion, gazebo, pergola, arch, arbour, and bower, romantic words evoking leisurely summer pastimes. Although we may feel nostalgia for a bygone elegance of the restrained variety, the history of garden structures shows an extreme lack of restraint that few of us would seek to emulate today.

In eighteenth-century England, garden architecture was popular, and ambitious structures were incorporated into natural surroundings. These elaborate playhouses for the wealthy, now referred to somewhat contemptuously as "follies," reflected a fascination with classical culture, the Orient, and the Gothic. Temples and mock ruins were located to give picturesque effect to a landscape that might also include artificial waterfalls, grottoes,

Arches can be used effectively to frame a focal point; in this garden the unique gate is compelling. CHARL DU TOIT

This old-fashioned gazebo provides a charming refuge from the midday sun.
JOHN BUYSSCHAERT

and caverns. The gardens of Princess Augusta at Kew, which were located on 40 ha (100 ac) of flat land, included a House of Confucius, a Gothic cathedral, a menagerie, 10 small temples or similar classically styled constructions, and 8 other buildings, including a Roman ruined arch, a mosque, an Alhambra, a Chinese open T'ing in the menagerie, and a pagoda.[21] All these buildings were built or restored between 1756 and 1763.

By the late eighteenth century, the picturesque English style of landscaping was carried to even further extremes on the continent. In the gardens of Count Hoditz in Silesia were a Chinese pagoda and temple, a Holy Grove, Druid caves with altars, a Christian hermitage, Indian pagodas, an antique mausoleum, and a town for dwarves (although dwarves being hard to come by, he had to make do with children).[22] It is no longer fashionable or practical to construct garden structures solely for ornamental purposes; they must be an integral part of the garden, supporting and complementing plantings, not overwhelming them, and in proportion to the available space.

There are many benefits to including structures in your garden. They provide vertical space upon which plants may grow (an advantage in small gardens) and can be attractive focal points or destinations at the ends of paths. Garden structures can also help establish microclimates and shield trees, shrubs, and perennials from the devastating effects of winter Chinook winds or summer hailstorms. Depending on your garden, budget, and the function you wish your structure to serve, you

A pergola casts light shade on a walkway or seating area, especially when covered with sheltering vines. CHARL DU TOIT

may erect something as substantial as a sheltering gazebo or as simple as a ready-made piece of trellis to screen and decorate a seating area.

If you wish to include structures in your garden plan, first consider what type of structure you require. Then, consider what materials best suit your garden design and complement your favourite plants, both climbers and those planted in the immediate vicinity. Do some research by touring prize-winning gardens or visiting the library or bookstores to find ideas that can be adapted to your style. Do-it-yourself books supply many plans as well as practical construction advice, or you can purchase easily assembled kits, either through garden centres or catalogues.

The transition from one garden room to another is marked by a small clematis-clad arbour. WINSTON GORETSKY

Remember to check the applicable local by-laws regarding building permits, set-backs, or height restrictions before you build any substantial structure. Finally, your garden is your sanctuary so indulge yourself and build that pagoda behind the peonies if you wish.

Gazebos. Gazebos, often called summerhouses, are ideally located on an eminence from which most of the garden may be viewed. With solid roofs and floors, gazebos provide the gardener with a place to escape from the midday sun or a prairie cloudburst while still enjoying the murmuring of bees or the fragrance the rain coaxes from flowers and earth. Ornate or large gazebos are best suited to expansive gardens, where they can be situated at a considerable distance from the house and will appear in proportion to the surrounding landscape. Gazebos may be also scaled down to fit

This Chinese-style pagoda is a folly built in the gardens of
Princess Augusta at Kew (1761). Grace Buzik

into smaller gardens and include space enough for only a few chairs
and a table.

There are many choices of materials and designs for your gazebo, from
the traditional white wooden gazebo complete with lattice-work, to
wrought-iron structures reminiscent of Victorian times. A wooden gazebo
stained in a soft shade of brown or grey for a slightly weathered look would
suit an informal garden, particularly one with a large proportion of indige-
nous prairie plants. Draped with native clematis or other hardy vines, it will
blend into the landscape as if it had been there for years. Gazebo roofs may
be pointed in Chinese pavilion style or domed, partially open or slatted and

∽ *Trompe l'oeil* ∽

Trompe l'oeil, which means "to trick the eye," is a technique used to create an illusion of greater space or depth than actually exists. *Trompe l'oeil* tricks in landscape design include gradually narrowing paths or borders to give false perspective, using plants with smaller leaves at a distance, and choosing background colours that tend to recede, such as blues, greys, and greens.

    Trompe l'oeil can also be whimsical and imaginative. Painted landscapes on walls can look like extensions of the garden and you can mimic the plants in the mural with shrubs or flowers in containers placed in front of it. Use an arch of trellis-work to frame a painted scene at the end of a path, as if you are peeking through a doorway to a secret garden. You can also create an illusory garden beyond a gate by mounting a mirror on a fence or wall, then building a false gate in front of the mirror. Your reflected garden will appear to be behind a gate, in another partly hidden garden room.

    Trompe l'oeil wall trellises are elegant deceptions, easily built and perfectly suited to small walled or fenced gardens or to balcony gardens. The trellis slats narrow toward the centre, as if receding into an alcove or tunnel. Plant flowering vines on your *trompe l'oeil* trellis, or mount a half-basket of a soft blue variety of trailing lobelia at the centre.

filled in with fast-growing climbers, or solid for greater protection from the elements.

If you wish to construct a gazebo near your house, the materials and design used should harmonize with, if not mimic, those characteristics of the house. Farther away from the house you have more latitude for creativity, even eccentricity, should you wish.

Pergolas. Pergolas are structures consisting of uprights joined with horizontal beams and

Constructed on a flat surface, a *trompe l'oeil* wall trellis gives the illusion of an alcove or tunnel; climbing vines will soften its edges. Grace Buzik

Even the smallest of gardens can be accented with a simple, informal arch.
VAL PRITCHARD

A formal brick archway announces the entrance to this beautiful Calgary garden.
LIESBETH LEATHERBARROW

cross-beams to form walkways. They are often used to link different areas of a garden. Usually vines are trained up and over this framework, providing light shade and privacy. The most practical type of pergola uprights for the average-sized garden are painted or stained wooden posts; however, metal posts or more monumental pillars of brick or stone may also be used. While rustic tree trunks either stripped or complete with bark are harmonious in a rural or informal garden setting, they will not last as long as other options.

If the uprights are spaced closely together, the pergola will be enclosed and tunnel-like; if you wish the pergola to be more open to the surrounding garden, space the uprights farther apart. The cross-beams may also be spaced closely if desired, providing additional plant support and a more roofed-in effect. The pergola must be high enough for an adult to walk beneath it, but the width is largely a matter of personal choice, as long as it is not so narrow as to appear completely unbalanced. Since the size of the pergola should be in proportion to the garden, a solution for small gardens is to modify the design by building the pergola against your house, thus creating a shaded gallery for either a walkway or a sitting area. No matter what style of pergola you choose, keep in mind that the uprights will be supporting not only the weight of the overhead beams, but also the climbing plants. Make sure that the posts are sturdy and set in concrete footings below the frost line and that heavy beams are bolted securely in place.

While pergolas are generally squared off in shape, tunnels and walkways may also be constructed as a series of linked, vine-draped arches. A graceful arched tunnel of wood or metal may frame a view of a sundial, statue, or even a simple bench. For the ambitious gardener with plenty of time and space, there is the sapling tunnel, created by a technique called pleaching. This involves training branches over a temporary wire framework to meet and interweave overhead.

A pergola-like structure that suits a small garden can be created by hanging chain or rope swags between uprights; if space permits, parallel rows can be set on either side of a path. As with a conventional pergola, train climbing plants up the uprights and along the swags.

Arbours. Arbours are generally simple, small structures consisting of a framework over which plants are trained to form a shaded green bower. An informal arbour may be constructed in a shaded corner against a backdrop of trees or shrubs by intertwining or weaving willow branches together and planting shade-tolerant vines to enclose the structure. A plain bench of wood or willow is all that is necessary to complete the picture. Arbours may also be made of painted trellis-work or metal and located in sunnier parts of your garden with roses or clematis trained over the framework. Relatively portable and adaptable to any style, they are a perfect choice for the tiny urban garden.

Arches. Arches are frequently used at the entrances to gardens, often in combination with decorative gates, and along pathways to help define individual garden rooms. They are particularly effective when used to frame a view, perhaps a well-composed monochromatic perennial bed or, in a smaller garden, a splendid container. Arches are generally lightweight, although sturdy enough to support climbing plants, and should be chosen to suit the style of your garden. If you wish to grow roses up the arch, you may prefer a traditional white wooden, trellis-work arch. Willow twig arches suit a wilder garden; those constructed of metal give a more formal effect and may be ornate or have clean, simple lines.

Trellises. The simplest kind of structure for your garden is a trellis. A trellis is a lattice or grid of slats, usually wooden, set in a frame and used as a screen or against a wall to support annual or perennial vines and other

---

∿ Trellising Tips ∿

Like successfully staked perennials, attractively trellised climbing plants will appear to be growing naturally, without sagging or conspicuous bindings. Consider the following tips if you have climbing plants in need of support.

- Ensure trellising systems are in place before you plant or as soon as climbers begin to grow in the spring.
- Some climbing plants, such as roses, need to be tied to trellises; as they grow, attach shoots securely with twine or with cushioned or plastic plant ties. Inspect plants regularly so you can tie up errant shoots while they are still pliable.
- Choose trellising material to suit the weight of the plants to be supported: strong nylon netting for annual vines, peas, or pole or runner beans; wooden, plastic, or heavy wire trellises for weightier stems, foliage, and blooms, such as honeysuckle, clematis, or roses.
- Remove tender climbing roses from trellises for the winter. Lay the canes on the ground and protect well with an insulating mulch after the first hard frost. Use tall hardy roses as climbers, such as 'John Cabot', 'William Baffin', and 'The Polar Star'. These do not require winter protection.
- Prevent cucumbers and squash from rotting by tying them onto horizontal or vertical trellises.
- Trellises do not have to be big; train nasturtiums up small trellises in containers. These may be purchased or you can construct your own with wood or willow twigs.
- Make portable hinged A-frame trellises of scrap lumber and wire mesh for the vegetable garden.
- Create teepees by lashing together the tops of bamboo poles and wrapping with nylon netting. Leave an opening between two of the poles for a children's hideaway. Plant peas, scarlet runner beans, or annual vines such as sweet peas, canarybird vine, black-eyed Susan vine, morning glory, or cup-and-saucer vine.
- Plant a small-flowered clematis under a tree and help it clamber up into the branches.
- Train self-clinging perennial vines such as Engelmann ivy on trellises, instead of allowing them to climb up house walls. When it is time to paint your house, the trellises can be temporarily detached from the wall and laid on the ground without removing the vine.

types of plants that may be trained as climbers. As they can be purchased or built to suit the available space, trellises are adaptable to small spaces; they may be set against walls or fences, or used free-standing as privacy screens and to provide enticing glimpses through to other areas of your garden. Trellis-work may also be incorporated into panels on fences or gates. The traditional patterns for trellises to support plants are often simple diamond or square designs, but if your trellis will not be obscured by flowers and foliage, you can choose a more ornate pattern or even an intricate fretwork design. At the opposite extreme, you can create an informal trellis by nailing or lashing together branches you have saved from tree pruning. Plastic trellises are also available; they require less maintenance than wooden ones, but are less aesthetically pleasing.

Trellis panels may form the basis for larger structures or garden rooms. Join them together to form a semi-enclosed area, either for seating or a special small garden within a garden. Less confined than a fenced-off area, the trellis room allows inviting glimpses inside.

Working with Landscapers

Many Calgary gardeners have the knowledge, confidence, desire, skills, and time to both design and implement their own garden landscape. There are others who lack experience and knowledge but love taking risks; they, too, usually try to develop a pleasing landscape without professional assistance. Then there are those who for a variety of reasons choose to hire professional landscapers.

Professional landscapers are trained to help you develop an attractive outdoor environment that complements your property and frames your home in much the same way a picture frame enhances a painting. People have many different needs and wants, and good landscapers will take all of them into consideration, tying them together into a unified whole. Not only will they provide you with the blueprints for a satisfactory design, complete with planting schemes, they will also be able to serve as contractors, providing the raw materials and skilled labour to implement your design, should you so desire.

Some landscapers are comfortable designing in any garden style; others develop and market a limited concept that can accommodate some personal preferences, but essentially remains a single bill of goods that may or may not fulfil your wishes. Keep that in mind when you interview landscapers. If you like the look being marketed by a landscaper, go for it. Otherwise, choose one with more flexibility who can understand your vision and incorporate your ideas.

'John Cabot', a hardy Explorer rose, can be trained to climb trellises and provides fragrant pink blooms all summer.

Whether you need the whole landscaping package (design and installation included), just the design blueprints to do the job yourself, or the design and installation of just one feature (such as a pathway or a deck), the process for selecting the right help is the same. First, have a clear idea of what you want and how much you are willing to spend. Then, find someone who will do the job for a reasonable price in a reasonable amount of time, making sure you check out his or her reliability, credentials, and references.

Before heading out in search of a landscaping professional, take some time to figure out and write down what your minimum requirements are so you can discuss them with prospective contractors. First, jot down some notes on how you intend to use your garden. Then, make a list of the hard landscaping features that you would like to include, such as decks, patios, and pathways, and make a rough sketch of where you would like them to go—if you have any preferences. Record the dimensions of the front and back yards on your sketch and where your house and garage are located. Pictures of the front and back yard showing current views of the house and its surroundings will also be helpful. If you are clear on the style of garden you would like to create (for example, formal, cottage, or prairie theme) or about a specific element you would like included in your design, take along pictures from books or magazines to illustrate your plans. Other information you should be prepared to provide includes what types of trees, shrubs, and plants are "must-haves" for you, whether you would like a high- or low-maintenance design, and your budget.

So, how do you choose a landscaper? The best starting point would be a recommendation from a friend or knowledgeable gardener. Otherwise, interview as many landscapers as you can, either in their workplaces or at seasonal home and garden shows, where many of them will have displays. Check whether or not they have graduated from a recognized horticultural institution, such as Olds College, or are members of the Landscape Alberta Nursery and Trades Association (LANTA), remembering that experience counts for something, especially when someone has lots of it. Ask to see pictures of completed projects to get a feel for their design styles and whether they appeal to you. Pay attention to the plant density when studying photos of their newly planted gardens. Good landscapers will plant shrubs and trees with mature size in mind, making provision to fill the necessary gaps with annuals and portable perennials until maturity has been reached and trees and shrubs fill their allotted spaces. The same holds true for perennials. Less-than-responsible landscapers plant enough trees, shrubs, and perennials in a given area to make it look lush at the time they are asking for their cheques! To an inexperienced customer this looks wonderful, but such dense planting usually leads to severe overcrowding and the subsequent need to remove many of the plants.

If you like what you see in the portfolios of individual landscapers, continue your initial discussions with them by describing the ideas you have in mind for your garden, using the notes and pictures you have brought with you. Take careful note of their responses; good landscapers will listen to you, be receptive to your ideas, and offer creative suggestions and solutions without overpowering you with personal preferences. Also enquire about their rates, both for putting a plan down on paper and for transforming the plan into reality.

Finally, ask for references and do the follow-up, interviewing previous customers to see if they found their landscapers to be reliable, accommodating, efficient, and on target for budgeting and scheduling. A quick call to the local Better Business Bureau and to LANTA to ask if any complaints have been registered against a particular company would also be worth your while. By the time you have interviewed several landscapers and discussed your plans with them, you should have enough information to make a well-informed choice.

TWO

The Decorative Gardener

Although a real garden is never "done," it does evolve to a point where you are confident that you are on the right track and that, in due course, the various design elements will come together in a pleasing way. When you have reached that stage (or sooner, if you have the opportunity), it's fun to spend some time thinking about the finishing touches, about what might appeal in terms of accents, ornaments, and furniture. For instance, a garden design can be strengthened by the addition of a unique focal point, enhanced by an unusual collection of terracotta containers, or enriched by the presence of a distinctive wooden bench. Ornaments that remain outside year-round also provide winter interest in the garden and a sense of constancy, a link from one season to the next. Water features in all shapes and sizes figure prominently in the history of garden adornment and capture your attention in a dynamic way, alive as they are with movement and sound; many features available today make a splash in even the smallest of spaces. So, too, a collection of containers, skilfully planted with simple or lavish combinations of colour, texture, fragrance, and form, can serve as a focal point, commanding your attention with its unique style and dazzling beauty.

The guidelines for choosing garden ornaments are few and simple. Most important, select objects that delight and satisfy you, that reflect your personality, and that reveal the spirit of your garden. A little goes a long way, however, and whatever you choose should work with the other elements of your garden, complementing its overall appearance.

Ornaments

Formal Ornaments. One source of inspiration for ornamentation is found in traditional garden designs that are lavish in their use of accents. Sculpture, wall medallions, sundials, and gazing globes are some of the many features that have given pleasure in landscapes through the ages and beg to be copied or modified for use in urban gardens.

Regretfully, there are some traditional ornamental garden features that do not adapt as well to the needs of the modern gardener. In the case of columns and obelisks, their majestic dimensions make them impractical for the average urban lot; the same holds true for grottoes—small natural or artificial caves often used to house some type of ornament, perhaps the statue of a god or goddess or a small water feature. In the case of decorative stone or brick walls, their cost is prohibitive for many Calgarians.

Statuary. A sculpture can serve as a dramatic focal point in a formal setting, making a bold gesture, or it can merge with the garden foliage in a less formal environment where its discovery comes as a welcome surprise. Simple walls and hedges make excellent backdrops for statuary, with small niches or decorative alcoves setting sculptures off to advantage in a more subtle way. Place formal sculptures at the centre of a circular lawn, at the end of a vista, or at the intersection of two paths; situate less formal figures under shrubs or large, architectural plants, among ornamental grasses, at the edge of a pool, or around the bend in a path.

Although original stone sculptures are almost impossible to find and expensive to purchase, well-made inexpensive replicas are available in garden centres and specialty shops. Many of these pieces have been modelled on classic European lines with flowing robes, nymphs, angels, and cherubs featuring prominently in their design. Such sculptures are logical additions to any formal landscape. Especially appealing to gardeners might be statues of Priapus (the Greek god of fertility and gardens), Flora (the Roman goddess of flowers), Venus (the Roman goddess of the rose and guardian of gardens), and Saints Phocas and Fiacre, both patron saints of the garden. However, don't limit your search for statuary to the purely classical. Modern sculptures enhance gardens of a contemporary character, just as the diminutive forms of woodland creatures and carved wooden sculptures are more appropriate in natural surroundings.

Most stone sculptures require very little upkeep, their appearance improving with age as they are exposed to the natural elements. As with all garden ornaments, you can leave them outside year-round if you are certain they won't crack or shatter during the numerous freeze-and-thaw cycles of a Calgary winter. If you are unsure about an object's durability, play it safe and bring it inside for winter's duration.

Sundials. Sundials have served both a practical and an ornamental function in gardens since the Middle Ages, although their invention dates back to ancient times. They are currently experiencing a revival in the gardenscape, having temporarily fallen out of favour at the turn of the century. There are two styles of sundials: those that are mounted horizontally on a low pedestal and those mounted vertically on a wall. Whichever you

Feeders help attract birds to the garden; festooned with wild cucumber vines, this one also has considerable ornamental value. MAUREEN IRETON

A favourite garden statue adds a focal point and character to your landscape year-round.
LIESBETH LEATHERBARROW

A traditional sundial is an eye-catching feature of this splendid Calgary rose garden. DON HEIMBECKER

choose, make sure you situate your sundial in a spot that remains sunny most of the day; otherwise, it will look out of place. If you plan to use your sundial to tell time, you will have to calibrate the angle of the gnomon (the sloping part that casts a shadow) for Calgary's latitude; instructions on how to do this are usually provided at the time of purchase.

Sundials make a great focal point in a symmetrical flowered, sunny courtyard, or on a terrace. They were traditionally used at the centre of knot gardens, collections of herbs grown in elaborate, symmetrical patterns and outlined by small clipped hedges. Sundials convey character when encircled by a profusion of herbs and roses, an old-fashioned plant combination that reinforces the sundial's place in history. The armillary sphere, a series of concentric metal hoops that show the progress of the planets across the sky, is an attractive alternative to the sundial.

Wall Decorations. As in any interior room, the walls enclosing your outdoor garden room offer fresh opportunity for accent. The ubiquitous wooden Calgary fence comes to life when adorned with an ornate medallion, a medieval-style stone mask or gargoyle, a tiled panel, a wooden wall planter, a ceramic sun face, or a wall-mounted fountain, each of which stands out when draped by the soft flowing lines of clinging annual and perennial vines.

Gazing Globes. An unusual but fascinating addition to garden decor is the gazing globe, a mirrored glass sphere

Ordinary bricks spring to life when adorned with a fanciful wall decoration. VAL PRITCHARD

Playful and unexpected, this grand chess set provides a welcome diversion on warm summer evenings. LIESBETH LEATHERBARROW

Whimsy is the key to this marvellous collection of *objets trouvés*. RENATA WICHMANN

ranging in size from 20–35 cm (8–14 in.) and prominently displayed on a pedestal or, less conspicuously, on the ground. It will capture images of the sky and surrounding garden over a wide range of angles. Use gazing globes singly to reflect images of colour, texture, and form in the garden and to give the illusion of space. Alternatively, arrange several in a pleasing cluster to create the mesmerizing effect of reflections within reflections within reflections. Because they are made from glass, gazing globes should not be placed where they are in danger of being broken, namely, close to a children's play area or under trees during windy weather when there is a danger of falling branches.

Informal Ornaments. Informal ornaments lack the history and definition associated with their more formal counterparts. Instead they mirror the personalities of their modern owners, who do not feel compelled by tradition when selecting the finishing touches for their gardens. Although informal objects most often grace the landscape in informal garden designs, they can introduce an element of pleasant surprise in a more formal setting when chosen and sited with care.

∽ Topiary ∽

Topiary is the art of clipping trees and shrubs into geometric or other decorative shapes. The Romans were enthusiastic practitioners of topiary, cutting fleets of ships and hunting scenes out of box and cypress. Pliny the Younger, a man who wrote of his garden with great delight, described clipped animals and box hedges cut out to spell names.[23] Not surprisingly, topiary was a feature of Italian Renaissance gardens, and the fashion spread to northern Europe. The Dutch were fond of topiary statues and the Dutch formal style was imitated in England, particularly when William and Mary acceded to the English throne in 1689 from Holland. Literary giants Alexander Pope and Joseph Addison were among those who railed against the excessive use of unnaturally clipped evergreens, and the practice fell out of fashion until the nineteenth century.[24]

Traditional topiary styles include domes, spirals, pyramids, and cylinders surmounted by balls, which today would appear out of place except in the most formal gardens. These days a gardener armed with a sharp pair of shears, imagination, and a sense of humour is more likely to add a touch of the fantastic with green sculptured animals or favourite objects inhabiting a less formal space. The best trees and shrubs for topiary are those recommended for hedges, as they tolerate the frequent clipping necessary to keep them in shape.

Some evergreen container-grown trees and shrubs are also suitable for clipping into shapes; however, they will not survive a Calgary winter outside so will need to be brought indoors. Try using dwarf cultivars of boxwood (*Buxus microphylla* 'Compacta', *B. m.* var. *koreana*) and yew (*Taxus baccata* 'Repandens', *T. cuspidata* 'Aurescens'). These can be overwintered indoors, but since they require a period of dormancy, they should be stored in a cold room with a winter temperature from 4° C to -2° C (39° F - 28° F). Myrtle (*Myrtus communis*) and rosemary (*Rosmarinus officinalis*) can also be used and will survive indoors at normal room temperatures; they do not require a period of dormancy.

Small-scale topiary may also be formed from wire and metal frames bent to create whatever shape you desire, stuffed with moss and planted with creeping plants such as English ivy (*Hedera helix*). English ivy will overwinter indoors; other favourite perennial groundcovers will not and therefore must be replanted in the topiary each year.

∽ Espalier ∽

Espalier, from the French "something to lean against," is a traditional method of training plants to grow in two dimensions, against walls, wires, or fences. Espaliered fruit trees were grown in walled towns in medieval Europe, when it was necessary to produce fruit within the town during sieges. As space was limited, the trees were grown flat against walls, where the reflected heat and increased exposure to sunlight and air resulted in earlier and larger fruit.[25] Because of these advantages, espaliered fruit trees became common in Europe, England, and, later, America. Espaliered apple trees produce fruit more quickly than standard trees, take up little space, and add year-round sculptural interest to the garden.

Espaliers may be grown on walls or trained to form free-standing fences. If an espaliered tree is grown against a wall, it is wise to leave about 15-cm (6-in.) clearance between the tree and the wall to allow room for circulation and working space; a wooden trellis or strands of heavy gauge wire strung between posts may be used to support the growing tree. A location that provides at least six hours of sunlight a day is necessary for espaliered fruit trees.

There are many different espalier patterns to choose from, some simple and some requiring much time, patience, and skill. You can even design your own free-form espalier if you wish.

In Calgary, apple or crabapple trees are the most reliable fruit trees to espalier. You can also try shrubs that produce flowers or fruit on old wood, such as Amur or Schubert chokecherry, cotoneaster, or wayfaring tree. Check in the library or bookstores for specialized books on growing and pruning espaliered trees.

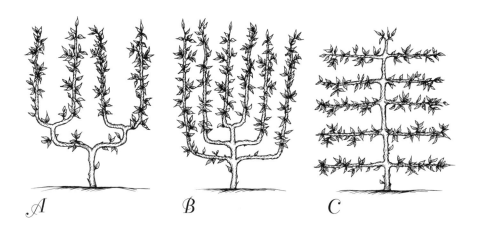

$\mathcal{A}$ $\mathcal{B}$ C

Simple espalier patterns for training the branches of fruit trees include: (a) double U, (b) palmette, and (c) horizontal T. GRACE BUZIK

These cedar trees have been clipped into decorative shapes and are a fine example of informal topiary.

LIESBETH LEATHERBARROW

Objets trouvés. The creative and innovative use of *objets trouvés*—found objects that don't necessarily have a history of adorning gardens—adds humour, whimsy, and endless possibility to informal landscapes. Again, understatement is the key to success. Too much of a good thing can end up giving the garden a cluttered or even tacky feeling.

Wooden folk art cutouts are popular *objets trouvés*; whether they portray a family of chickens strutting across the lawn or a bouquet of tulips permanently arranged in a favourite container, they are a delight in country-style gardens with a rural or pastoral ambiance. A collection of old gardening implements left carelessly abandoned throughout the garden to weather naturally, an old straw bee skep, or a worn pair of leather boots are also in keeping with a rural theme. The paraphernalia of bird lovers are also eye-catching in the natural garden, with bird-baths, feeders, and an assortment of nesting boxes making a splendid display against a verdant backdrop. You are limited only by your imagination in your search for the unexpected but perfect *objet trouvé*. Explore antique stores, flea markets, jumble sales, art and craft fairs, and import shops—you never know what treasures you might find!

Natural Objects. Garden ornaments need not be restricted to the artificial, manufactured type. Many natural objects and plants can provide the ideal resting place for your eyes as you wander through the garden. A dry stream bed meandering across the property, realistically constructed with pebbles, cobbles, and small boulders, can have as much visual impact as a real stream, yet requires no maintenance once it has been constructed. Similarly, a ribbon of groundcover such as thyme, bordered by cobbles on its "banks," creates the illusion of a water feature and will inevitably capture your attention as it transects the lawn. Topiary, created by pruning plants into geometric or realistic three-dimensional shapes, results in the addition of living sculptures to the landscape; as such, they make charming focal points in a formal setting. Espaliered fruit trees, those trained into pleasing two-dimensional shapes, usually against a flat surface such as a wall or a fence, are also pleasures to behold. Even a small pile of rounded boulders, a fallen log, or a forgotten stump in a woodland garden can make the difference between the ordinary and the special.

Garden Furniture

All gardeners should have at least one spot where they can steal a moment to sit and enjoy the fruits of their labours, to smell the roses, to contemplate the universe, to curl up with a book, or just to rest their feet. Such a seating arrangement can be purely functional, purely decorative, or a bit of both. It can be as simple and inexpensive as an upended log placed beneath a tree in the far reaches of the garden, or as sophisticated as one of the many lovely outdoor furniture sets available today, perfect for dining alfresco on a patio or deck.

As well as suiting the mood of your garden, furniture must also meet your maintenance requirements. Wooden country-style benches and Adirondack chairs left to weather naturally to a soft silver-grey will blend with the landscape in cottage and woodland gardens, offering a subtle invitation to take a time out. Other than the periodic application of a water sealant to prevent rotting, they require no care; they may also be left outside during the winter. In addition, bent willow and unpainted wicker furniture are perfect in the informal garden, though wicker must be sheltered from inclement weather in both summer and winter unless it is specifically labelled for outdoor use.

The same natural-look furniture painted pristine white or some other bright colour will contrast vividly with the background, calling attention to itself and issuing a clear invitation to sit and relax. Painted furniture requires a commitment to annual upkeep and winter protection.

Cast cement and artificial stone benches are long-lived and fairly maintenance free. They can be simple or ornate and look at home in a formal setting. Though cement or stone benches are often cold and hard to sit on, many gardeners find it worth their while to sacrifice a bit of comfort for visual appeal. A small portable cushion will relieve the discomfort, and a pot of colourful annuals and perennials perched at the end of a stone bench adds the finishing touch to an enchanting vignette.

Reproduction wrought and cast iron furniture are other excellent choices for the formal garden, evoking images of romance and days gone by. Although longer-lived when offered winter protection, either may be left outdoors in the winter garden, where it can work

Rustic bent-willow furniture is perfectly suited to this shaded woodland garden retreat.
Calgary Horticultural Society

magic under a light dusting of snow. Unfortunately, they too require some maintenance. Check for rust spots in the spring and paint just these spots or the whole piece of furniture, as required, with paint specially formulated for cast or wrought iron.

Moulded resin furniture is popular as it requires no upkeep and is comfortable to sit on. It is also light and usually stackable, making it easy both to move around the garden and to store in winter. Because of its style, resin furniture is suitable for contemporary gardens; its modern lines would look out of place in most other garden settings.

A garden is meant to be viewed from many vantage points, so when positioning your outdoor furniture, don't limit yourself to the one logical location close to the house. Why not place another seat in a special place where you can enjoy the early morning or late afternoon sun, at the top of a flight of stairs, at the end of a path, in front of a warm wall, at the edge of a pond, or in the midst of an inviting cluster of scented plants? Then, having chosen and furnished your favourite spots, remember to take the time to enjoy them, to revel in the scenery that surrounds them, and to take a well-deserved break from the everyday hustle and bustle of living!

Containers

Container gardening—ancient Egyptian, Roman, Greek, and Chinese gardeners did it; medieval and Victorian gardeners did it; and, increasingly, modern-day gardeners are doing it too. Container-grown plants have enjoyed popularity throughout the ages for good reason; their low maintenance, cleanliness, convenience, and mobility all contribute to their appeal and success. From the colourful impact of bright flowers welcoming visitors and passers-by on a front step to a small bounty of vegetables and herbs on a balcony, container gardens open up endless planting and design possibilities.

Grouping carefully planted pots can transform a patio, terrace, or balcony almost instantly. Use container plantings to soften the sharp edges of a pool, deck, or wall. If areas of your garden are bare or boring as seasonal flowers fade, fill in the gaps with vigorously blooming bulbs, annuals, or perennials in containers. Container-grown plants can form a good basis for "vertical gardens" through the use of wall pots, window boxes, and hanging baskets, which add interest to stark, unsightly walls and fences. If garden space is limited or non-existent, an entire flower or vegetable garden may be planted in containers and located on a balcony or rooftop.

For those who enjoy growing plants normally unsuited to the Calgary climate or soil, containers provide semi-controlled conditions as soil mixtures may be matched to the individual plant's requirements. Provided they are not too heavy, containers may be relocated to sheltered spots, or even brought indoors, to better survive the vicissitudes of the average Calgary summer.

Containers suitable for growing plants come in a wide variety of styles and materials. No matter what you choose, make sure they have adequate drainage holes. You may select from containers made of clay, wood, metal, concrete, plastic, stone, fibreglass, or glazed ceramic. When choosing a material, keep in mind that timber and metal containers require some maintenance; clay, concrete, and glazed ceramic containers are susceptible to frost; and those popular wooden barrels may have stored toxic materials, making them unacceptable—check before you buy! It is wise to stick with pots of one style or material when planning an arrangement; introduce variety by combining pots of different heights, shapes, and designs within the chosen style. An odd number of planters in a grouping is more pleasing to the eye than an even number.

The size of container you choose depends on the type of plants for which it is destined. Annuals do well in pots 23–30 cm (9–12 in.) deep, perennials prefer pots deeper than 30 cm (12 in.), and shrubs and trees require still bigger containers.

Large pots should be positioned before they are filled with soil; otherwise, they will be too heavy to move. Experiment with a number of different locations and arrangements, viewing them from all angles in the garden and the house (even from upstairs!) before making a final decision. When the perfect spot has been chosen, place the containers directly on a hard, level surface, supported by blocks or in saucers.

Containers to Enhance Garden Style. The containers you choose should enhance your garden style. Few garden themes cannot be evoked through the use of container gardens, and some of the most adaptable are woodland, formal, oriental, western, and cottage styles.

Woodland. If you have a tree- and shrub-filled garden with ferns, violets, Jacob's ladder, and Solomon's seal underfoot, you may want to opt for woodland-style containers. Planters made of cedar or other woods are good choices, as are twig baskets or half-barrels. Hollowed-out stumps or logs and old watering cans provide a little whimsy in the woodland garden.

Formal. For a more urban or formal garden, there are many types of planters from which to choose. To emphasize a formal look, you must use restraint in the number of container varieties selected, or the formality quickly relaxes. Consider limiting the selection of flower colours, too, unless you prefer the juxtaposition of a riot of colours against a formal container. Urns on either side of a doorway, each filled with a monochromatic arrangement of plants, will enhance and define an entrance. Use strategically placed urns as a focal point at the end of a garden path or at the centre of a formal

Hen and chicks sprout from the hub of an old wagon wheel, surrounded by a magnificent display of container-grown plants. VAL PRITCHARD

A collection of shade-loving begonias and ferns tumbles from an over-turned wooden barrel. IRENA BURNS

Formal planters can be used successfully in an informal setting; these pots accentuate the browns and greys of the surrounding stones. CALGARY HORTICULTURAL SOCIETY

garden. There are also faux lead and copper planters that will fit nicely into a formal scene, as will planters with cherub and garland motifs. Classic terracotta pots will pick up the warm earth tones of the brick facing on your house.

Oriental. If your urban look has a strong emphasis on foliage and evergreens, you may want to evoke an oriental feeling. Reasonably priced ceramic pots from Chinatown can be planted with foliage and grasses or used to create a small, above-ground water feature. Another idea is to lay three small rocks on a bed of sand in a small, flat ceramic tray, and using fork tines, rake around them for a miniature Japanese sand garden.

Western. Perhaps living under big blue Alberta skies leads to a preference for a prairie theme. A half-barrel filled with prairie wildflowers or grasses fits this style, as do a few hen and chicks or other succulents winking from a bleached steer skull or filling up old cowboy boots. For a south-western look, select terracotta pots painted either in Navaho patterns or a Mexican motif.

Cottage. The original English cottage garden was created by people of the working class who did not have the money to spend on ornaments or containers for their gardens. Today, the make-do philosophy, originally born out of necessity, allows for plenty of whimsy and charm, yet is environmentally responsible in its emphasis on recycling. Wicker baskets make delightful containers and small vines can be trained to twine up the handles. An old bird cage can take on new life as a hanging planter. The make-do cottage style, however, can become a hodge-podge rather than a theme, depending on your personal taste and tolerance for clutter. If this starts to happen, unify disparate containers by spray-painting them to coordinate with each other or with your house trim.

Unique and Unusual Containers. Selecting containers to fit a theme requires forethought, but it does not have to be all serious. Containers can be a playful addition to the garden; your creativity and sense of humour are the only limiting factors. One Calgary Horticultural Society garden competition winner had a set of old worn work boots laid casually at the back door as if someone had returned from a hard day's work. From the tops and peeking through a hole in the toes and sides of the tongue of the boots were several hen and chicks.

Other unique ideas may be found in Calgary gardens. One featured a lawn chair elegantly displayed—set on the lawn with a seat of groomed turf. The seat had been hollowed out and a shallow tray inserted for growing grass. Another garden casually showed jeans presented as if hanging out to dry, with flowers growing from the pockets, worn-out knees, and waistband. If you live on a lake or a river, you can enhance that voyageur setting by letting an old leaky canoe take on a new life as a planter. You might set the canoe in a lake of thyme or other groundcovers. The selection of containers expands when you keep in mind that containers do not themselves have to be capable of holding soil. Garbage or freezer bags, punctured for drainage, can be used to line wicker and twig baskets or to hold the soil to conform to a container shape. Pots can also be placed in a container to protect the actual planter.

Container Plantings. After you have chosen containers to enhance your garden style, it is time to select plants, keeping in mind the planned location of the container to determine if you will

When choosing plants for delicately painted oriental pots, emphasize foliage texture rather than bloom colour. Liesbeth Leatherbarrow

The choices for unusual containers are limitless; these old boots are a product of imagination at work. Myrna Ross

Rectangular planters overflow with a stunning display of schizanthus, marigolds, geraniums, lobelia, and Swan River daisies in vivid rainbow hues. Liesbeth Leatherbarrow

∾ Growing Media for Containers ∾

When choosing a growing medium for your pots, you have two choices—soil-based or soil-less. Each has distinct advantages and disadvantages. A good soil-based mixture consists of a combination of sterilized loam, peat, sand, and nutrients. It holds the moisture well, has good drainage, and requires feeding less regularly than a soil-less medium. Do not use garden soil in containers. It is too heavy and will become hard and crusted on the surface, making it difficult to determine when to water. A slow-release fertilizer may be added to soil-based mixes.

The soil-less medium is peat-based and very lightweight. It usually also contains vermiculite and perlite. Soil-less mixtures are available for purchase pre-mixed, or you may mix your own to suit your needs and preferences. The lightness of a soil-less mixture makes it ideal for filling large pots on balconies or roofs where weight can be a concern. However, this is not an advantage for large plants, which become top-heavy and therefore blow or tip over more easily. A soil-less mixture will also not hold moisture as well as a soil-based growing medium, so plants should be watered more frequently. Do not allow soil-less mixtures to dry out completely, as they can be very difficult to moisten again. Container plants in this type of growing medium require frequent feeding with a liquid fertilizer. Some commercially available potting mixes include beads of a gel-like substance that help retain moisture, or you may purchase these separately and add them yourself.

∾ Sample Container Plantings ∾

Pink/purple theme for a medium container in semi-shade

Godetia (*Clarkia amoena*)
Heliotrope (*Heliotropium arborescens*)
Swan River daisy (*Brachycome iberidifolia*)
Trailing lobelia, mixed colours (*Lobelia erinus*)
White daisy (*Chrysanthemum paludosum*)

Yellow theme for a large container in a sunny location

Canarybird vine (*Tropaeolum peregrinum*)
Fried egg plant (*Limnanthes douglasii*)
Gazania (*Gazania*)
Orange/yellow daisy (*Ursinia anthemoides*)
Purple heart (*Setcreasea pallida*)
Purple sage (*Salvia officinalis* 'Purpurea')
Yellow cosmos (*Cosmos bipinnatus*)
Yellow sanvitalia (*Sanvitalia procumbens*)

need sun-loving or shade plants. Whether you are planning a scheme for the entire garden or a single planter, pay attention to plant height, breadth, and colour; contrast in foliage shape, texture, and size; scent; and seasonal interest.

In a formal arrangement, the height of plants can be the same or similar. Informal arrangements are often planted from back to front in the following order: tall, medium, short, groundcover, and trailing. The groundcover and trailing plants at the front soften the rim of the container and add breadth and body to the arrangement.

When considering what flower colours to include in a planter, avoid too many contrasts as this confuses the eye. Usually a combination of two or three bright colours, balanced by green foliage and highlighted by white, gives a pleasing effect. A scheme limited to varying shades of one colour can also have visual impact, but then careful attention must be paid to selecting a variety of shapes in the flowers and leaves. Do not choose plants that are too close in colour to the container and keep the background in mind. Strong contrast shows plants to their best advantage and prevents the possibility of "losing" the arrangement through camouflage.

There are a number of effective combinations of foliage shape, texture, and size that are worth trying. Mix tall, spiky, or broad tongue-like shapes with denser, lower-growing ovals, circles, and pointed shapes. Place short, compact, formal foliage plants in the same container as less formal sprawling plants. Combine hard, shiny evergreen leaves with soft, thick, hairy leaves. Do not limit yourself to annuals; many favourite perennials perform admirably in containers and can be heeled into a flower bed to overwinter. The possibilities are endless.

Variety and continuity of bloom can be maintained in an area of a garden by rotating through a series of pots containing plants of seasonal interest. Such a sequence might be: spring bulbs and perennials; summer annuals, tender bulbs, and perennials; autumn bulbs and perennials; and, finally, containers filled with evergreen boughs, berries, and everlastings to provide colour and texture during the winter.

Alpine Troughs. If you enjoy hiking in the mountains, you have probably marvelled at the exquisite beauty of diminutive alpine plants that grace montane meadows in profusion despite the harsh growing conditions. Their delicate foliage and dainty flowers belie the ruggedness of their existence; the varied palette of their bloom colours casts a gentle glow on both grassy inclines and rocky talus slopes.

Although you can't bring the mountains to your backyard, you can re-create miniature alpine landscapes in hypertufa troughs. These troughs are constructed of a mixture of cement, perlite or vermiculite, peat moss, Fibermesh (a cement strengthener), and an optional concrete colourant, which is packed in moulds and allowed to dry and cure. The finished

Easy-to-make alpine troughs are ideal containers for growing specialized alpine plants. VAL PRITCHARD

troughs can be square, rectangular, bowl-shaped, or free-form. Do not plant your troughs until they are completely cured, which takes at least one month from pouring. Uncured, the high lime content in the hypertufa will leach into the soil, where it has the potential to kill your alpines.

When choosing alpines for your troughs, remember that many of these miniature plants can be accommodated in a small space. Look for the same range of colours, forms, and textures as you would for a herbaceous border. The variety among alpine plants is truly amazing, so you will have no trouble creating pleasing combinations.

When the trough is ready for planting, fill it with a specialized, free-draining, gritty soil mix. Be sure to incorporate distinct levels in your design, through the use of small rocks and terraces, to mimic an alpine environment and provide the nooks and crannies that alpines love. Then, plant your new alpine collection and cover the soil surface with small stone chips. The chips will keep the soil cool, the moisture out, and prevent direct contact between the soil and the plants' crowns.

Plants in new troughs will grow vigorously at first, drawing upon the natural supply of nutrients in the fresh soil. This growth spurt ends after a year, at which time you should begin a regime of supplemental springtime feeding. Adding bone meal or a fertilizer high in phosphorus (high middle number) to the soil will help maintain healthy plants.

∾ Alpine Plants to Grow in Troughs ∾

Columbine (*Aquilegia jonesii*)
Draba (*Draba incerta*)
Jacob's ladder (*Polemonium viscosum*)
Lewisia (*Lewisia pygmaea*)
Lungwort (*Mertensia viridis*)
Moss campion (*Silene acaulis*)
Rock jasmine (*Androsace* spp.)

Sandwort (*Arenaria obtusiloba*)
Saxifrage (*Saxifraga bronchialis,
S. cochlearis minor, S. paniculata minutissimum*)
Spring gentian (*Gentiana verna*)
Townsendia (*Townsendia exscapa*)

Alpines in troughs need special attention to survive Calgary's drying winter Chinooks and extremely cold temperatures. Try burying your trough in the ground and covering it with a pile of leaves, straw, or evergreen boughs; alternatively, leave your trough *in situ* and surround it in its entirety with a thick layer of leaves, straw, or evergreen boughs. To prevent rodents from taking advantage of this cosy bed and enjoying mid-winter snacks on your alpines, wait until the ground has frozen to cover them. Secure the coverings with twine or burlap.

Winter Containers. Although most gardeners only think of container plantings as attractive additions to the summer garden, they also can be used to advantage in the winter landscape. An artful arrangement of colourful deciduous and evergreen branches in a simple clay pot lends beauty and seasonal interest to the front entrance of your home. A light dusting of snow adds to the charm of your display.

ᧉ Materials for Winter Containers ᧉ

Start collecting suitable materials for your winter container during the spring and summer when you are attending to pruning chores in your garden.

Evergreen branches

Blue Colorado spruce (*Picea pungens* 'Glauca')
Cedar (*Thuja* spp.)
Juniper (*Juniperus* spp.)
Mugho pine (*Pinus mugo*)
White spruce (*Picea glauca*)

Deciduous branches for bark

Amur chokecherry (*Prunus maackii*) - polished cinnamon-gold
Birch (*Betula* spp.) - black
Golden elder (*Sambucus nigra* 'Aurea') - golden/green
Pincherry (*Prunus pennsylvanica*) - reddish brown
Red-twigged dogwood (*Cornus sericea, C. stolonifera*) - red
Winged burning bush (*Euonymus alata*) - corky, ridged

Deciduous branches for fruit, seeds, and leaves

Buffaloberry (*Shepherdia argentia*) - reddish orange berries
Cotoneaster (*Cotoneaster lucidus*) - dark blue berries
Highbush cranberry (*Viburnum trilobum*) - red berries
Russian olive (*Elaeagnus angustifolia*) - persistent, silvery green foliage
Sea buckthorn (*Hippophae rhamnoides*) - bright orange berries
Sumac (*Rhus typhina*) - velvety red seed clusters

Use the twigs and branches you collect to stake floppy perennials until the fall, at which time you can retrieve them for your winter container arrangement.

Choose a favourite container or flower box and empty any leftover planting medium. Your chosen container can be of any size and made of any material. Even clay and ceramic pots will withstand the rigours of winter if they are not filled with moisture-laden potting soil.

Think big when you start placing branches in your container. Convention has it that a dried flower arrangement should be about two and a half times the size of its container. Winter containers can support an even bigger cluster. Start by placing evergreen branches around the perimeter of the pot to provide a framework and stability for your creation, and fill this framework in with deciduous branches. Some perennial seed pods and capsules and ornamental grasses may be added, but keep in mind that many of these will become soggy in repeated snow-and-melt cycles. If you are whimsical by nature, select an inexpensive bird-shaped Christmas ornament to perch jauntily on a branch; many of these ornaments are very realistic and can provide an appropriate finishing touch. A word of caution to those who dwell where deer are frequent visitors: Deer are often starving during severe winters and will not hesitate to munch on or even demolish the proffered delicacies.

There are also other ways to enhance an otherwise bare front step, patio, or deck during the winter months. You might consider showing off a collection of pine cones in a shallow container. Or why not plant up a few plastic pots in the spring with everlasting annuals such as statice or strawflowers? Let them reach maturity during the course of the summer and then place them, plastic pot and all, into a decorative container for display on a deck or patio. The everlastings will withstand the ravages of winter quite well and look delightful when rimmed with frost or capped with small mounds of sparkling snow after a light snowfall.

Small Water Features

The presence of water as an ornamental element of a garden is irresistible to most gardeners. Trickling or splashing, the music of water attracts and soothes, and invites birds and other wildlife into the garden. The addition of a water feature also opens up planting possibilities by introducing a new type of habitat. While the idea of a water garden seems to be universally appealing, the prospect of installing a large pond can be daunting, both in terms of expense and labour. In addition, finding the ideal location or space for a pond is often difficult in small urban gardens.

Fortunately, the ambitious pond or stream project is not the only option for bringing the benefits of water into the average-sized city garden. There are dozens of small to positively tiny water gardens that can suit the style of any garden. Garden centres, specialty shops, and mail-order companies offer a huge range of ready-to-install water features, from small pools to wall fountains, complete with all the necessary hardware for efficient operation. The creative gardener can also find innovative ways to include water as part of a garden's design, often by recycling materials already on hand.

Small water features have many advantages in addition to being adaptable to any size of garden. Their cost is low, many of them are portable, and perhaps best of all, you can put in more than one, each different in design and function. This allows you to incorporate in the garden both the beauty of still, reflective water and the liveliness and auditory delight of moving water. You may desire a water garden primarily for growing aquatic plants, as well as one designed to attract birds.

Container Water Features. The simplest water features are containers such as wooden half-barrels, stone troughs, or ceramic or metal bowls. Containers can be sunk into the garden or left above ground. Half-barrels should be waterproof, and some available at garden centres will be ready to fill with water. Alternatively, install PVC plastic as a liner, or paint the interior of the barrel with a nontoxic waterproofing product. You can also try packing clay in any gaps between barrel staves and filling the barrel with water; the wood should swell enough to eliminate any leaks.

Large glazed ceramic or waterproofed terracotta pots can also serve as water features for decks or patios in a grouping with other containers. However, be extremely careful that you do not exceed the weight tolerance of structures such as balconies or decks. For an impromptu, occasional water feature for a special alfresco dinner, float a few beautiful blossoms (such as rose-form begonias) in an elegant large bowl. Still-water containers in sunny locations are ideal homes for water lilies, which are not happy in rapidly moving water.

Container water features may also be equipped with small submersible pumps to circulate the water to waterspouts or tiny fountains. Water may be circulated through a series of containers, falling from one half-barrel to another at a lower elevation or pouring from an urn or jar tipped on its side into a small pond or other decorative container. In Calgary's climate, container water gardens should be emptied for the winter and those containers likely to be damaged by freezing stored indoors or in a heated garage over the winter.

Pebble Water Features. The pebble water feature is another easily constructed, informal way to bring water into a small garden. This technique holds appeal for parents of young children due to the extremely low water level required. A pebble pond can also be a depository for childhood rock or shell collections as it can be filled with either large cobbles, small stones, or shells, selected for their interesting colours and textures, and

Delightful informal ponds can be designed to enhance gardens of any size. LIESBETH LEATHERBARROW

enhanced and brightened by the water flowing over them. In-ground pebble ponds can be very tiny, with water bubbling through the stones circulated by a pump submersed in a reservoir below. A layer of heavy wire mesh supports the stones above the reservoir. Pebble water features may also be created in containers, and look particularly attractive catching the spill from a wall-mounted fountain.

Informal Ponds. Informal ponds are suited to natural gardens and are irregularly shaped; the most successful are designed to appear as though they were always a part of the landscape. These ponds offer the gardener the opportunity not only to grow aquatic plants but also to surround the pond with bog-loving species in specially prepared areas. The variety of plant life will attract birds, fascinating insects, and maybe even frogs. In a tiny pond, ledges and stones provide the shallow areas required by these welcome visitors.

A small informal pond may be tucked into any size of garden, but for the most natural effect try to conform to the garden's topography and site the

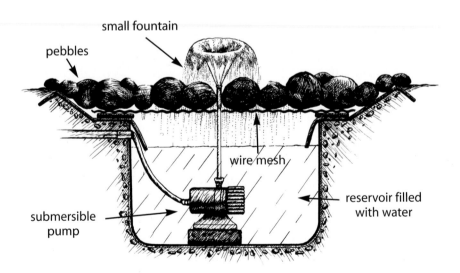

Pebble water features bring the sound of running water to very small spaces and are quite safe for young children. GRACE BUZIK

～ Creating a Bog Garden ～

A bog garden provides the environment preferred by the moisture-loving plants that grow at the edges of lakes and streams in natural settings. You may create a bog garden around the margins of an informal pond or it may be completely self-contained. The perimeters of most artificial ponds remain dry due to liners that prevent seepage. It is usually necessary to specially prepare all areas where you wish to grow bog plants.

Artificial ponds and bogs appear most natural when they are situated in low-lying areas where water would naturally accumulate. It is also a perfect use for an area that drains poorly. Keep in mind that most bog plants prefer full sun. To create a bog, excavate a saucer-shaped depression to a depth of approximately 60 cm (24 in.) in the centre. Line the hole with heavy plastic that has been perforated in several places to allow water to seep away gradually. Mix the topsoil you have removed with compost, moistened peat moss, or well-rotted manure and return it to the hole. Choose hardy plants recommended for marginal plantings, many of which are native to Alberta. These provide a wide array of flowers and foliage shapes and textures for your bog garden. Check the soil regularly during dry spells, adding water to keep it moist. Weeds also find bog garden conditions to their liking and should be removed promptly. Bog gardens may also be created in wooden half-barrels or ceramic or stone containers. These containers should have some provision for gradual drainage or a removable plug.

Hardy perennials for Calgary bog gardens

Arrow arum (*Peltandra virginica*)
Blue water iris (*Iris laevigata*)
Bogbean (*Menyanthes trifoliata*)
Cattail (*Typha latifolia*)
Marsh marigold (*Caltha palustris*)
Palmate-leaved coltsfoot (*Petasites palmatus*)
Scouring rush (*Equisetum hyemale*)
Water iris (*Iris versicolor*)
Water plantain (*Alisma plantago-aquatica*)
Yellow flag (*Iris pseudacorus*)

pond in a low area where water would naturally accumulate. Pond liners should be well camouflaged with natural materials, usually stone, which helps to establish a solid perimeter. In very small informal ponds, it is appropriate to confine the hydrotechnics to a gently bubbling "spring" or to add a stone frog with character, doubling as a waterspout.

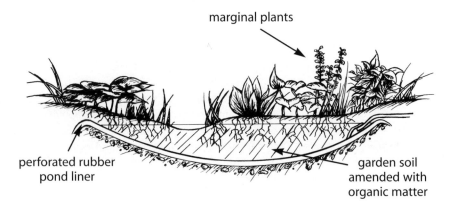

marginal plants

perforated rubber
pond liner

garden soil
amended with
organic matter

SELF-CONTAINED BOG GARDEN

Cross-section of a bog garden for moisture-loving plants. Grace Buzik

Formal Ponds. A formal pond differs from an informal pond in that it is geometrically shaped and the materials used in its construction are not chosen to appear as a natural part of the landscape. If you have spent any time immersed in gardening history books, the mention of formal ponds evokes geometrically precise lines and dreams of European holidays. Formal ponds have been focal points of the great gardens of the world: Persian paradise gardens with cooling fountains; the elegant still pools of Renaissance Italy reflecting classical statuary; and the grand pools of seventeenth-century France, parterre-surrounded and alive with splashing and sparkling water from elaborate fountains. Despite this illustrious history, the formal pond can also be a focal point sized in proportion to any small garden or garden room.

A small formal pond may be raised above ground level or set into the ground, and can be as simple as a square or rectangular gap between paving stones. It can be surrounded by low hedging or narrow flower beds and edged with brick, stone, decorative tiles, or wood. Your formal water garden may be a still water-lily pond tucked into a corner or a dramatic focal point. If you choose to make it a dominant feature in the garden, add moving water, even something as subtle as a tiny bubble fountain. Different fountain heads create high or low jets of water, glittering gems in the air, or a smooth glassy effect. A fountain spilling into a small pool in the centre of a courtyard should be selected as carefully as any sculpture for your home. Keep your eyes open for unusual and original fountains to make your water feature unique.

∾ Small Water Lilies ∾

Water lilies add a touch of the tropics to any water garden. The smallest water lilies require 15 cm (6 in.) of water above the soil level; larger varieties need greater depth. Bricks may be used to raise planting baskets to the desired level. Choose hardy rather than tropical water lilies; dwarf or compact varieties suit small containers and ponds. Even hardy water lilies will not survive freezing and should be brought inside for winter unless you have a deep pond that does not freeze completely during the winter. Try the following varieties of small hardy water lilies; one plant should spread enough to adequately cover a 60-cm (24-in.) diameter pool or tub.

Hardy water lilies for small ponds

Nymphaea 'Albatross' - white
N. 'Aurora' - yellow-apricot, turning to red
N. 'Froebelii' - crimson
N. 'Graziella' - golden-orange
N. 'James Brydon' - pink
N. 'Joanne Pring' - deep pink
N. 'Laydekeri Lilacea' - pale mauve
N. 'Odorata Minor' - white
N. pygmaea var. *helvola* - yellow
N. pygmaea var. *rubra* - pink, turning to dark red

Canals and Rills. Two formal water features not often used but highly adaptable to small-scale gardens are canals and rills. Narrow canals symmetrically flanking a small garden will make it appear longer; crosswise, they will give the impression of greater width. Like paths, canals are most effective if they lead to a focal point. Rills are small channels usually set in brick or stone that connect small formal ponds or link them with other features of the garden, such as a seating area or pergola. If you wish, you may incorporate small steps into the beds of canals and rills to provide a pleasing and gentle rippling movement. To prevent leakage, line the channels of these water features with heavy PVC plastic over a bed of sand before adding the decorative stones or bricks.

Wall Fountains. Even the smallest of gardens can be enlivened by the sound of splashing water with a wall fountain. Requiring little more than a vertical surface, the wall fountain can be surrounded by trellised flowering vines to create a water garden in the most confined spaces. The best wall fountains for restricted areas are those that come in one piece, the water falling into an attached basin, but many decorative fountains are available without a basin, allowing you to design your own catchment pond. Wall fountains require a small submersible pump to circulate water from the pond up through a hose to the fountain spout. To hide the mechanics, you will need access to the back of the wall the fountain is to be mounted upon, or a recess in the wall; alternatively, you can tuck the hose behind trellising and disguise it with plantings.

Wall fountains offer wonderful decorative opportunities, from traditional lions, gods, and gargoyles to unusual custom-made masks. Most wall fountains suit raised and geometrically shaped ponds, and they can provide a striking focal point in a small Mediterranean-style patio or courtyard. However, wall fountains also have a place in informal gardens: a tiny, rocky in-ground pool surrounded by shade-loving hostas or ferns would be a green oasis beneath a fountain in a cool corner.

A classic wall fountain, bordered by baskets of bright annuals, spills water into a mossy pool. MAUREEN IRETON

THREE

The Sensuous Gardener

Gardens for Visual Impact

For most people the sensual appeal of a beautiful garden is first experienced through sight. Artists have known for many centuries that a well-composed garden is a subject of enduring interest for painting and, more recently, a favourite topic for photography. However, you do not need to be an artist to create a garden picture that is a pleasure to behold, whether it is a tranquil, green haven of contrasting textures framed by trees, a floral tapestry of bright and warm colours, or a cool white garden that glows ethereally in the moonlight. Like each artist, each gardener may have a unique vision and style, and although it is necessary to work within individual limitations of space and the climatic limitations of the Chinook zone, there are few garden concepts not adaptable to Calgary conditions.

This lavish perennial border is ablaze with dramatic mid-summer colour. FRANK SCOTT

Planting for Colour. Planting for colour is a good way to accommodate your favourite plants in a pleasing garden design. As you plan your garden, take into account the background colours already present in your house, garage, or fences. Then consider the range of colours you enjoy most and the mood you wish to establish. For a cool, quiet, and restful atmosphere, you may wish blues to predominate; festive, warm colours such as red, orange, and yellow are more stimulating and brighten and cheer Calgary's short summers. As white flowers are often wonderfully scented and shine at dusk, consider a white garden if you love to sit outside on soothing summer evenings after a busy day.

Colour is affected by the intensity of light, which changes with the seasons, especially in northerly latitudes. Bright sunshine can make pastel shades appear washed out; light colours suit north-facing areas and brighten shade with reflected light. Colours that are strong or "saturated," that is to say, pure colours, absorb more light than those that are less pure or weaker versions of the colour and they are at their richest in bright light. Sunny south- or west-facing locations show these flowers to best advantage as they tend to retreat in shade.

Certain colours also seem to suit certain seasons. Yellow is a refreshing and cheerful harbinger of spring after a long dreary winter, but can be overpowering in large doses in the glare of mid-summer gardens. Summer is a season of bold contrasts and deep green foliage. Fall is the time to match the mood of nature with russets, reds, and oranges. Winter gardens rely on the magic of white frost and snow to bring alive the greys, browns, and reds of bark and berries, seed heads and grasses. It is possible to change the colour scheme of your garden by season, taking into consideration the usual blooming times of plants. This is easiest to do by planting separate areas for each season, but if your garden is small, it can also be accomplished in a single flower bed with coordinated plantings that bloom consecutively from spring to fall. Needless to say, the latter method requires considerable planning as the timing of bloom is all-important. Keep careful records on how your chosen plants perform, and take particular note of bloom times in your garden. These will vary somewhat from what is recorded in charts and books, depending on the microclimate that prevails in your chosen flower bed. Don't hesitate to replace plants whose colour and bloom times are slightly out of balance with the master plan. A pleasing design depends as much on trial and error as it does on careful preparation.

In designing your garden, you may choose flower beds of harmonizing or contrasting colours or explore a monochromatic theme. Monochromatic gardens, those in variations of one colour, are striking and the most effective means to use colour to set a mood. Keep in mind that in the monochromatic garden it is important to vary plant forms, texture, and density. The form or shape of a plant can be erect or sprawling, gently rounded or spiky, and the range of textures provided by flowers and foliage is boundless. Within a colour group you will find solid, substantial flowers with large single leaves and delicate clouds of blooms with airy foliage. Although it is always a good idea to repeat certain groupings or types of plants for a unified effect, exploring the wide variety of plants within the range of your chosen colour will prevent monotony. Gardeners should heed the caution against dogmatism provided by Gertrude Jekyll, the English gardener, painter, and writer credited with designing the first monochromatic gardens.

> It is a curious thing that people will sometimes spoil some garden project for the sake of a word. For instance, a blue garden, for beauty's sake, may be hungering for a group of white Lilies, or for something of palest lemon-yellow, but it is not allowed to have it because it is called the blue garden, and there must be no flowers in it but blue flowers. I can see no sense in this; it seems to me like fetters foolishly self-imposed. Surely the business of the blue garden is to be beautiful as well as to be blue.[26]

Blue Gardens. Blue gardens are particularly suited to the foothills country of Alberta. Cool and relaxing, blue can evoke the intensity of the prairie sky or the hazy, almost purple hues of distant mountains; it also creates an illusion of space ideal for a small garden. Fortunately, a wide selection of blue flowers thrives in the Calgary area, ranging from the pure deep blue of the gentian to the dainty blue-striped white petals of the striped squill. There are also blues that tend towards shades of lilac, lavender, and purple. In designing your blue garden, it is best to separate the clear, intense blues, such as the gentians or Himalayan blue poppies, from the softer shades. This can be accomplished by using foliage in shades of grey or silver, which is especially flattering to blue flowers. Try not to use too much dark green foliage as it will dull the effect of blue blossoms. Gold-leaved hostas work well with blue.

As Gertrude Jekyll pointed out, blue gardens benefit from touches of lighter colours to relieve the eye. White and cream are refreshing amidst blue, and pale yellow flowers can also be used to separate and set off strong blues and purple-blues, preventing them from overwhelming their less powerful neighbours. Some blue flowers have built-in lighter contrasts: just think of the white bees, or centres, of blue delphiniums. Blue flowers bloom throughout the growing season, from early bulbs such as striped and Siberian squill through to fall Michaelmas daisies.

Red Gardens. Red gardens are hot and vibrant. Red is the colour of excitement, and beds planted in red leap forward to claim your attention. Red needs space and too much red can be overpowering in a small garden; however, if you have the space, a sunny corner will glow with rich red flowers. There are some pure, saturated red flowers, such as the

Sweet William and cottage pinks are underplanted with thyme, perfect companions for a fragrant pink theme garden. LIESBETH LEATHERBARROW

Golden Marguerites and yellow Asiatic lilies proclaim the sunny nature of a yellow border. KATHERINE PEDERSON

'Champlain' Explorer Series rose, but most reds are mixed to some degree with other colours. Yellow makes bright scarlet reds turn towards the orange shades, the colour of many red geraniums; a touch of blue creates crimson reds, such as the 'Ville de Lyon' clematis. White lightens red to pink. As with most warm and cool versions of any colour, these shades do not always combine happily with each other or with the pure reds. Dark purple foliage harmonizes with red flowers, and light green provides a striking contrast. Although bright red in a garden is warming and cheering, many gardeners prefer to use softer shades for large flower beds, reserving red for accent and contrast. Pink and plum are also in the red family and are more adaptable to small urban gardens.

Pink Gardens. Pink gardens can be soft or coolly romantic or warm and tropical. A touch of blue creates cool pinks ('Silver Cup' lavatera); yellow warms pink to shades of peach and apricot ('Alchymist' hardy shrub rose). Try not to use too many pastel pinks together; instead, incorporate several shades of light to dark shades of pink, separating cool and warm pinks. Darker shades of magenta (rose campion) and blue-tinted pinks into the range of violet ('Prairie Night' bee balm) work to deepen pale cool pinks ('Blue Pearl' impatiens), and white brightens the planting. Coppery pink shades ('Miss Willmott' potentilla) flatter warm peach or apricot pinks, and because it is already present in these colours, a touch of light yellow is appropriate.

Yellow Gardens. Yellow is bright, eye-catching, and cheerful, the colour of sunshine. Like red, however, yellow alone can be too much for a small garden. Use yellow to brighten otherwise dark areas, not forgetting the many plants with yellow or variegated foliage that give a subtler effect in shade without flowers. If you wish to plant a yellow garden, use plenty of pale yellow (woolly yarrow), as well as saturated bright yellows (marsh marigold), and add generous amounts of white or cream to soften the effect. Also consider using some of the many white flowers that have yellow centres or stamens, such as daisies. If you love strong yellows, consider creating a sunrise or sunset garden, combining them with reds and oranges to pick up the warm glow of the sun's rays at these times of day.

White Gardens. White gardens reflect all the light that strikes them. White is the easiest colour to work with in the garden as it can be used with any other colour. Combined with grey and green foliage, white flowers are fresh and cool, clean and elegant. Monochromatic white beds should include creamy white flowers as well as pure white, so as not to appear stark. Texture and shape are important in white gardens as there is less variance in flower colour to capture interest. Because of its high reflective value, white is a good choice for shady areas and is incompa-

rable on moonlit nights, although soft pinks and icy blues will also illuminate a midnight stroll. The selection of white flowers for Calgary is wide, and almost all the favourite hardy perennials used by Calgary gardeners have a white form. Plants with white-and-green variegated foliage can also be integrated into a white garden.

Elegant white tulips are the focus of this early-summer white garden.
JOHN BUYSSCHAERT

Silver-grey Gardens. Silver-grey plants are often included in white gardens, to enhance pastel pinks and blues or to set off a bold shade of magenta. The colour can range from a bright, almost white silver to softer greys that border on blue or green. If you wish to plant a silver-grey bed, explore the wide range of plant shapes and foliage textures within this colour range to avoid a monotonous or flat look. Small touches of lavender, blue, or green will enliven these plant-

ings. The silver-grey garden is well suited to the dry conditions in Calgary since many of these plants are natives of arid regions. The grey shades are caused by a coating of small hairs that shield leaves from the intense sun in hot summer climates.

Green Gardens. Many gardeners take green for granted; however, the possibilities of an all-green garden are rarely exploited. Green is lush, verdant, and restorative: the bright green of emerging spring leaves energizes, whereas the deep blue-green of spruce

A successful green theme garden such as this one relies on considerable variation in foliage texture and colour to make an impact. HELEN JULL

soothes. Green is the colour of shade and the colour gardeners most associate with unspoiled natural landscapes. Green can provide neutral buffer zones between clashing colours, but it can also make a wonderful study in a garden all by itself. There are greens in shades from almost yellow to almost blue, grey and silver greens, hard shiny greens, and soft fuzzy greens. Foliage size, shape, and texture are immensely varied and allow the gardener great possibilities to play with form in designing the garden. White-striped or variegated foliage brightens dark green, and there are even flowers from yellow to white shades of green. The gardener concentrating on green can work on either a large scale with trees and shrubs, or a small scale in a flower bed using grasses, groundcovers, or other perennials with attractive foliage. The best thing about green is that a suitable choice of evergreens keeps green interest in the garden year-round.

Harmonizing and Contrasting Colours. While monochromatic gardens are elegant and artistic, many gardeners prefer a combination of harmonizing or contrasting colours. Harmonizing colours are side by side on a colour wheel, for example, blue and purple; contrasting colours are opposite on the wheel, for example, red and green. You will find it easiest to use plants that harmonize for the basis of your plan, adding contrasting colours where emphasis or a focal point is required. Colour schemes involving pairs of contrasting strong colours directly opposite each other on the wheel, such as blue and orange, red and green, or violet and yellow, will create the most striking colour effects in your garden; if you wish, the contrast can be toned down by using a paler shade of one of the pair. Avoid using too many contrasting colours as contrast can be tiring to the eye. Instead, aim for a ratio of two-thirds cool to one-third warm colours in your perennial border.

Even working with two or three carefully selected colours may be too restrictive to gardeners with a more casual approach to planting. Many avid gardeners habitually fall in love with special plants that do not fit into carefully planned planting schemes. If this is your style of gardening and you would like to accommodate every colour of the rainbow, you can try arranging the colours as in a spectrum. Be aware, however, that this technique may require more space than is readily available in most city gardens. For more random plantings, it is most effective to surround strong colours with plenty of green and white to avoid clashes with their neighbours. Small gardens should be restricted to one or two dominant primary colours, with the planting completed with lighter tones of harmonizing or contrasting colours. If you wish to include as many colours as possible, remember that small dots of red or yellow in a bed of blues, violets, and pinks may be enough to achieve the desired effect.

Although colours do move in and out of fashion, there are no right or wrong colours and even the way you combine them is largely a matter of personal taste. Your garden may differ from that of your neighbour as a Van Gogh differs from a Monet. In a large garden with several different "rooms" or areas there is greater scope for varied colour themes, but you can still achieve unity through repetition of certain elements or plant groupings.

∾ Plants for Colour-theme Gardens ∾

Perennials. Try the following reliable hardy perennials in your colour-theme borders. Some specific cultivars and hybrids are noted here, and there are many others available at your local garden centres and in catalogues.

Blue

Bellflower (*Campanula* spp.)

Catmint (*Nepeta* x *faassenii*, *N. mussinii*)

Cranesbill (*Geranium* x 'Johnson's Blue')

Delphinium (*Delphinium* spp. and blue hybrids)

Gentian (*Gentiana cruciata*, *G. septemfida*)

Globe thistle (*Echinops ritro*)

Grape hyacinth (*Muscari* spp.)

Himalayan blue poppy (*Meconopsis betonicifolia*)

Michaelmas daisy (*Aster* spp.)

Monkshood (*Aconitum napellus*)

Pincushion flower (*Scabiosa caucasica* 'Clive Greaves')

Sea holly (*Eryngium* spp.)

Siberian squill (*Scilla siberica*)

Speedwell (*Veronica* spp.)

Striped squill (*Puschkinia libanotica*, *P. scilloides*)

Red

Asiatic lily (*Lilium* x *hybrida* 'Corina', 'America', 'Firecracker', 'Conquistador')

Bee balm (*Monarda didyma* 'Gardenview Scarlet')

Blanket flower (*Gaillardia* 'Burgundy')

Clematis (*Clematis* 'Ville de Lyon')

Coral bells (*Heuchera sanguinea*)

Helenium (*Helenium autumnale* 'Moerheim Beauty')

Maiden pinks (*Dianthus deltoides* 'Zing')

Maltese cross (*Lychnis chalcedonica*)

Oriental poppy (*Papaver orientale*)

Rose (*Rosa* 'David Thompson', 'Adelaide Hoodless', 'Champlain')

Yarrow (*Achillea millefolium* 'Paprika')

Pink

Beardtongue (*Penstemon barbatus*)

Bee balm (*Monarda didyma* 'Beauty of Cobham', 'Marshall's Delight', 'Prairie Night')

Cheddar pink (*Dianthus gratianopolitanus* 'Pike's Pink')

Cranesbill (*Geranium cinereum* 'Ballerina', *G. macrorrhizum* 'Ingwerson's Variety')

Fleabane (*Erigeron speciosus* 'Pink Jewel')

Fleeceflower (*Polygonum bistorta* 'Superbum')

Meadowsweet (*Filipendula rubra*)

Musk mallow (*Malva moschata*)

Potentilla (*Potentilla fructicosa* 'Miss Willmott')

Rose (*Rosa* 'Alchymist', 'John Davis', 'Morden Blush', 'Prairie Dawn', 'Therese Bugnet')

Rose campion (*Lychnis coronaria*)

Yellow

Cinquefoil (*Potentilla recta* 'Warrenii')

Daylily (*Hemerocallis* 'Stella d'Oro')

False sunflower (*Heliopsis helianthoides* 'Summer Sun')

Foxglove (*Digitalis grandiflora* syn. *D. ambigua*)

Giant scabious (*Cephalaria gigantea*)

Globeflower (*Trollius europaeus* 'Lemon Queen')

Golden corydalis (*Corydalis lutea*)

Golden groundsel (*Ligularia steno-cephala* 'The Rocket')

Golden Marguerite (*Anthemis tinctoria*)

Goldenrod (*Solidago* hybrids)

Marsh marigold (*Caltha palustris*)

Woolly yarrow (*Achillea tomentosa*)

White

Delphinium (*Delphinium* 'Galahad')

Dittany (*Dictamnus albus*)

Goatsbeard (*Aruncus dioicus*)

Lungwort (*Pulmonaria* 'Sissinghurst White')

Meadow rue (*Thalictrum aquilegifolium* 'Album')

Phlox (*Phlox paniculata* 'David')

Rose (*Rosa* 'Blanc Double de Coubert', 'Henry Hudson')

Shasta daisy (*Chrysanthemum* x *superbum* or *C. maximum*)

Sneezewort (*Achillea ptarmica* 'The Pearl')

Snow-in-summer (*Cerastium tomentosum*)

Sweet woodruff (*Galium odoratum*)

Silver-grey (foliage)

Archangel (*Lamiastrum galeobdolon*)

Bethlehem sage (*Pulmonaria saccharata* 'Argentea')

Dead nettle (*Lamium maculatum* 'Beacon Silver', 'White Nancy')

Lambs' ears (*Stachys byzantina*)

Lavender (*Lavandula angustifolia*)

Mullein (*Verbascum nigrum*)

Pussytoes (*Antennaria* spp.)

Sage (*Artemisia schmidtiana* 'Silver Mound')

Silver sage (*Salvia argentea*) (biennial)

Wormwood (*Artemisia ludoviciana* 'Silver King')

Green (foliage)

Bugbane (*Cimicifuga racemosa*)

Golden marjoram (*Origanum vulgare* 'Aureum')

Lady fern (*Athyrium filix-femina*)

Lady's mantle (*Alchemilla mollis*)

Ornamental rhubarb (*Rheum palmatum*)

Ostrich fern (*Matteucia struthiopteris*)

Plantain lily (*Hosta* spp.)

Plume poppy (*Macleaya cordata*)

Sheep's fescue (*Festuca ovina glauca*)

Spurge (*Euphorbia epithymoides*)

Pink and purple (colours beside each other on the colour wheel) harmonize beautifully to create a restful mood in this perennial garden.
Renata Wichmann

Annuals. There are many exciting new annual cultivars and hybrids appearing at garden centres every year. Here are a few suggestions for annual colour-theme gardens.

Blue

Ageratum (*Ageratum houstonianum*)
Bachelor's button (*Centaurea cyanus*)
Larkspur (*Consolida ambigua*)
Lobelia (*Lobelia erinus compacta,
   L. erinus pendula*)
Love-in-a-mist (*Nigella damascena*)
Pansy (*Viola* x *wittrockiana*)
Petunia (*Petunia* x *hybrida*)
Phlox (*Phlox drummondii*)
Salvia (*Salvia farinacea*)
Sweet pea (*Lathyrus odoratus*)

Red

Amaranthus (*Amaranthus caudatus*)
Carnation (*Dianthus caryophyllus*)
Celosia (*Celosia cristata, C. plumosa*)
Coleus (*Coleus blumei*)
Fuschia (*Fuschia* x *hybrida*)
Geranium (*Pelargonium* x *hortorum*)
Nasturtium (*Tropaeolum majus*)
Nemesia (*Nemesia strumosa*)
Petunia (*Petunia* x *hybrida*)
Poppy (*Papaver* spp.)
Zinnia (*Zinnia elegans*)

Pink

Balsam (*Impatiens balsamina*)
China aster (*Callistephus chinensis*)
Clarkia (*Clarkia unguiculata*)
Cosmos (*Cosmos bipinnatus*)
Godetia (*Clarkia amoena*)

Impatiens (*Impatiens wallerana*)
Lavatera (*Lavatera trimestris*)
Petunia (*Petunia* x *hybrida*)
Evening (night) scented stock
   (*Matthiola incana*)
Verbena (*Verbena hortensis*)

Yellow

Calendula (*Calendula officinalis*)
Canarybird vine (*Tropaeolum pere-
   grinum*)
Dahlberg daisy (*Dyssodia tenuiloba*
   syn. *Thymophylla tenuiloba*)
Lantana (*Lantana camara*)
Marigold (*Tagetes erecta, T. patula*)
Nasturtium (*Tropaeolum majus*)
Pansy (*Viola* x *wittrockiana*)
Portulaca (*Portulaca grandiflora*)
Strawflower (*Helichrysum bracteatum*)
Sunflower (*Helianthus annuus*)

White

Angel's trumpet (*Datura* spp.)
Annual baby's breath (*Gypsophila elegans*)
Candytuft (*Iberis* spp.)
Four o'clock (*Mirabilis jalapa*)
Lavatera (*Lavatera trimestris*)
Moon vine (*Ipomoea alba*)
Snapdragon (*Antirrhinum majus*)
Spider flower (*Cleome hasslerana*)
Statice (*Limonium sinuatum*)
Sweet alyssum (*Lobularia maritima*)

Contrasting yellow pansies and purple lobelia (colours opposite each other on the colour wheel) are striking against a cool green backdrop.
LYNNE COLBORNE

Planting for Visual Texture. In addition to selecting and grouping plants for colour attributes, the gardener should seek an appealing combination of visual textures. Too much of any type of foliage or flower is monotonous; try to use a variety of fine-, medium-, and coarse-textured plants in your garden.

Fine-textured plants have small leaves and a delicate appearance, such as most ferns, or a soft surface, such as lambs' ears. Fine- to medium-textured plants work well as groundcovers. At the opposite end of the spectrum are coarse-textured plants—those with large leaves (ornamental rhubarb) or spiky leaves or flowers (sea holly). Many medium-textured plants inhabit the middle range between fine and coarse. Use coarse-textured plants sparingly as accents in larger groupings of fine- and medium-textured plants. Vary the visual texture of foliage by planting shiny-leaved plants next to those with dull leaves, and plants with rounded, uniformly shaped leaves next to those with strap-like, jagged, or irregularly shaped leaves. Evergreens can be soft or spiky; include some of each type for textural interest in the winter garden. Don't forget to also consider the shapes and sizes of blossoms. Combine those plants with flowers on racemes (delphinium), with daisy-like blossoms (feverfew), bell-shaped blossoms (Canterbury bells), or with softly plumed blossoms (astilbe).

Planting for Moonlight. A garden created to look wonderful by the light of the moon might not seem an obvious goal for gardeners in Calgary. After all, it doesn't get dark here until late during the summer, and many of us are already dreaming sweet dreams before the moon even rises. As a result, most Calgary gardens are beautifully designed for daytime visual delight and sensation, with little thought being given to evening and night-time viewing. However, not all Calgarians have the luxury of time during the day for enjoying the fruits of their gardening labours. Many spend precious daylight hours working hard at home, away from home, or in the garden. Others sleep during the day, work the late shift, and return home when daylight has faded. For all of you who are not able to take a time out from busy days and for those who like to take one final late-evening stroll through the garden before calling it a day, consider this: many plants look and smell their best by moonlight!

So-called night gardens were fashionable during the nineteenth century when ladies and gentlemen preferred to view their gardens in the mist or by night to protect their fair skins from the harsh light of the sun. Today, night gardens are making a comeback to accommodate hectic lifestyles or, more simply, to extend the hours of viewing pleasure; fortunately, many beautiful effects can be created in the garden for late-evening enjoyment. The wise selection and placement of plants, strong structural design elements, and the addition of artificial light to the landscape are keys to a successful night garden design.

Creating a garden that is a pleasure to behold as daylight fades and darkness descends need not be a complicated affair. It also need not preclude the existence of plant arrangements that are attractive by day. In fact, many of the plants that add interest to flower borders and beds during traditional viewing hours work equally well at night. Often all it takes to add night-time beauty to the garden is the regrouping and relocation of existing plants, the addition of one or two plants that perform exclusively in a nocturnal environment, and a fresh way of looking at old garden friends in a new light!

When selecting plants for the night garden, remember that not every plant needs to be a night-time performer. Just ensure that you have sufficient variety to provide a balanced and enticing visual display, especially along pathways and in other areas that are easily accessible or easily viewed from inside the house. Strive for continuous bloom succession in the night garden so there will be something to catch your eye, no matter what the time of year.

Flower and foliage colours are two important design elements to consider in the development of a night garden. Brightly coloured plants in shades of red, orange, and gold are surrounded by a radiant glow in the warm light of the late-afternoon sun before they recede and disappear into inky blackness. As such, they perform admirably at bridging the gap between day and night. Later, cool-coloured flowers in shades of blue, mauve, purple, and pink reflect the early evening light and shine with an almost fluorescent brilliance before they too vanish into the background. As darkness finally falls, drifts of white and other pale-coloured blossoms take centre stage; they are visible as ghostly shadows in even the dimmest of natural light conditions, but stand out boldly by the light of the moon, hovering mystically against shadowy backgrounds.

Silvery foliage does a wonderful job of capturing and reflecting moonbeams, thereby creating drama in the evening landscape. More eye-catching still is variegated or multicoloured foliage; the dark parts of each variegated leaf recede and become invisible while the light markings seem to advance and float mysteriously in the dark.

Evening-scented annuals and perennials and those that bloom exclusively in the evening are a must for the night garden. Many of the plants that smell good at night are also light coloured to attract late-night pollinators such as moths, beetles, and bats, and they will still be visible when the sun disappears beyond the horizon.

Remember that lighting and structures in your garden can also add interest to evening strolls. Lighting, whether natural or artificial, accents individual plants or groups of plants, casts interesting shadows, and generates sensational silhouettes. In fact, the interplay of light and shadow helps create the enchanted, almost magical distinction of a night garden. Light-coloured structures stand out and help define the darkened landscape; dark structures fade into oblivion. Arbours and trellises can frame the moon or be silhouetted

~ Plants for Night Gardens ~

Bright flowers for late afternoon. Brightly coloured flowers (reds, oranges, and yellows) glow in the warm late-afternoon light and bridge the gap between day and night.

Cardinal flower (*Lobelia cardinalis*)

Daffodil (*Narcissus* spp.)

Leopard's bane (*Doronicum caucasicum*)

Marigold (*Tagetes* spp.)

Narrowleaf zinnia (*Zinnia linearis*)

Orange lilies (*Lilium* spp.)

Red geraniums (*Pelargonium* spp.)

Red salvia (*Salvia splendens*)

Statice (*Limonium sinuatum*)

Sunflower (*Helianthus* spp.)

Thread-leaved coreopsis (*Coreopsis verticillata* 'Moonbeam')

Cool flowers for early evening. Cool-coloured flowers (blues, mauves, and magentas) reflect early evening light and seem to fluoresce before fading away.

Bee balm (*Monarda fistulosa*)

Clematis (*Clematis* spp.)

Coleus (*Coleus* x *hybridus*)

Glory-of-the-snow (*Chionodoxa luciliae*)

Peach-leaved bellflower (*Campanula persicifolia*)

Sage (*Salvia officinalis*)

Shirley poppy (*Papaver rhoeas*)

This intriguing landscape, with its superb use of fine-, medium-, and coarse-textured plants, invites exploration. WINSTON GORETSKY

Pale flowers for darkness. Pale-coloured flowers (whites, creams, pastel yellows, and pinks) remain visible, even after darkness falls.

Astilbe (*Astilbe* spp.)
Baby's breath (*Gypsophila paniculata*)
Candytuft (*Iberis sempervirens*)
Cleome (*Cleome hasslerana*)
Goatsbeard (*Aruncus dioicus*)
Potentilla (*Potentilla* spp.)
Snowdrop (*Galanthus nivalis*)

Snowdrop anemone (*Anemone sylvestris*)
Species lily (*Lilium* spp.)
Spirea (*Spirea* spp.)
Sweet alyssum (*Lobularia maritima*)
Sweet woodruff (*Galium odoratum*)

Silvery or variegated plants for reflections. Plants with silvery foliage or variegated leaves capture and reflect light in fascinating ways.

Dusty miller (*Centaurea cineraria*)
Goutweed (*Aegopodium podagraria*)
Honesty (*Lunaria*)
Lambs' ears (*Stachys byzantina*)
Lavender (*Lavandula angustifolia* spp.)
Lavender cotton (*Santolina* spp.)
Lungwort (*Pulmonaria* spp.)
Ornamental kale (*Brassica oleracea*)
Plantain lily (*Hosta* spp.)

Ribbon grass (*Phalaris arundinacea picta*)
Russian sage (*Perovskia atriplicifolia*)
Sage (*Artemisia* spp.)
Sage (*Salvia officinalis*)
Snow-in-summer (*Cerastium tomentosum*)
Yarrow (*Achillea* spp.)

Night bloomers

Angel's trumpet (*Datura*)
Evening primrose (*Oenothera biennis*)
Four o'clock (*Mirabilis jalapa*)
Night phlox (*Zaluzianskya capensis*)

Night-scented plants

Blue-flowered petunia (*Petunia* spp.)
Evening primrose (*Oenothera biennis*)
Four o'clock (*Mirabilis jalapa*)
Lilac (*Syringa* spp.)
Mignonette (*Reseda odorata*)
Nicotiana (*Nicotiana sylvestris*)
Night-scented stock (*Matthiola bicornis*)
Sweet rocket (*Hesperis matronalis*)

A delightful weathered lantern creates atmosphere, as well as serving the practical purpose of lighting the garden at night. VAL PRITCHARD

against it. Ponds reflect moonbeams, producing subtle back-lighting effects on neighbouring plants. Even a backlit tree with an unusual shape can provide an excellent backdrop for your night garden.

Finally, on a practical note, if you are prone to taking a late-evening constitutional through your garden, remember to keep pathways free from obstacles and overhead branches trimmed to prevent accidents.

Nocturnal Illumination. The night-time play of artificial light on fluttering leaves, on highly textured bark, or on gnarly tree branches can introduce an air of mystery and drama into your garden. This is easily accomplished by the thoughtful placement of a small number of light fixtures, each selected for a specific reason, to create a desired effect.

The potential for artificial light in the night garden is often not realized in Calgary because the long hours of summer daylight and the characteristically cool evenings seem to preclude the need for it. What is often overlooked is that Calgarians do have ample opportunity to enjoy the artistic effects created by dancing lights and shadows, especially early and late in the gardening season when nights are long. There is also no reason why an outdoor lighting system can't be designed to highlight garden beauty year-round, providing visual pleasure from indoor and outdoor vantage points alike.

Flooding the garden with light is not recommended, except for security reasons; too much light can make healthy plants appear sickly or artificial. However, there are several more-subtle lighting techniques that can be used either uniquely or in combination to highlight garden features.

Up-lighting. Up-lighting, as its name suggests, consists of directing a beam of light upwards, usually originating in concealed fixtures secured at ground level. This technique is often employed to accent garden structures and deciduous shrubs and trees with wide, open growth habits. Naked skeletons of trees in winter are also excellent candidates for up-lighting. Up-lighting creates fascinating shadow patterns, imparts a glow to leaves and branches, and reveals contours that go unnoticed in ordinary light.

Artistic variations on the up-lighting theme include silhouetting, shadowing, and spotlighting. Silhouettes and shadows are created most effectively against a solid backdrop such as a light-coloured fence or wall. To create silhouettes, conceal a light source at ground level between the backdrop and neighbouring plants, directing the beam upwards at the backdrop; when viewed from a distance, the individual shapes of adjacent plants will be silhouetted against the backdrop. To create shadows, conceal the light source at ground level in front of plants that are backed by a fence or wall, directing the beam at an angle towards the plants. The resultant shadows projected onto the backdrop can be striking, especially for plants with unique, shapely foliage. To draw attention to a particular landscape detail or

∾ Installing Garden Lighting ∾

For those of you who would like to try designing and installing your own outdoor garden lighting, consider the following pointers.

🌹 Obtain an electrical permit from the municipality and arrange for an inspection upon completing your wiring project.

🌹 Make sure your design is compatible with the existent house wiring and that it will not cause an electrical overload.

🌹 Turn off the electricity at the house when working with outdoor electrical equipment.

🌹 Work in a dry garden.

🌹 Use weatherproof wiring, outlet boxes, plugs, sockets, connections, fixtures, and bulbs; insulate according to regulations.

🌹 Bury electrical cables at least 45 cm (18 in.) deep to avoid damage from spades or pitchforks. Accidentally severing a live electrical cable on a 120-volt line can cause severe electrical shock. Also determine whether the type of cable you are burying needs to be sheathed or has been rated for burial without protection.

🌹 Make a map of your underground wiring for future reference in case of a break or short circuit.

🌹 Protect above-ground wiring with a conduit, especially when it lies in a location where it may be easily damaged.

🌹 Always use a rubber gasket between the bulb and the socket in outdoor light fixtures; this gives a water-tight fit, preventing moisture from leaking into the sockets.

Solar-powered outdoor lighting systems are also available. They consist of a panel that collects the solar energy, and rechargeable batteries in which the collected energy is stored. Many of these systems turn on automatically after dusk and light your garden until the batteries have discharged. They are easy-to-install, self-contained units with no plugs or wires to connect. As such, they have a great deal of portability and flexibility, allowing you to light corners that are a long distance from conventional power sources. For a solar-powered system to be effective, the collector panel must receive strong, direct sunlight for a large part of the day. Although the initial start-up costs are high, no additional expenses are incurred once the system is up and running.

structure, such as an elegant statue, a fountain, or an ornate bird-bath, use a spotlight installed at ground level.

Down-lighting. Down-lighting is another effective means for lighting the garden, one that more closely approximates the behaviour of natural light. As its name suggests, beams of light are directed downwards onto trees, shrubs, and flower borders from concealed locations situated as high as possible above the garden. When designed with sensitivity, a scheme of down-lighting can realistically reproduce the soft diffuse glow of the full moon, projecting mysterious shadows on the garden floor below. When carried out on a smaller scale, using low, hooded fixtures instead of those mounted up high, down-lighting is a valuable tool for featuring low plants and structures or for defining the edges of a walkway. This technique is sometimes called contouring.

Side-lighting. Side-lighting is a technique that employs low-level light fixtures that cast a wide beam spaced at regular intervals along the edges of driveways, paths, and walkways. These fixtures create pools of light that make fascinating patterns on the ground and guide you safely to your destination.

Lighting Kits. Until recently, the installation of outdoor electrical lighting was an elaborate and somewhat expensive affair, requiring a permit, the purchase of numerous individual electrical components, and the services of an electrician—at the very least for making or inspecting the final connection to a household's 120-volt electrical line.

For complex lighting needs, this custom design route is still the best way to go, whether you employ an electrician or do the job yourself. It affords you the greatest flexibility in terms of variety and quality of materials available, and the effects they can achieve. However, during the past decade, inexpensive low-voltage lighting kits, suitable for use by the average homeowner, have appeared on the shelves of gardening centres and hardware stores, making simple outdoor lighting a viable option for most people. These kits usually consist of a step-down transformer that converts the regular 120-volt line current from the house to a safe 12 volts, a timer, a half-dozen fixtures available in a variety of shapes, spikes for securing fixtures in the ground, and an adequate length of plastic-covered wire. Such kits are a good buy since they are inexpensive, easy and safe to install, and the fixtures come in a variety of shapes and sizes. Unfortunately, most of the fixtures are made of plastic, so in the long run they may not hold up as well as their more expensive metal counterparts. They also only provide coverage for a limited area; if your plan is to install decorative lighting to illuminate a large space or several locations, you will likely have to buy several kits.

Before purchasing a kit, make sure it has been approved by the Canadian Standards Association (CSA). When you are ready to install it, be sure to wire all the lamps in daylight so you can see clearly what you are doing, and don't plug the transformer into the household outlet until the entire system has been wired. Even a low-voltage electrical fixture can give you a small shock.

Lighting Fixtures. There are many attractive outdoor lighting fixtures available for the garden; choose a style that you like and that will serve the purpose for which it is intended. Post lights or globe lights mounted on posts up to 2.5-m (8-ft) high will beautifully illuminate a driveway, an entrance way, or a seating area. Bullet lights, which consist of a simple lamp in a protective casing, and floodlights are best for up-lighting and down-lighting shrubs, trees, and large plants in the border. Low-set mushroom-shaped lights shed a wide circle of light downwards and are excellent for lighting paths, walkways, low border plants, and groundcovers. Tiered lights glow softly to side-light a path, steps, and ground-hugging plants.

The bulbs you use in your fixtures will depend in part on their rating and in part on the effect you wish to create. The two types of light bulbs most commonly used are halogen and incandescent. Halogen lights most closely approximate natural light conditions; incandescent lights shed a warmer, softer glow. To reduce the likelihood of attracting insects with your outdoor lamps, purchase yellow-tinted bulbs as insects are repelled by them. When deciding what strength of light bulbs to choose, first check the fixture rating and do not exceed it. Then take into account that low-wattage bulbs throw a soft, diffuse light over a limited area, whereas high-wattage bulbs are useful for spotlights or for illuminating a larger area of the garden.

Regardless of whether you choose to light your night garden with a low-voltage kit or a high-voltage custom system, think of your design in terms of painting a picture with light and shadow to create an effect that is natural and dramatic at the same time.

Gardens for Touching

From time to time gardeners need to be reminded that there is much more to be enjoyed in gardens than what can be seen. By reaching beyond the obvious effects of visual impact, the other wonderful, though often more subtle, sensations evoked by every element of the garden can be discovered. If you have good eyesight, these discoveries are a bonus; if you have limited eyesight, they are essential.

Experienced gardeners know that the act of creating and maintaining a garden is, by its very nature, a tactile one. Gardeners use their hands to dig, plant, water, and pick their way through every growing season. The smooth curve of a well-worn trowel handle, the damp crumbly texture of freshly turned earth, and the cool mist of a sprinkler on a hot summer's day—these are all sensations that feel good to the touch and give satisfaction time and time again.

The pleasures of touching need not be restricted to the practical aspects of implementing a garden plan. Whether you are hard at work, making daily rounds, or simply passing through, take the time to get in touch with the "feel of things." Plants can withstand many a gentle rub along the way, and most herbs require these moments of direct contact to reveal their fragrant secrets.

The same varied textures of blossoms, foliage, and bark that create pleasing images in the garden also make for fascinating touching. Mosses and tulip petals feel like velvet; ornamental grasses have a papery feel; ferns, astilbe, and meadowsweet are feathery to the touch; lambs' ears, sages, and pussytoes are soft and fuzzy; sedums, hen and chicks, and wintergreen are distinctly leathery; and the seed heads of ligularia and clematis are amazingly silky. Even the smooth barks of Amur chokecherry and birch and the rough bark of elms beg for the occasional caress. Place these plants and others like them within easy reach in the garden, where you and your visitors are likely to pause for a lingering touch. By the same token, sharp and prickly plants, though beautiful to behold, should be placed towards the back of the border or off the beaten path to avoid skin irritation or minor injury. Sea holly, roses, junipers, spruce, and yucca fall into this category.

As you learn to explore with your fingertips, encourage your children to do the same. By developing a touching garden and giving permission to touch, you can create an entertaining opportunity for children to learn about living plants. Let them pick the velvety blossoms of snapdragons and learn to make them "snap." Show them how to sip sweet nectar from the annual

❧ Plants for Touching Gardens ❧

Plants pleasant to the touch

Amur chokecherry (*Prunus maackii*) - bark

Astilbe (*Astilbe* spp.) - flowers and foliage

Birch (*Betula* spp.) - bark

Buttercup (*Ranunculus acris* 'Flore Pleno') - children's games

Clematis (*Clematis* spp.) - seed heads

Daisy (*Chrysanthemum* x *superbum*) - children's games

Elm (*Ulmus* spp.) - bark

Fern (all types) - foliage

Golden groundsel (*Ligularia* spp.) - seed heads

Grass (all types) - foliage

Lambs' ears (*Stachys byzantina*) - foliage

Meadowsweet (*Filipendula rubra*) - flowers and foliage

Moss (all types) - foliage

Pussytoes (*Antennaria* spp.) - foliage

Sage (*Salvia officinalis*) - foliage

Salvia (*Salvia splendens*) - children's games

Snapdragon (*Antirrhinum majus*) - children's games

Stonecrop (*Sedum* spp.) - foliage

Tulip (*Tulipa* spp.) - flowers

Wintergreen (*Gaultheria procumbens*) - foliage

Plants unpleasant to the touch

Juniper (*Juniperus* spp.)

Rose (*Rosa* spp.)

Sea holly (*Eryngium* spp.)

Spruce (*Picea* spp.)

Yucca (*Yucca filamentosa* spp.)

scarlet salvia trumpets, which can be easily removed without affecting the overall beauty of the plants. Offer daisies to make flower chains and the game "loves me, loves me not" or buttercup blossoms to determine one's affinity for butter. Or why not enlist their help picking small fruits and vegetables, both hands-on activities that will familiarize them with the texture or "feel" of plants?

A word of caution about poisonous plants: Having created a touching garden, it would be best not to grow them at all. However, if you must, then know what you have, identify them as being out of bounds for touching (and tasting), and plant them in locations that are difficult or impossible for children and pets to reach.

Gardens for Fragrance

Of all stimulants to the senses, fragrance is the most capricious to detect, the most elusive to define, and the most complex to describe. In the garden, as elsewhere, it also has the singular ability to evoke memories, more so than any other sensation. Distinctive scents wafting gently on the breeze can transport you instantly through time to places, events, or individuals who have special meaning.

With a bit of ingenuity and careful plant selection, you can use the perfumes of plant blossoms and foliage to weave an understorey of magic in your garden. The process of choosing fragrant plants to grow is a personal one, and as with all areas of garden planning, you will likely go through several versions before you get it just right. Many factors can influence your choices. Not only do you need to identify the particular fragrances that appeal to you (for example, spicy, fruity, minty) and buy accordingly, but you also need to think about how you use your garden and when. This will help you determine where to plant your fragrant treasures for maximum enjoyment.

Plants exude fragrance to attract pollinators—bees, butterflies, moths, and other winged creatures whose activities are essential for plant reproduction. Plant fragrances themselves are determined by the composition of their essential oils, harboured in glands at the base of petals or within leaves. Often, dozens of different essential oils within one plant combine to give it a complex but exquisite characteristic essence.

The essential oils of flowers are slowly and naturally discharged into the air from a petal's surface—the warmer the air temperature, the more rapid the release. Also, the higher the humidity, the more intense the blossom scent; gardens are particularly fragrant after a light rain or watering. In contrast, the scented oils of leaves are released only as the cell walls are broken, when the leaves are gently rubbed or crushed. For a single species to have

The silky seed heads of *Clematis tangutica* make it just one of the many irresistible plants that appeal to the sense of touch. MAUREEN IRETON

both flowers and leaves that are fragrant is unusual; in most cases it will be either the flowers or the leaves that delight us. French marigolds, sages, and lavender are among the small number of plants whose leaves and blossoms are both pleasantly scented.

Sometimes the best way to discover what flowers smell like and which scents appeal to you the most is to bury your nose in blossoms or gently rub leaves with the tips of your fingers. Do this discreetly in the gardens of friends, public gardens, or local nurseries.

Some scents simply defy description. Roses smell like roses, and lilacs—well, they smell like lilacs. You need to experience them to decide whether or not you like them. Other scents are familiar and easy to define. Cottage pinks, wall flowers, stocks, and the biennial sweet rocket are distinctly clove scented; heliotrope smells of vanilla to some and almonds to others; lemon verbena, lemon balm, lemon-scented geraniums, and dittany all have lemon-scented foliage; sweet alyssum and some honeysuckles smell of honey (though some would say that sweet alyssum reminds them of freshly mown hay as do the dried leaves of sweet woodruff and the hay-scented fern). Even if you can't describe in words what you are smelling, you'll know whether a particular scent appeals to you or not.

When you visit your local nursery to select plants and you aren't sure which cultivar is the best bet for fragrance, remember the words *fragrans* or *odoratum* in the botanic name provide a clue. Generally speaking, cultivars with single rows of petals or naturally occurring doubles are more fragrant than hybridized doubles (during hybridization, the second row of petals generated can replace a flower's fragrance). Another rule of thumb is the lighter the flower colour, the stronger the scent; many white-flowered plants are fragrant at night. Usually white blossoms are the most strongly perfumed, followed by off white, pink, mauve, yellow, and purple. Blue, orange, or red flowers usually have little or no scent. However, as with every rule, there are exceptions. In the case of roses, usually the red ones are the most strongly scented. Finally, plants that bloom early in the spring or late in the fall are very fragrant in order to attract pollinators that are characteristically sluggish at those times. Prudent research into book and catalogue descriptions, word-of-mouth recommendations, and experience over time will help you sniff out the less obvious choices.

If you spend a large part of your time working in the garden, you can plant for fragrance in virtually any sunny spot that is sheltered from prairie breezes and winds. Your daily garden chores will at one time or another bring you into close proximity with all your scented plants, and you can enjoy them at will. Of course, scented plants displayed next to garden paths and entrance ways are more accessible to both you and your visitors, as are those situated in raised beds and containers artfully arranged adjacent to seating areas. Take advantage of the prevailing wind direction to focus airborne scents where you are most likely to pause and savour them.

～ Grouping Fragrant Plants ～

While appealing to some, the blending of multiple scents in a small area is overwhelming to others. In fact, you will probably enjoy your garden the most when the individual fragrant components are kept distinct, separated either in space or by the timing of their release. When choosing garden sites for your fragrant purchases, group like-scented plants to combine and enhance their effect. To introduce a diverse selection of perfumes into the garden and at the same time minimize their interaction,

🌹 leave generous spaces between plants with dissimilar scents

🌹 interplant day-scented and night-scented bloomers; early-season and late-season bloomers; or plants that hug their fragrances to themselves and those that offer their perfumes up on a gentle breeze

Fragrant Plants. *Tried and True Perennial and Annual Favourites.* In its simplest form, fragrance gardening begins in the summer flower border with well-known, tried-and-true favourites spaced judiciously to separate their spheres of influence. Tender and shrub roses are probably the most universal choice for imparting fragrance to the garden. These can be planted in a bed of their own or included in an established flower bed. Try cottage pinks, carnations, sweet Williams, sweet alyssum, mignonette, annual candytuft and lupins, or verbena at the front of the border. In the mid-section, plant old-fashioned peonies (pink and white are the most fragrant) or pale lavender heliotrope against a background of the taller Russian sage or garden phlox.

Hardy Bulbs. Fragrant spring-flowering hardy bulbs deserve a place in the garden, either in the border, naturalized in the lawn, or in a woodland setting. Some daffodils and tulips impart a delicate fragrance to the air, as do grape hyacinths, the honey-scented snowdrops, and the diminutive *Iris reticulata*. Martagon and trumpet lilies grow from hardy bulbs and provide reliable colour and fragrance all summer long. Choose martagon lilies for early in the season and trumpet hybrids for the mid-season. Oriental lilies are also fragrant, blooming late in the season; they require plenty of protection to survive Calgary winters. Species lilies, ancestors to the hybrids, are also deliciously perfumed. An added benefit of growing lilies is that they do well in dappled light. As such, they are one of the few scent options not requiring full sun, although sweet-smelling lily-of-the-valley, sweet woodruff, and some hostas will perfume shady corners.

Tender Bulbs. Exotic tender bulbs are a must for the fragrant garden, especially when planted in pots placed adjacent to seating areas. Their heady and unfamiliar perfumes lend an aura of romance and mystery to the surrounding air. Look for freesia, peacock orchid, *Amarcrinum*, baboon flower, perfumed fairy lily, sea daffodil, or spider lily at your local garden centre or order them from a reputable catalogue, remembering that they will not survive a Calgary winter outdoors. However, when planted in pots they are easy to bring inside for overwintering, and may also be given an indoor head start in early spring.

Trees and Shrubs. Trees and shrubs are essential ingredients for the well-planned garden, and there are several fragrant varieties that are hardy in the prairies. Many evergreens, whether pine, spruce, or fir emit an agreeable resinous scent familiar to those who love the smell of Christmas trees in their living room. This fine aroma becomes particularly noticeable when the atmosphere is hot and humid, a condition that admittedly does not often prevail in Calgary, but when it does, the resultant scent can take your breath away. Balsam poplar, little-leaf linden (planted in a sheltered spot), Russian olive, hawthorn, ornamental crabapple, and Nanking cherry all do well in Calgary and make a fragrant statement when they bloom. Lilac, mock orange, honeysuckle, some daphnes, and many shrub roses do the same, especially when massed around an entrance or positioned strategically under a window or in the perennial border.

Vines. Vines should be used much more often as vertical accents in the garden. A few scented ones are worth growing on trellises bordering a patio or framing a bedroom window, cloaking a pergola, or draped artistically over an archway. Annual sweet peas are everyone's favourites, with the purple varieties of the old-fashioned original Spencer-type the most fragrant.

~ Plants for Fragrant Gardens ~

Annuals and perennials

Annual candytuft (*Iberis umbellata*)
Annual lupin (*Lupinus hartwegii* spp.)
Carnation (*Dianthus caryophyllus* 'Grenadin Series')
Cottage pink (*Dianthus plumarius*)
Garden phlox (*Phlox paniculata*)
Heliotrope (*Heliotropium arborescens*)
Hosta (*Hosta* spp.)

Lily-of-the-valley (*Convallaria majalis*)
Mignonette (*Reseda odorata*)
Peony (pink and white) (*Paeonia* spp.)
Russian sage (*Perovskia atriplicifolia*)
Sweet alyssum (*Lobularia maritima*)
Sweet William (*Dianthus barbatus*)
Sweet woodruff (*Galium odoratum*)
Verbena (*Verbena hortensis*)

Hardy bulbs

Daffodil (*Narcissus poeticus* 'Actaea', *N. tazetta* 'Minnow', *N. cyclamineus* 'Tete-a-tete')
Grape hyacinth (*Muscari* spp.)
Iris (*Iris reticulata*)

Lily (*Lilium* spp.)
Snowdrop (*Galanthus nivalis*)
Tulip (*Tulipa* 'Best Seller', *T.* 'General de Wet', *T.* 'Angelique')

Exotic tender bulbs

Peacock orchid (*Acidanthera bicolor*)
Amarcrinum
Baboon flower (*Babiana*)
Freesia (*Freesia*)

Perfumed fairy lily (*Chlidanthus fragrans*)
Sea daffodil (*Hymenocallis*)
Spider lily (*Crinum*)

Trees and shrubs

Balsam poplar (*Populus balsamifera*)
Crabapple (*Malus* spp.)
Daphne (*Daphne cneorum*)
Fir (*Abies* spp.)
Hardy roses ('Blanc Double de Coubert', 'Therese Bugnet', 'Henry Hudson', 'Jens Munk')
Hawthorn (*Crataegus* x *mordenensis*)
Honeysuckle (*Lonicera* spp.)

Lilac (*Syringa* spp.)
Little-leaf linden (*Tilia cordata*)
Mock orange (*Philadelphus* spp.)
Nanking cherry (*Prunus tomentosa*)
Pine (*Pinus* spp.)
Russian olive (*Elaeagnus angustifolia*)
Spruce (*Picea* spp.)

Vines

Annual sweet peas (old-fashioned original Spencer-type) (*Lathyrus odoratus*)

Hardy 'Explorer' roses 'John Cabot', 'William Baffin' (trained as climbers)

Plants with scented foliage

Basil (*Ocimum basilicum*)

Bee balm (*Monarda didyma*)

Borage (*Borago officinalis*)

Chives (*Allium schoenoprasum*)

Chrysanthemum (*Chrysanthemum* spp.)

Curry plant (*Helichrysum angustifolium*)

Dill (*Anethem graveolens*)

Lavender cotton (*Santolina chamaecy-parissus*)

Lemon verbena (*Aloysia triphylla*)

Mint (*Mentha* spp.)

Parsley (*Petroselinum* spp.)

Rosemary (*Rosmarinus officinalis*)

Rue (*Ruta graveolens*)

Sage (*Salvia* spp.)

Scented geranium (*Pelargonium* spp.)

Tarragon (*Artemisia dracunculus sativa*)

Thyme (*Thymus* spp.)

Wintergreen (*Gaultheria procumbens*)

Night-scented plants

Blue-flowered petunia (*Petunia* spp.)

Evening primrose (*Oenothera biennis*)

Nicotiana (*Nicotiana sylvestris*)

Honeysuckles (*Lonicera* spp.)

Four o'clock (*Mirabilis jalapa*)

Evening (night) scented stock (*Matthiola longipetala*)

Species lily (*Lilium* spp.)

Sweet rocket (*Hesperis matronalis*)

The evocative perfume of tender roses, such as this delightfully scented grandiflora rose, 'Gold Medal', is well worth the extra effort required to protect them during a Calgary winter. Don Heimbecker

Regretfully, there are no true climbing roses that survive our Calgary winters, but several fragrant shrub roses can be trained over a trellis or pergola to look like climbers, with stunning visual and aromatic impact. Try the Explorer roses 'John Cabot' or 'William Baffin'. Other vines, although themselves unscented, can help create the still, protected microclimate that serves to intensify the perfumes of fragrant plants.

Plants with Scented Foliage. No fragrant planting scheme is complete without a good collection of the plants that boast an astonishing array of aromatic foliage—herbs. Their leaves need to be pinched or rubbed gently to release their scented oils, so plant them within easy reach. For maximum impact, plant herbs by the back door, spilling over the edges of a garden wall or path, or in pots on the deck. Think about including the proverbial parsley, sage, rosemary, and thyme in your herb collection; then pick your favourites among such standards as basil, mint, dill, rue, tarragon, chives, lemon verbena, borage, curry plant—the list is endless. Also save a corner for some potted scented geraniums and lavender cotton, and don't forget that bee balm, chrysanthemums, and wintergreen gladly release their scented oils when you brush past them.

Night-scented Plants. Finally, take advantage of the many plants that wait until nightfall to share their fragrant secrets. This will be especially appealing if you are away from home all day, which leaves the evening as the only available time for working in and enjoying the garden. Plant them near seating areas, adjacent to well-travelled paths, or under an open window, where their fragrance will linger even after you have gone to bed. Night-scented plants to choose from include sweet rocket, evening (night) scented stocks, evening primrose, nicotiana (especially *Nicotiana sylvestris*), four o'clocks, blue-flowered petunias, and species lilies. Honeysuckles also are at their most fragrant at nightfall.

Gardens for Tasting

Few gardening pleasures are as rewarding as the sweetness of your own just-picked strawberries, tomatoes, or baby carrots, or the fresh flavours of the first chives or mint of the season. The archetypal garden is one that tempts us to taste, and to many gardeners, the garden that does not please the palate is incomplete.

For the first settlers in Calgary, gardens were an important source of food, and large crops of root vegetables often sustained families over the long winter. Today, most urban gardeners have neither the space nor the time required to maintain large plots of potatoes or thickets of raspberry canes. Many no longer need or even desire this type of garden (although admirable large vegetable gardens are planted in Calgary every year). But even though the utility garden has largely given way to the ornamental garden, you can still enjoy the culinary delights that come with cultivating a tasting garden. Fruit, vegetables, and herbs, which include favourite edible flowers, can all be integrated into a garden of any size. If you consider edible plants as part of the complete design of your garden and incorporate them according to aesthetic qualities, they will be both functional and beautiful, nourishing body and soul.

Plants for tasting should be easily accessible, so plant edible flowers, herbs, and salad greens along paths, at the front of mixed borders, and in pots or planters on a deck, patio, or balcony. If it is necessary to plant tall herbs, such as lovage or angelica, at the back of a flower bed, lay stepping stones to allow you to reach these plants without setting foot in the soil. (Even if your garden is purely ornamental, it is wise to plan for access to all plants for pest patrol, deadheading, and other maintenance.)

Ideally, the tasting garden should be free of all pesticides and herbicides. If you must use chemical controls, choose those that are recommended for use on edible plants, and read labels carefully to determine when it is safe to harvest plants that have been sprayed.

The practical benefits of incorporating edible plants in your garden include convenience, freshness, and the opportunity to choose from many more herb, fruit, and vegetable varieties than are commonly available for purchase at supermarkets or even farmers' markets. But there are also less tangible rewards. There is an undeniable satisfaction to be found in even a limited self-sufficiency, and as you taste your transient summer garden, you share in the experience of those past gardeners whose toil was as much due to necessity as a desire to create beautiful surroundings.

Edible Perennials. The least labour-intensive means of establishing a tasting garden is by planting edible perennials.

Vegetables. Although most vegetables are annuals in Calgary, there are perennial vegetables that are happy to be tucked in among the flowers, and they will provide you with culinary pleasure for years with a minimum of fuss. Asparagus takes about four years to become fully productive, but when the time comes to harvest those delectable tender spears for a spring dinner, it is well worth the long period of anticipation. In addition, asparagus has lovely ferny foliage that turns golden in the autumn. Rhubarb is another spring treat that makes a handsome addition to a mixed border with its large leaves and red stalks.

Herbs. Many perennial culinary herbs display striking shapes, textures, and colours in both flowers and foliage. They are also very attractive to bees and butterflies. Bee balm, a tea herb, has shaggy red, pink, purple, or white blossoms on tall plants suitable for the middle of borders. Watch for hummingbirds hovering over your bee balm; it should attract any in the neighbourhood! Smaller herbs for the front of the border include thyme, with purple or pink flowers, and feverfew and chamomile adorned with daisy-like blooms in white and yellow. The foliage is also varied and decorative. Lovage is an impressive celery-flavoured herb for the back of the border. It can reach 2 m (6 ft), not including the flowers—vigorous umbels that often shoot up to 3 m (10 ft). Tarragon and winter savory have narrow leaves, and sorrel resembles spinach. There are golden, purple, and tri-colour (purple, cream, and green) varieties of sage, but these require winter protection in Calgary as they are not as hardy as the reliable common sage. Other attractive foliage herbs include low-growing golden oregano, variegated white-and-green marjoram or lemon balm, and gold-and-green and silver-and-green thyme. With the exception of lovage and lemon balm, which grow well in partial shade, all these herbs prefer a sunny location and should be mulched for the winter.

Most culinary herbs are well behaved, but there are two desirable perennial herbs that require caution—horseradish and mint. They should not be planted in mixed borders because of their aggressive tendencies and the difficulty of eradicating them once established. Instead, plant them in areas where they can be confined, such as in the narrow beds between a house and a sidewalk or lawn. Horseradish is deep rooted and will grow from the tiniest piece of root left in the ground. However, if you are fond of this herb, the flavour and sinus-clearing power of freshly ground horseradish root are incomparable. Mint is indispensable in a tasting garden, so do not allow its reputation to deter you from planting a patch.

If you wish to include tender perennial herbs such as rosemary or bay in your tasting garden, it is easiest to plant them in pots so they may be brought inside for the winter. This saves on the labour involved in planting them in the spring and digging them up in the fall.

Edible Annuals. Tomatoes and annual herbs such as basil are also well suited to pots, which can be moved around at your convenience and brought inside for protection from hail or frost. Basil is extremely sensitive, often wilting at temperatures several degrees above freezing and sulking during protracted periods of wet weather; if grown in your vegetable or flower garden, it will not thrive unless it is planted in a sunny, sheltered spot and protected with plastic row covers. There are exciting new cultivars of this most desirable herb introduced every year, but a recommended cultivar of basil for Calgary is African blue basil, which is more cold-tolerant (but not frost-tolerant) than other basils, can easily be propagated from cuttings, and is an attractive container plant with purple flower spikes and purplish blue stems and leaf veins. The flavour is pleasant but not the same as that of the Italian-style basils, so you may wish to try two or three varieties. The best cold- and frost-tolerant herb you can grow in Calgary is parsley, either the decorative curly or flat-leafed varieties. It is not unusual for Calgary gardeners to still be harvesting parsley in late October or early November, long after other garden edibles, except some root vegetables, have succumbed to frost.

If you have a vegetable patch, include some annual herbs that self-sow, the next best thing to perennials. Borage, chervil, and dill cast their seeds about

This herb garden, gratifying to both the eye and the palate, is conveniently located a few steps from the back door. LIESBETH LEATHERBARROW

with enthusiasm, reappearing each year; summer savory reproduces itself with more restraint. Extra seedlings are easily transplanted or shared with less fortunate gardening friends. Herbs may also be used in the vegetable garden as companion plants to repel pests or enhance growth.

Fruit Trees and Shrubs. On a larger scale, a well-placed specimen of an apple, crabapple, or chokecherry tree is a fine focal point for your tasting garden. Plant these trees away from decks or patios to avoid the mess created by falling and rotting fruit. Incorporate fruiting shrubs, such as currants, raspberries, Saskatoons, Nanking cherries, and highbush cranberries, into your landscape invitingly within reach of paths.

Children's Tasting Gardens. Tasting gardens are another enjoyable way to introduce children to gardening. Children love picking and eating fruit, vegetables, and herbs from their own gardens. Try hardy alpine strawberries, which do not send out suckers and will produce plenty of small strawberries all summer long. They also self-seed to produce even more plants the following year, if not completely picked clean! There are small varieties of round or finger-shaped carrots ideal for snacking, and herbs such as chocolate mint or the many fruit-flavoured varieties such as apple, pineapple, or lemon mint are appealing for children to nibble on. Dainty star-shaped blue borage flowers easily pull off their stems and can be frozen in ice cubes for cold drinks on hot summer days, the flowers turning pink as the ice melts. Add a few edible flowers such as violas, nasturtiums, or calendula, and the children's potage garden will be complete. A note of caution: Do not include poisonous plants in a garden where young children will be playing and tasting. Children should also be taught not to eat any plants without asking permission from a responsible adult, as herbicides or pesticides may cause even edible plants to become dangerous to eat.

This exuberant child's garden, planted by an eight year old, overflows with edible flowers and herbs (nasturtium, calendula, bachelor's button, and parsley). LIESBETH LEATHERBARROW

~ Plants for Tasting Gardens ~

Herbs

Angelica (*Angelica archangelica*)

Basil (*Ocimum basilicum*)

Bay (*Laurus nobilis*)

Bee balm (*Monarda didyma, M. fistulosa*)

Borage (*Borago officinalis*)

Bronze fennel (*Foeniculum vulgare* 'Purpureum')

Chervil (*Anthriscus cerefolium*)

Chives (*Allium schoenoprasum*)

Cilantro (*Coriandrum sativum*)

Dill (*Anethum graveolens*)

Golden oregano (*Origanum vulgare* 'Aureum')

Lemon Balm (*Melissa officinalis*)

Lovage (*Levisticum officinale*)

Marjoram (*Origanum majorana*)

Mint (English, spearmint, peppermint, chocolate, pineapple, lemon) (*Mentha* spp.)

Parsley (curly and flat-leafed) (*Petroselinum crispum, P. hortense*)

Roman chamomile (*Chamaemelum nobile*)

Rosemary (*Rosmarinus officinalis*)

Sage (common, tri-color, purple) (*Salvia officinalis*)

Sorrel (*Rumex acetosa*)

Summer savory (*Satureja hortensis*)

Tarragon (*Artemisia dracunculus sativa*)

Thyme (golden, green, silver) (*Thymus vulgaris*)

Variegated marjoram (*Origanum vulgare* 'Variegata')

Winter savory (*Satureja montana*)

Fruit Trees and Shrubs

Apple (*Malus* spp.)

Chokecherry (*Prunus virginiana* 'Schubert')

Crabapple (*Malus* x *adstringens* cultivars)

Cranberry (*Viburnum* spp.)

Currant (*Ribes* spp.)

Gooseberry (*Ribes* spp.)

Nanking cherry (*Prunus tomentosa*)

Raspberry (*Rubus* spp.)

Saskatoon (*Amelanchier alnifolia*)

~ Edible Flowers ~

The following common garden flowers are edible, as are the blooms of culinary herbs such as basil, chives, oregano, rosemary, sage, and thyme.

Calendula (*Calendula officinalis*)

Daylily (*Hemerocallis* spp.)

Geranium (including scented) (*Pelargonium* spp.)

Hollyhock (*Alcea rosea*)

Nasturtium (*Tropaeolum majus*)

Ornamental onion (*Allium* spp.)

Pansy (*Viola* x *wittrockiana*)

Pinks (*Dianthus* spp.)

Rose (*Rosa* spp.)

Viola (*Viola* spp.)

Gardens for Sound

Yet another layer of sensual enjoyment to be derived from the garden comes from the wide range of natural sounds produced within its confines. The next time you are out weeding or bent to some other gardening task, take a well-deserved break, close your eyes, and simply listen. First try to filter out the cacophony of neighbourhood voices, lawnmowers, and traffic, and then let the murmur of rustling leaves, the gentle hum of honey bees, and the warbling of avian visitors surround you. The harmony of these natural sounds in the garden is guaranteed to give you a feeling of peace and tranquility, and a heightened sense of having created a natural haven from the bustle of everyday living. What's more, by recognizing the possibilities of "gardening for sound," you, the gardener, can take a few simple steps to enhance your auditory pleasure.

Foliage. Foliage in the garden provides endless opportunity for the hiss and swish of prairie breezes. The deciduous leaves of shade trees, shrubs, and vines rustle pleasantly when the breezes blow. Even evergreens such as spruce and especially pines whisper invitingly in the wind.

If you think your garden is too small for growing trees, remember that columnar varieties of some common trees can be found to fit your space. In a breath of air, their fluttering leaves are as audible as those of their bigger cousins. Try Swedish columnar aspen, the columnar variety of Scots pine, columnar Siberian crab, or Sutherland caragana, all of which grow with an erect, non-spreading habit. Other compact trees that are attractive and will not outgrow limited spaces include trembling aspen, hawthorn, and Russian mountain ash. Large shrubs such as Nanking cherry, double-flowering plum, highbush cranberry, and lilac can be trained into small trees to fit small gardens.

If trees are truly not an option for you, plant ornamental grasses strategically, either in the ground or in pots; they will rustle in the slightest of breezes to create the effect of the wind blowing through wide expanses of prairie grass. Quaking grass, golden brome, and ribbon grass are all useful for this purpose, but may require some containment as they can be invasive.

Bees. There is no sound as pleasant as the buzz of honey bees as they go about their daily business of collecting nectar and pollinating flowers. They are a living presence and good company on a quiet day. Honey bees favour certain plants over others, so choose several of these and plant them in attractive clumps throughout the garden to ensure the presence of their industrious drone. Hyssop, anise hyssop, bee balm, asters, columbines, and daisies are just a few of the many plant species that are attractive to bees. Incidentally, it is legal to house active bee hives within the city limits.

Birds. Bird song and chatter create a wild chorus that is music to the ear. Since birds are attracted to spaces most closely resembling their natural habitats, you can make a large variety of birds welcome in your garden by offering an assortment of natural foods. The seed heads of ornamental grasses and composite flowers such as asters, daisies, and sunflowers are excellent sources of nutrition for seed-loving birds; trees and shrubs (both deciduous and coniferous) supply the grubs, insects, berries, and pinecone seeds favoured by others. Trees and shrubs also serve as nesting sites, protection from predators, and, in some cases, a pantry for collected seeds. Finally, you can install a simple bird-bath or, if you wish,

---

∼ Plants to Attract Bees ∼

Honey bees seem to prefer plants that range in colour from blue to white. Choose from the following.

Anise hyssop (*Agastache foeniculum*)	Forget-me-not (*Myosotis*)
Aster (*Aster* spp.)	Globe thistle (*Echinops ritro*)
Basil (*Ocimum basilicum*)	Hyssop (*Hyssopus officinalis*)
Bee balm (*Monarda* spp.)	Jacob's ladder (*Polemonium* spp.)
Bellflower (*Campanula* spp.)	Lavender (*Lavandula angustifolia*)
Blue-eyed Mary (*Omphalodes verna*)	Lobelia (*Lobelia erinus*)
Borage (*Borago officinalis*)	Monkshood (*Aconitum* spp.)
Catmint (*Nepeta* spp.)	Oregano (*Origanum* spp.)
Columbine (*Aquilegia* spp.)	Ornamental onion (*Allium* spp.)
Coneflower (*Echinacea purpurea*)	Poppy (*Papaver* spp.)
Cornflower (*Centaurea* spp.)	Sedum (*Sedum* spp.)
Daffodil (*Narcissus* spp.)	Siberian squill (*Scilla siberica*)
Daisy (*Chrysanthemum* spp.)	Summer savory (*Satureja hortensis*)
Delphinium (*Delphinium* spp.)	Thyme (*Thymus* spp.)
Feverfew (*Chrysanthemum parthenium*)	Valerian (*Valeriana officinalis*)
	Veronica (*Veronica* spp.)

a more elaborate water feature with running water to help entice birds for your listening enjoyment.

Water. Most of us find the sound of running water soothing to the soul, and although the installation of a pond may not be on your "to do" list, there are a few simple alternatives worth considering. A self-contained wall-mounted fountain, complete with a circulating pump, is inexpensive and easy to run and maintain; mount one close to your favourite outdoor seating area. A small circulating pump and fountain installed in a half-barrel is another inexpensive way to create the sound of splashing water. For more ideas on simple, inexpensive water features, see the section on small water features in chapter two.

The soothing sound of water splashing over rocky ledges is both restful and rejuvenating. Val Pritchard

FOUR

The Traditional Gardener

The first settlers to arrive in Calgary brought with them gardening wisdom passed down through many generations. This information was essential as survival often depended upon growing enough food to nourish a family over the winter. Traditional gardening techniques are based on observation, experience, and common sense. Before synthetic pesticides, herbicides, or fertilizers—the "quick fixes" of modern horticulture—gardeners relied on natural processes and naturally occurring substances. While most of the advancements of modern agriculture are undoubtedly beneficial to large-scale food production, many home gardeners are returning to time-honoured techniques that recognize nature as a partner rather than as an adversary. Many methods of planting, pest control, and water conservation adopt the experience of the past to safeguard the gardens of the future.

Phenology

Phenology is the study of the timing of recurring biological events in relation to plants and animals and how these events are connected to climatic conditions. People who work close to the land have long observed native plants and animals for cues to the progress of the seasons to determine when it is time to plant, prune, or harvest. Times for the flowering or leafing-out of a plant species vary from place to place, and even in the same place, they vary from year to year. As the result of these and similar observations, calendars were developed based on natural phenomena rather than on arbitrary dates.

The study of phenology has a fascinating history. The Japanese have recorded the date of the annual appearance of the cherry blossoms since A.D. 812. These records are kept in the imperial court archives. The term *phenology* was first used by Swedish botanist Carolus Linnaeus (Carl von Linné), who pioneered methods of compiling information on plant cycles and climatology and established a network of phenological stations in Sweden. In England, six generations of the Marsham family of Norfolk kept detailed phenological accounts from 1736 to 1925. The oldest part of the document was discovered under the floor of an old mill in 1924. The Marshams recorded the leafing-out dates of 13 trees, including hawthorn, birch, beech, oak, and horse chestnut, and the flowering dates of snowdrops, wood anemone, and hawthorn. They also noted the movements of several migratory birds and the first croaking of frogs.[27]

If you keep a garden journal, you will undoubtedly have recorded your own phenological data. Who can resist triumphantly recording the appearance of the first precocious little snowdrop or crocus, or the unexpected deep purple of the little bulbous spring irises thrusting through the brown mulch in an otherwise drab garden? The tedium of Calgary winters makes spring record-keeping a pleasure; the challenge is to continue to faithfully record the signals of the changing seasons throughout the busy gardening year.

It is useful to track certain indicator plants in relation to the weather over the course of several years. Their times of leafing-out and bloom in the microclimate of your garden may be different from

---

∼ A Time to Plant ∼

These time-honoured planting tips for the Calgary region are based on phenology.

🌸 Plant lettuce and radishes when the early blue violets bloom.

🌸 When the buffalo beans are in bloom, sow lettuce, peas, sweet peas, and poppies; plant out onions and pansies.

🌸 Pansies, snapdragons, and other hardy transplants may be set out in the garden when native poplars and willows leaf out as this signals the end of hard frosts; however, light frosts may still occur.

🌸 Plant potatoes when the poplars start to leaf out.

🌸 Plant lettuce, spinach, beets, carrots, and other cool-season vegetables when dandelion and honeysuckle bloom.

🌸 When the Saskatoons are in bloom, sow broad beans, carrots, turnips, beets, spinach, calendula, and clarkia; plant out petunias, snapdragons, cabbage, broccoli, and potatoes.

🌸 When the green ash trees leaf out, it is time to plant out tender perennials and annuals.

🌸 When the first daylilies start to bloom, set out tomato and pepper plants.

🌸 Plant corn, cucumbers, pumpkins, and squash when the lilac blossoms fade.

those in the gardens of neighbours or friends across town. In addition, the flowering dates of the earliest-blooming plants (March to April) will vary far more than the flowering dates of the later-blooming ones (June to August). After several years of observation, you will become familiar with the biological sequences in your own garden and be better able to apply what nature is telling you to your own gardening practices.

The timing of spring development in Calgary is largely controlled by temperature accumulation; after warm winters, expect early spring leafing and flowering. The common lilac is a familiar Calgary shrub to use as a natural calendar. The leafing-out of the lilac is a signal to sow cool-season vegetables such as lettuce, peas, and spinach; when the lilac blooms, it's time to fertilize the lawn and plant warm-season crops such as bush or runner beans and corn. Conventional wisdom has it that lilacs do not bloom until the risk of frost has passed; therefore, it should also be safe at this time to plant out tomatoes, peppers, and tender annuals. When the lilac flowers fade, the soil should be warm enough to plant out squash and cucumbers, which are best started indoors in the short Calgary growing season.

Heirloom Gardening

Heirlooms—family treasures passed on from generation to generation—provide us with a much-needed and appreciated link to the past. They give us a sense of who we are and where we come from, and they are often the key to a successful future. It may seem strange to think of vegetables, fruits, flowers, and their seeds as heirlooms, but immigrants newly arrived in North America cherished the seeds so carefully transported from their homeland. They were essential for survival in an unfamiliar place where few native-grown foods were to be found. From the beginning, varieties of vegetables and fruits grown from the settlers' own supply of seeds provided sustenance for the body, just as surely as their flower gardens yielded nourishment for the soul. And like heirloom photographs, paintings, and jewellery, these living riches were reverently passed on from generation to generation.

Plants in early gardens were pollinated naturally with the help of insects or wind. This process, called open pollination, usually led to plants being cross-pollinated with pollen from the same or related plants, resulting in healthy variation in plant offspring. Those who tended the gardens would then, when the time was right, collect seeds for the following year's growing season, making intuitive choices to save seeds from the biggest, the tastiest, or the prettiest of their vegetables and flowers. The consequence of this selective process was the development of plants with traits that were favourable to local growing conditions and to the taste preferences of the local population.

The Case for Heirloom Gardening. Sadly, in modern times many of the plant varieties so treasured in days gone by have disappeared from the face of the planet, never to be seen again. This is a concern to many conservationists, not only for its historic significance, but also because it represents the irreversible loss of genes, the chemical blueprints in plants that define their unique combinations of characteristics. The resultant decline in genetic diversity, a condition essential to the healthy evolution of all living things, can have serious consequences in the future, especially when it comes to food crops.

North American gardeners fell out of the habit of saving seeds around the turn of the century when scientific advances led to modern techniques of hybridizing plants. During hybridization, scientists choose plants with recognized and desirable characteristics, such as disease or drought resistance, and pollinate them by hand for several generations (self-pollination), with uniformly identical or pure offspring the outcome. These pure strains are then crossed with each other to produce new strains that are superior in some desirable way to the parent plants. First-generation hybrids (or F1 hybrids) show a remarkable increase in productivity, referred to as hybrid vigour. At the same time, seeds harvested from F1 hybrids are often sterile and never as productive as the parent plants. In addition, many F1 hybrid offspring, known as F2 hybrids, may bear little or no resemblance to their parents.

The new hybrids with their uniform and hand-picked characteristics were a boon to food producers, consumers, and seed companies alike. Food producers were pleased to be able to grow plant varieties that not only showed increased productivity, uniformity, and disease resistance, but could also withstand the rigours of mechanical harvesting and long-distance transportation to markets. Consumers were excited about the great variety of food to be found on the grocery store shelves. The seed producers, having developed exciting new varieties of vegetables, fruit, and ornamental plants, could withhold the parentage of their creations and thus carve out lucrative markets for themselves as exclusive seed sources.

It is obvious that the advent of hybrids on the growing scene was a good thing; we have all enjoyed the results and should be thankful for their existence. However, they are not without shortcomings. Mass plantings of identical hybrid plants make them susceptible to epidemics, which can be disastrous in food crops. According to Carolyn Jabs, author of *The Heirloom Gardener*, "Of the world's 80,000 edible plants, humans use only a few for food. Scientists estimate that prehistoric people ate about 1500 wild plants, ancient societies cultivated at least 500 major vegetables, and the modern world depends on about 30 plants for 95% of its nutrition."[28] In addition, the process of breeding plants for selected attributes was often carried out at the expense of pre-existing desirable traits such as fragrance; many fine traditional annuals and perennials have lost their exquisite scents in the pursuit of bigger, brighter, and fancier blooms. Finally, the appeal of hybrids, which encouraged many to jump on the bandwagon to the exclusion of all else, has led to the abandonment and eventual extinction of many wonderful old plant varieties.

It is important to know that bioengineers, the scientists responsible for selective hybrid breeding programs, can only combine and recombine genes; they can't invent new ones. So once specific genes and the characteristics they define are lost through extinction, genetic diversity (the variation of genes in the gene pool) has been diminished forever. This could come back to haunt scientists in the future as they struggle to develop plant varieties for coping with ever-changing, unpredictable environmental conditions. Kent Whealy, founder of the Seed Savers Exchange in the United States, reports that fewer than 20 percent of the pea and bean varieties listed in American catalogues at the turn of the century have survived to today. In the case of apple trees, over 8000 varieties were available for cultivation at the turn of the century; in 1981, only 1000 of those varieties could be found.[29] Although these numbers refer to studies carried out in the United States, they demonstrate the degree to which old plant varieties are vanishing from the earth. Possibly, the very genes that might allow plants to endure the growing conditions of the future have vanished. We'll never know for sure, but collectively we should be doing our best to keep as many options open as possible, which includes preventing the further extinction of plant varieties and the essential genetic information they harbour.

The concern for maintaining genetic diversity as insurance for the future has led to the heirloom gardening movement, which strives to locate and preserve original, open-pollinated seed varieties. To this end, organizations have sprung up across North America. These include seed exchanges, whose members undertake to grow and share heirloom seeds; "live museums," such as Heritage Park, where staff are intent upon creating and maintaining period gardens representative of the past; seed storage laboratories, which serve as repositories for heirloom seed collections; and seed companies that are once again including heirloom, open-pollinated seed varieties in their catalogues.

Individuals too can take up the cause, making valuable contributions both out of conviction for scientific need and for intellectual satisfaction. For many, understanding and preserving the past are compelling, as is the notion of becoming a heritage plant collector—and the ensuing anticipation of the chase and thrill of uncovering an old, forgotten, and sometimes unidentifiable plant variety. Not only do individuals often make discoveries missed by the authorities, but by creating their own period gardens, practising sound seed-collecting techniques, and sharing seed stock with friends, they also ensure the distribution of heirloom plants and seeds to future generations of gardeners.

Creating an Heirloom Garden. To create an accurate period garden in the Calgary area, say for the turn of the century, is a challenge. How can you determine what was typical for the time when so much about gardening character was, and still is, determined by the cultural background of the gardeners? A large number of ethnic origins are represented among Calgarians and Albertans, all of whom practised different gardening traditions. Few original gardens have survived the ravages of time to serve as models for the heirloom gardener, and detailed plant lists for reference are few and far between. Unless you are lucky and come into the possession of seeds that have been passed down through the generations, you must rely on regional, period seed catalogues to learn what was being grown and assume that locals were ordering from those catalogues. If, through careful research, you are able to come up with a wish list of seeds for your period garden, tracking them down will take some effort.

Many interesting discoveries are waiting to be made, especially in isolated rural areas. If you would like to take up the search, get involved by interviewing local old-timer gardeners about seeds that have been passed down from generation to generation and about their memories of favourite plants of the past. You can also read old agricultural journals, seed lists, and catalogues for seed and plant descriptions to help you identify any new findings in the field. If you are on a quest for a particular plant variety, centre your investigations on current seed catalogues specializing in heirloom plants, classified ads in gardening magazines, and seed exchange lists.

Once you have your precious seeds in hand, you must take care to provide optimum growing conditions, usually described on seed packets, and to practise sound seed-collecting techniques. To collect seeds that will grow true-to-type in succeeding generations, you must also minimize the possibility of cross-pollination from related plants. To do this, separate your heirloom plants spatially from related plants, or plant related varieties that reach sexual maturity at different times. Then, when the time is right, pollinate your heirloom plants by hand. It is also useful to be familiar with vegetative plant propagation techniques so you can sample existing heirloom plants, trees, and shrubs for your collection (with permission, of course), particularly if their seeds are difficult or impossible to germinate.

The move towards heirloom gardening is gaining momentum in Calgary and in Alberta, and as more concerned citizens become aware of its importance, participation will likely increase. Generations to come will be thankful for the efforts made to uncover and preserve the treasures from a rich horticultural tradition.

∾ An Historic Apple Tree ∾

This extract is based on an article by Henry Lefebvre that appeared in *Calgary Gardening* (vol. 10, no. 3, 1996).

Last year, I had the privilege of meeting Mrs. Sally Elder, an energetic lady of 91, at the home she has lived in for 64 years. We were to talk about the 53-year-old apple tree in her garden and whether I could take some cuttings (scions) from it for propagation through grafting.

Mrs. and Mr. Elder purchased this 'Hibernal' apple tree from Beaverlodge Nursery in 1942, and subsequently won First Prize at the 1946 Calgary Horticultural Show and Second Prize in 1948 with its apples. Despite its age, the tree is still strong and productive. This past September, Mrs. Elder offered me several apples for sampling. The apples, 8–10 cm (3–4 in.) in diameter, were very appealing—yellow with shades of red, and very tasty and crisp. It is an early variety and, typically, does not keep very long. For comparison, it is crisper, tastier, and prettier than 'Heyer 12'. It is also known to be among the hardiest of apple cultivars.

According to S. A. Beach's *Apples of New York* (State of New York, Department of Agriculture, 1905), 'Hibernal' is a Russian variety, and considered then by some as "representing probably the hardiest type of the Russian race of apples. . . . The strong growth makes it especially desirable as a stock for top-grafting. . . . The fruit is large, irregular, skin thick, greenish-yellow with red on the sunny side. . . . The flesh is acid, juicy and good for cooking." These comments were referenced to various sources dating from 1880 to 1903! Over the years, 'Hibernal' has been used extensively as rootstock because of its winter hardiness.

Organic Gardening

The philosophy of growing plants organically is relatively new to the modern world of agriculture and horticulture, although it has been routinely practised since the beginning of time by people in tune with nature's cycles of renewal and replenishment. Briefly stated, organic gardeners choose to work with nature, imitating its processes; they add organic materials to the soil to maintain its structural quality and fertility, and they encourage, as much as possible, the use of natural methods of pest, disease,

At Heritage Park, gardeners propagate heirloom plants by including them in gardens whenever possible. LESLEY REYNOLDS

and weed control rather than synthetic chemical ones. If, on occasion, chemicals are needed to solve a particular gardening problem, organic gardeners always try to select those made from natural products. Although these too can be toxic to insects and humans, they are less so than synthetic chemicals and will break down relatively quickly into substances that are harmless to the environment.

Many horticultural practices derive from the evolution of agricultural practices; the temporary absence and the subsequent re-implementation of an organic gardening strategy is no exception. As populations started growing rapidly in the mid-nineteenth century, there was an accompanying

A bountiful harvest is reaped annually from this organic garden; healthy plants can be maintained without synthetic fertilizers or pesticides. VAL PRITCHARD

need for reliable food sources; unfortunately, those who worked the land lost sight of nature's continuous cycle of growth, death, and decay that had sustained diverse plant communities continuously and without intervention since the early days of plant evolution. They also lost sight of the fact that nature's single most important building block for healthy plant growth has always been (and will continue to be) a healthy soil, liberally supplied with living microorganisms and organic matter to ensure that plants reap its considerable benefits. Instead, some agriculturists and scientists adopted the view that soil was a medium whose primary purpose was to keep plants in place. Crop production became a chemical process with all plant needs being provided through external sources.

This philosophy was reinforced by the discovery in the early 1900s of industrial processes for manufacturing artificial fertilizers, pesticides, and herbicides, and since then there has been no looking back for the synthetic chemical industry. By the mid-twentieth century, however, evidence was beginning to mount that chemicals were not the panacea they were meant to be. True, on the one hand, crop yields had increased, quality had improved, and insect, weed, and disease disasters no longer posed a threat to people's livelihoods. On the other hand, agricultural and horticultural chemicals were becoming serious ground and surface water contaminants, chemical residues in grains, produce, and livestock were compromising people's health and wildlife populations, and the indiscriminate addition of chemical fertilizers and pesticides to the soil was killing valuable soil microorganisms. The destruction of these microorganisms led to a drastic deterioration in soil quality and structure, which, in turn, contributed to serious soil erosion problems.

At about this time, a small group of farmers, worried about the negative effects of chemicals in the environment, began what has become the organic movement. Using the results of a study by Charles Darwin about living soil organisms, farmers and gardeners recognized the importance of returning nutrients to the soil and the role soil organisms, organic matter, and humus play in growing plants successfully. They viewed their growing environments as living systems requiring the recycling of organic wastes, and they believed synthetic fertilizers and pesticides were fatal to the environment. For many years these pioneers were considered to be radical and little attention was paid to their ideas and methods. Now all of that is changing, as more and more people who work the soil recognize that excellent results can be achieved in the garden by following nature's example. Among the techniques employed by the increasing numbers of organic gardeners are integrated pest management, companion planting, and crop rotation.

Integrated Pest Management. The variety and accessibility of pesticides and herbicides in the gardening marketplace can give the impression

∽ Going Organic ∽

Making the switch to organic gardening is quite straightforward and doesn't need to be done all at once. Simply decide where you would like to devote your initial efforts and the rest will follow. There are several key elements to becoming a successful organic gardener, and it pays to become conversant in all of them for optimum results.

🌹 **Recycle organic waste.** Organic home and garden waste can be turned into compost. Healthy soil is essential for a chemical-free garden, and compost is essential for maintaining a healthy soil. Not only does compost supply and release a reserve of nutrients for plants when they need them, it also improves soil drainage and water retention, helps increase the volume of air in the soil, increases the activity and number of beneficial soil microorganisms, feeds and encourages earthworms, prevents soil erosion, stops nutrient loss through leaching, acts as a buffer against toxins in the soil—the list of benefits is endless.

🌹 **Keep the soil healthy.** Amending your soil with compost and other organic matter may take time, but such additions will create a soil rich in humus, which, in turn, will nurture healthy plants. Use organic fertilizers to help supply nutrients that are in short supply until you have restored the health of your soil.

🌹 **Keep the garden clean.** A clean garden helps protect plants against insect pests, weeds, and disease. Remove and dispose of diseased plants in the garbage as soon as you notice them and before they have a chance to infect the rest of the garden. Check new plants for insects and disease before bringing them home.

🌹 **Learn to manage pest problems.** Use a variety of preventive tactics to control pests before they damage your garden. To this end, encourage beneficial bugs by growing a diversity of flowering nectar and pollen-rich plants, discourage bad bugs, and practise crop rotation and possibly companion planting to prevent infestations.

🌹 **Practise disease prevention.** The best prevention consists of employing good cultural practices, practising good sanitation, taking advantage of plants' built-in defences by planting disease-resistant cultivars, and rotating crops in vegetable gardens.

🌹 **Practise weed prevention.** Eradicate any existing weeds by hand-pulling or mechanical means. Continue your control efforts by pulling weeds before they go to seed and by mulching to prevent weed seeds from germinating.

🌹 **Use natural pesticides.** It is better to stay away from pesticides completely; however, if you do need to resort to them, choose natural rather than artificial pesticides.

🌹 **Have realistic expectations.** Don't strive for perfection; be tolerant!

that the only good garden is an unblemished garden, free of any undesirable insect or weed intruders. Such perfection is not achieved without a cost to your garden environment. A garden is alive, a host to an incredible number of organisms that do not live in isolation. For this reason, chemicals can have far wider implications than the gardener intends. Both direct and indirect contact with garden chemicals are almost always injurious to a person's health; chemical residues found on many foods can be extremely harmful or even fatal to chemically sensitive people; liberal and indiscriminate use of pesticides kill beneficial insects as well as harmful ones, and also the birds that feed upon them; and many pests have developed a resistance to the effects of certain pesticides, which makes their use worthless. Increasingly, gardeners are thinking twice before reaching for the pesticide or herbicide bottle to deal with an insect or weed problem, realizing that chemicals are a last resort, not the first line of defence.

What does the term *pest* mean in reference to gardens? A pest may be defined as any insect, plant disease, weed, or animal that has an adverse effect on desirable plants. It is a meaningful term only with reference to people; pests are only pests because they share humans' preferences for certain ornamental plants, fruits, and vegetables.

The ecology of a garden involves fascinating life cycles and relationships, most of which are best allowed to continue uninterrupted. However, since a garden is also a creation of the gardener—a manipulated environment—the checks and balances nature provides to deal with pests may be inadequate and will need to be supplemented. So, if the use of chemical pest controls is to be discouraged, what can home-owners do to protect their garden investments of time and money from unwelcome visitors?

Integrated pest management offers a solution to this dilemma. This approach to controlling pest damage is "integrated" because it involves coordinating many strategies: promoting plant health and pest prevention through cultural methods and plant selection; physical or mechanical controls; biological controls; and, if necessary, the limited and informed use of chemical controls. The keys to successfully employing integrated pest management in your garden are vigilance, knowledge, and tolerance.

Insect and Animal Pest Control. As you make your way around your garden, watch for potential insect problems; be aware of potential pests and the plants they prefer. When you notice damage to plants, identify the culprit, and consider its life cycle and the amount of damage it will inflict. Learn when the pest usually makes an appearance in your garden. If you catch it early, it can probably be easily washed or picked off. Be prepared to accept a certain level of damage in the interest of maintaining a chemical-free garden. While they can be aesthetically offensive, caterpillars, leaf miners, and aphids will not kill most healthy plants.

Beneficial Insects. Many biological controls naturally reduce the populations of insect pests. Identifying and understanding beneficial insects that prey on pests are important principles of integrated pest management. Beneficial insects protect plants from harmful insects, either by attacking and devouring them (predators) or by laying their eggs in the pests and killing them when the larvae hatch (parasites). It is usually the hungry larvae of insects that do the most damage to plants; correspondingly, the larvae of beneficial insects are often the most efficient at consuming "bad bugs." The adults and larvae of ladybugs, lacewings, mealy bug destroyers, spined soldier bugs, and praying mantis are well-known predators of aphids, chinch bugs, whiteflies, and many other insects. Ground beetles prey on soil-dwelling pests such as cutworms. Certain wasp larvae and nematodes are examples of beneficial parasites. The wasp larvae are effective controls for loopers, leaf rollers, hornworms, bagworms, webworms, and codling moths; the nematodes (tiny roundworms that live beneath the soil's surface) protect against root weevils, cabbage root maggots, beetle grubs, and other subterranean pests. Learn to identify these beneficial insects and their larvae and do not harm them.

Make your garden a friendlier place for beneficial insects by catering to some of their needs. Parasitic wasps feed on flower nectar they can retrieve only from small, shallow flowers such as those of the carrot family, including dill, parsley, angelica, or fennel, which all have flowers arranged in umbels. Herbs with small flowers also attract desirable bugs. Try sage, thyme, oregano, mint, lavender, and rosemary. Annuals such as cosmos, petunias, strawflowers, zinnias, nasturtiums, marigolds, and sunflowers are also good sources of food. Sugar and yeast mixtures spread on plants encourage lacewings and ladybugs. Shelter can be provided for insects such as nocturnal ground beetles by mulching flower beds.

Beneficial insects can be bought in large quantities from some suppliers and released into the garden as a pest control measure, but remember that there are no guarantees the insects will stay in your yard. Carefully time the purchase and release of beneficial insects into your garden as the insects or eggs should not be stored for longer than a few days. Release insects or place eggs in the garden in late spring or early summer when there is an appropriate food source available, locating them near their preferred prey. Wet down the garden first to provide moisture for the insects and avoid releasing them during the hottest parts of the day.

Insectivorous Birds. Biological pest control is also provided by the many species of insectivorous birds that spend all or part of the year in Calgary. The addition of sheltering trees, water, and feeders will attract many birds to your garden. True, some birds are considered pests, such as bossy house sparrows or bullying magpies (which drive away more desirable songbirds) or even melodic but fruit-thieving robins, and it is difficult to discourage these persistent visitors. However, if you study the nesting requirements of desirable birds such as chickadees, wrens, and flickers (which nest in cavities) or flycatchers and warblers (which prefer dense shrubbery), you can modify your garden accordingly. It is also the responsibility of every gardener to exercise extreme caution when using insecticides, which are toxic to birds, and preferably to avoid them entirely. In addition, if insect populations are reduced too greatly, an important food source for birds is lacking. It is worth tolerating a few chewed leaves or a bumpy lawn for the continued well-being of the birds that bring so much life, colour, and delight to our gardens.

Microorganisms. Biological control can also be achieved by using microorganisms. Garden insect pests have no inherent ability to ward off disease, so by artificially increasing the levels of anti-pest bacteria already naturally present in the garden, the pests themselves become diseased without endangering the environment. Each type of such bacteria attacks the larvae of a specific bug, so a gardener can target individual bugs for control without harming beneficial insects or the birds that feed upon them. *Bacillus thuringiensis* (Bt) is one such bacterium available commercially; several varieties of Bt are effective against potato beetles, mosquitoes, corn borers, cabbage worms, tomato hornworms, leaf rollers, gypsy moths, and blackflies. Bt produces a toxic protein crystal that binds to the gut of the caterpillar, causing it to stop feeding almost immediately and to die within a few days. Bt may also be harmful to butterfly larvae, so make sure you spray only those plants infected with undesirable caterpillars. Another microorganism commercially available is *Bacillus popilliae*, or milky spore disease, which, once established, is an effective control for grubs. These bacterial controls, available either in dust form or as liquid concentrates or powders to be mixed with water and sprayed on leaves, are best applied when caterpillars are small. The advantages of Bt and similar bacteria are twofold: they affect only specific insects and residues break down quickly.

Botanical Insecticides. Not all insecticides are based on synthetic chemicals. Botanical insecticides are derived from roots, flowers, or leaves of plants. They break down quickly in sunlight and water (unlike synthetic chemicals) and are short-lived, both positive characteristics. On the negative side, they are generally broad spectrum and kill a number of types of insects, not just a specific one. Rotenone, pyrethrum, nicotine, ryania, and sabadilla are all botanical pesticides. Rotenone and pyrethrum are toxic to fish and should be kept away from waterways. Rotenone also kills bees and is poisonous to humans in large amounts. Botanical insecticides are sold under specific brand names, so consult an expert at a local gardening centre to help you select the appropriate product. They should be treated with the same respect and caution due synthetic chemical insecticides. Also be aware that some of the more recently developed synthetic chemicals are actually safer than their natural equivalents; again, it is best to check with an expert regarding the relative safety of these products.

Soaps and Oils. Many gardeners are turning to soaps and oils as relatively safe methods of insect control. These work only if they contact the body of the pest, and they must be applied frequently to control large insect populations. Non-detergent soaps, when used in conjunction with other control measures, can be effective against aphids, spider mites, mealy bugs, and whiteflies. Use a commercially available insecticidal soap, as common laundry or dish soap can damage some plants. Dormant oil is another useful product. It is sprayed on trees during the winter, before buds begin to break, to smother and kill the eggs of pests such as aphids, scale, and mites. Dormant oils can damage trees that have leafed out, but some newer spray oils have been developed for use during the growing season against pests such as aphids, scale, whiteflies, mealy bugs, and mites; they may also help control some caterpillars. Some plants, for example, raspberries or blue spruce trees, should never be sprayed with oils. All sprays should be applied carefully, according to directions.

Diatomaceous Earth. Soft-bodied pests such as aphids, slugs, and spider mites may be deterred by sprinkling diatomaceous earth, a razor-sharp dust, on and around garden plants. It cuts their bodies as they attempt to cross it, which eventually results in dehydration and the death of these pests. Be aware that it can also harm useful garden inhabitants, such as earthworms.

Good Cultural Practices. Most garden pests and diseases can be kept to acceptable levels simply by using good cultural practices, which include maintenance routines and careful plant selection. Since healthy plants are much better able to survive the depredations of pests, make sure the plants in your garden receive adequate water and nutrition. Check new arrivals carefully for signs of insects or disease. Keep your garden clean by picking up and disposing of garden debris—fallen leaves and fruit, stacked boards or rocks, sweepings, and cuttings—as these all provide potential hiding places and homes for pests. It is true that a year-round organic mulch also provides cover for a variety of pests, slugs especially, but the benefits of mulch are so considerable that gardeners may decide to risk pest infestations. If so, perhaps a greater degree of vigilance for the first appearance of bugs and disease will help avoid disaster. Leaves and fruit, especially those that are diseased, should be removed from plants and disposed of immediately. Conscientious sanitizing of pruning tools, using a fresh 10 percent bleach-and-water solution or a disinfectant, also helps prevent the spread of infection and disease.

Barriers. Barriers are a safe way to prevent insects from damaging certain plants. Floating row covers of lightweight fabric can be laid over hoops or cages to exclude harmful pests from plants while allowing light and water through. Weigh down the fabric at the edges with boards, bricks, or soil to prevent it from lifting in the wind. These covers are particularly useful in vegetable gardens to exclude pests such as the carrot rust fly and cabbage loopers and worms, which attack cole crops such as broccoli, cabbage, and cauliflower. Floating row covers should be laid down early in the growing season to prevent insects from laying eggs near susceptible plants. Check covered plants regularly to make sure you have not trapped any pests inside that may have been overwintering in the soil. Row covers also help retain heat during cool Calgary nights. If you have previously had problems with cutworms, make collars from milk cartons or tin cans with the ends removed and sink them in the earth around young vegetable plants. Sticky bands around tree trunks can help deter those pests that must climb up to lay eggs or feed, such as cankerworms. To apply, wrap a 10-cm (4-in.) band of waterproof paper snugly around the trunk, leaving no crevices for insects to crawl through, and coat it with a product commercially available for this purpose. Remove bands each year after they are no longer required, to expose the trunks to air, and reapply as necessary. As many insects fly into trees, this method will not be effective unless you know what insect you are dealing with and what time of year it will be climbing.

Hand Picking. Pests that are big enough to see and present in small enough numbers can usually be removed from plants by hand. Slugs, caterpillars, weevils, beetles, and grubs can all be controlled by hand picking. Wear gloves or use tweezers for this task if you are the squeamish sort, placing the pests in a lidded container for disposal. A strong spray of water into trees and perennials can help dislodge mites and aphids, as well as remove dust from plants. Prune off any galls (hard abnormal growths on trees caused by insects) as soon as you notice them. Galls are particularly noticeable on the tips of spruce trees, where they harbour the cooley spruce gall aphids; other gall-forming insects attack poplars, willows, and other trees and shrubs. You may also spy hard brown bands around twigs; these are egg bands from which forest tent caterpillars will hatch and they should be removed.

Resistant Plants. Over the years botanists have successfully developed varieties of plants that are resistant to certain diseases and insects. It is worthwhile to spend some time researching which plant varieties are pest resistant, so you can then choose these strains for your garden.

Weed Control. Weeds are the survivors of the plant world. They adapt to a wide range of growing conditions; are efficient at using whatever water, light, and nutrients they can get; and are often disease and pest tolerant. Many annual, biennial, and perennial weeds reproduce prolifically, producing large quantities of seed that can lie dormant in the soil for years, if necessary. Perennial weeds may spread by stolons above ground, or underground by creeping invasive rhizomes. Some weeds, such as quack grass, produce chemicals that are toxic to or inhibit the growth of other plants, a process called allelopathy. Weeds can also be poisonous to humans or animals; the spotted water hemlock is so toxic that the roots of one plant can kill a cow. However, weeds do have a few redeeming features: they provide habitat for some beneficial insects and butterflies, and some are even edible.

Integrated pest management techniques are as important for controlling weeds as they are for controlling insect and animal pests. Gardeners remove weeds for aesthetic reasons or because they harbour pests and compete with desirable plants for space and water, but the problems weeds cause beyond the borders of urban gardens are also powerful arguments for responsible weed control. This is why the Alberta Department of Agriculture administers laws passed by the province that define what is considered a weed and classifies weeds according to the severity of damage they cause to agriculture and the environment.

Restricted, Noxious, and Nuisance Weeds. Restricted weeds are particularly pernicious and are the group the Province of Alberta is seeking to eradicate completely. According to the *Weed Control Act*, they must be destroyed to prevent the spread, growth, ripening, or scattering of the restricted weed. Noxious weeds are those weeds that must be controlled to prevent spreading. When a notice to remedy a restricted or noxious weed problem is issued, the weed inspector includes a statement of the action to be taken to fulfil these requirements. There is also a long list of nuisance weeds that should be prevented from spreading or scattering seeds. The level of enforcement for a nuisance weed problem depends on the severity of the infestation.

The City of Calgary also has by-laws regarding the control of weeds listed as restricted, noxious, and nuisance. These by-laws aim to create a minimum standard of property maintenance within the city and to reduce the spread of weeds generally. Roving weed inspectors keep watch for problems and issue notices to property owners, giving them six days from the receipt of the notice to rectify the problem. Inspectors also respond to complaints received from citizens regarding weed infestations and take a proactive approach with home-owners to help rectify the situation and prevent future problems. There is zero tolerance of restricted weeds and a high level of enforcement of applicable laws and regulations whenever these plants are discovered.

Many noxious or restricted weeds have been introduced from other parts of the world and, hence, have no natural controls here. They aggressively out muscle vulnerable native species of plants, many of which are already threatened by loss of habitat, and this, in turn, affects those creatures that depend on native plants for survival. There are examples of this within Calgary: purple loosestrife, which destroys the ecological balance of wetlands by choking out native species, has been removed from sites along the Bow River.

∾ Restricted and Noxious Weeds ∾

Restricted weeds

Diffuse knapweed (*Centaurea diffusa*)
Dodder (*Cuscuta* spp.)
Eurasian water milfoil (*Myriophyllum spicatum*)
Nodding thistle (*Carduus nutans*)

Red bartsia (*Odontites serotina*)
Spotted knapweed (*Centaurea maculosa*)
Yellow star thistle (*Centaurea solstitialis*)

Noxious weeds

Bladder campion (*Silene cucubalus*)
Blue weed (*Echium vulgare*)
Canada thistle (*Cirsium arvense*)
Cleaver (*Galium aparine* and *Galium spurium*)
Common tansy (*Tanacetum vulgare*)
Cypress spurge (*Euphorbia cyparissias*)
Field bindweed (*Convolvulus arvensis*)
Field scabious (*Knautia arvensis*)
Hoary cress (*Cardaria* spp.)
Hound's-tongue (*Cynoglossum officinale*)
Knawel (*Scleranthus annuus*)
Leafy spurge (*Euphorbia esula*)

Oxeye daisy (*Chrysanthemum leucanthemum*)
Perennial sow thistle (*Sonchus arvensis*)
Persian darnel (*Lolium persicum*)
Purple loosestrife (*Lythrum salicaria*)
Russian knapweed (*Centaurea repens*)
Scentless chamomile (*Matricaria maritima*)
Spreading dogbane (*Apocynum androsaemifolium*)
Stork's bill (*Erodium cicutarium*)
Tall buttercup (*Ranunculus acris*)
Toadflax (*Linaria vulgaris*)
White cockle (*Lychnis alba*)

Weeds are opportunistic plants that out compete most of the plants gardeners enjoy growing, and they can never be totally eliminated from the landscape. However, many cultural techniques may be employed to prevent weeds from detracting from the health and beauty of your garden. Consider the following steps you can take to stop weeds from gaining a foothold.

Barriers. When establishing a new garden, make sure that all weeds are completely destroyed before you seed a lawn or lay sod. Lay landscape fabric down before you construct paths or patios to prevent weeds from seeding in cracks. You may also wish to install barriers of the same materials under fences, and then cover these areas with a decorative mulch. All gardeners should make sure they do not import weeds into the garden with new purchases; check for any foreign seedlings in tree, shrub, perennial, or annual containers.

Tilling and Mulching. Once plants in a garden are well established and healthy, weeds are less likely to be a problem, but they will still blow in to settle on any available patch of earth. Do not till the soil more than is necessary as buried weed seeds germinate if brought to the surface, and the stolons and rhizomes of perennial weeds may be cut up into pieces, each capable of starting a new plant. Newly emerged seedlings should be pulled or hoed out before they have a chance to set seed or spread, disturbing the soil as little as possible; spreading or tap-rooted perennials require more muscle power and you may need to dig deeply to completely remove them. The use of mulches on shrub and flower beds and in vegetable gardens can smother annual weeds and prevent seed germination; mulches also deter, but may not eliminate, more persistent perennial weeds.

Watering Practices. Target your watering on desirable plants by using soaker hoses and drip irrigation systems to direct water precisely where it is needed, rather than watering large areas from above with sprinklers. This not only conserves water, but it also deprives the weeds of moisture.

The Destructive Power of Heat. Since small compost piles may not achieve a high enough temperature to kill weed seeds, do not compost weeds after they have set seed. Perennial weeds with persistent root systems, such as toadflax, should be dried out thoroughly before composting or discarding.

If you have a large weedy area, such as a vegetable patch, you can use the sun's heat to destroy weed seeds and stolons and rhizomes near the surface of the soil. This process, called solarization, can also kill disease-producing organisms and soil pests. In early summer, remove all weeds from the area and moisten the soil thoroughly. Since soil moisture must be maintained throughout the process, you may wish to lay a soaker hose over the area. Cover with black plastic sheeting, and bury the edges of the plastic in the soil to seal them so no heat can escape. Leave the plastic on for four to six weeks, and a few weeks longer if the weather has been cool or cloudy. Since some beneficial soil organisms will also be killed, apply a layer of compost to reintroduce these to the soil before planting. Because solarization takes time, it is practical only if you can afford to have the area out of cultivation for the better part of a growing season.

Weeds also have a habit of invading cracks in paths or other paved areas. Boiling water should kill these, but it may need to be applied several times to get rid of perennial weeds. Neglected, out-of-the-way perimeter areas of the garden with poor or compacted soil will also be a haven for these unwelcome visitors. Weeds will have less of a chance to invade your garden if you amend the soil and plant a groundcover in such areas.

Weeds in Lawns. Weeds in established lawns can best be controlled by keeping your lawn healthy enough to crowd them out. Dig out weeds as soon as you spot them. If a portion of the lawn is badly infested with weeds, it may be less frustrating in the long run to dig up that area and start again. Remove all weeds, level the site, water, and wait a week or two for weeds to germinate. Pull these weeds and repeat this procedure to be sure that most weed seeds have germinated.

Attitudes to Weeds. As with insect pests, it is wise to have a small amount of tolerance for weed pests and avoid incautious spraying with herbicides harmful to people, animals, and desirable plants. Total weed eradication is impossible, and, after all, children need places where they can pick a few dandelions to present proudly to their mothers or collect daisies for a necklace.

Integrated pest management principles encourage a wider understanding of the intriguing and often amazing life forms inhabiting your garden. They can provide an effective and reasoned approach to dealing with pest problems that will result in a healthier environment for all the plants and animals you welcome into your garden.

∿ Edible Weeds ∿

Several weeds commonly found in the Calgary area are edible. Make sure you are able to positively identify these weeds and do not eat any edible weeds unless you are certain they have not been sprayed with herbicides.

Chickweed (*Stellaria media*)
Dandelion (*Taraxacum officinale*)
Lamb's-quarters (*Chenopodium album*)

Purslane (*Portulaca oleracea*)
Shepherd's purse (*Capsella bursa-pastoris*)
Stinging nettle (*Urtica dioica*) - cooked

Companion Planting. For gardeners, the traditional concept of companion planting is simple—select plant combinations to accomplish specific goals such as pest control, enhanced growth, or physical protection to contribute to a garden's health. The idea is not a new one. Throughout time, people who have worked the land have observed the relationships between neighbouring plants, noting in particular that some plants seem to have insect-repellant qualities. Not surprisingly, the earliest plants to be recommended by the Greeks and Romans for this purpose were aromatic ones with strong, bitter flavours. Early growers reasoned that insects would react to them adversely, in the same way people did, and so chose to concentrate their observations on herbs with those qualities. Native cultures made similar observations, noticing that the bitterest herbs had the strongest insecticidal and repellant properties. Interestingly, ancient societies did not actually practise the art of companion planting, even though they recognized its value; they simply could not afford the space required to do so effectively. Instead, they created their own sprays and dusts made from these beneficial plants and applied them to target crops in a manner reminiscent of modern-day chemical pest and disease control. It fell to the herbalists from the fifteenth century onwards to promote the concept of companion planting. They found that wormwood consistently repelled flies and flea beetles, heliotrope repelled ants, geum repelled clothes moths, and burning loosestrife discouraged fleas, snakes, and gnats.

Today, organic gardeners are adamant in their support of companion planting as a natural form of insect management—especially in the vegetable garden—since it deters harmful pests without adversely affecting beneficial organisms, rather than killing indiscriminately as many synthetic chemicals do. However, documented repellant qualities of most plants are based entirely on testimonials made by generations of gardeners whose words of wisdom have become firmly entrenched in the annals of gardening lore. As with all lore, there is a basis of truth for these observations, but few claims are backed by conclusive scientific evidence. To complicate matters further, many of the supposed beneficial effects of a companion plant can be explained by other factors that influence plant growth, such as change in crop location, natural fluctuations in pest populations, and evolving microclimates. In some cases, the very opposite of the reported benefit of a plant holds true, with plants thought to repel certain insects actually attracting them. Explanations for such inconsistencies are tenuous at best; there are just too many variables in the science of growing plants for comprehensive statements to be made without the scientific data to support them. Despite these inconsistencies, researchers are finally beginning to realize the validity of companion planting and are initiating studies to sort out the complex chemical and physical relationships involved.

The complexity of the relationships between companion plants means the results of scientific studies will be a long time in coming. That's not to say, however, that you should regard companion planting as a procedure unworthy of implementing in your garden. The strategy is definitely worth pursuing, but it will require some research on your part and some careful record-keeping to determine what works for your unique growing environment. Refer to one of the many excellent books available on companion planting and try recommended combinations to help you solve pest problems, be prepared to experiment, and keep in mind that what works for someone else might or might not apply to the growing conditions in your garden.

Plants as Repellants and Camouflage. Evidence is accumulating that companion plants work in many different ways. They may repel harmful pests using toxins, odours, or physical barriers, or act as deterrents by discouraging feeding by insects and the subsequent laying of eggs. For example, catnip has a compound that repels up to 17 varieties of insects; nasturtiums are effective against whiteflies, southernwood against cabbage butterflies, and potatoes against Mexican bean beetles. Hairy, spiky, and thorny plants sport obvious physical barriers to harmful insects. Plants with strong odours sometimes mask the odour of a target plant and hide it from a pest that favours it; French beans or clover grown with brassicas have been shown to reduce aphid populations, root fly attacks, and caterpillars to varying degrees using this camouflage technique.

Plants as Traps and Decoys. Some plants serve as an alternate food source for pests or have other characteristics that attract them, and they can be used to lure pests away from more valued plants. Decoy plants represent a refinement to this diversionary tactic; they are actually harmful to the pests they attract, often making them sick or unable to lay eggs. Many crops have been recommended as traps over the years: goldenrod for cucumber beetles, nasturtiums for aphids, and sunflowers for corn earworms.

Trap-and-decoy cropping is not easy. To do it well, you need to know quite a bit about pests and how they feed, move, and colonize. The best way to learn these details is by consulting reference books about local pests and by observing their behaviour in your own garden. Also, don't lose sight of the fact that some pests may simply be attracted to a particular plant in the absence of anything more appealing in the vicinity; they will most certainly move on once they detect the presence of a more palatable plant.

Nursery Plants. One useful companion plant is the nursery plant that attracts and harbours beneficial insects. These beneficial insects may be predators or parasites that actively destroy harmful insects, or they may be pollinators such as bees, whose presence is essential for plant fertilization, especially for fruit trees and in the vegetable garden. Nursery plants not only provide the nectar and pollen that attract beneficial insects; some-times, they also serve as an alternate food source for beneficials, sustaining them in the absence of prey. Other times, nursery plants simply offer shade and shelter to beneficials and create the cool, moist soil conditions favoured by beetles and spiders, two important members of the insect pest patrol. Interestingly, the very conditions that promote populations of beneficial insects and arachnids are those least favoured by insect pests. This allows the beneficials to increase their populations in a non-competitive environment, which, in turn, results in better pest control in the garden. The wider the range of plants you grow, the wider the range of beneficial insects that are attracted to help you keep the upper hand over pests.

The Importance of Balance. Some companion plants help others if they are present in small proportions, but then hinder or harm them as their proportions increase and they compete for light, water, or nutrient reserves. For example, a light groundcover of weeds among vegetable crops makes it harder for insects to locate their host plants, resulting in smaller populations of insect pests; however, when the weeds are allowed to take over, this benefit all but disappears in the ensuing competition.

The chemical secretions and residues from a plant's leaves and roots can be beneficial to some neighbouring plants and harmful to others, and sometimes even harmful to themselves. For example, dandelion roots exude a chemical that controls fusarium wilt in tomatoes. Buttercup root secretions inhibit the growth of clover. Clovers give off root secretions that inhibit seed from germinating, both their own and seed from other plants. Ethylene gas, on the other hand, a substance given off by many plants, causes slower and therefore sturdier growth in neighbouring plants, resulting in increased wind resistance; ethylene also causes premature ripening, which may be advantageous in some crops.

For some plant pairs, companion planting offers obvious physical benefits. Select tall plants to provide shelter from the sun and wind to shorter plants; or grow groundcovers at the base of plants such as clematis, whose roots need to be sheltered from the heat of the sun. Root channels that are left in the soil, lined with nutrients from the break-down of once-inhabitant roots, are of great benefit to the plants that follow, both in terms of soil structure and available nutrients. Many companion plants get along well together because they root in different soil layers, thus reducing one form of competition between them. The deep-rooters bring up minerals from their depth to where shallow-rooters can benefit, and the breakdown products of shallow-rooters are eventually washed down to depths where deep-rooters can benefit from them. Many of the advantages described here, and others like them, will accrue whether you engage in diverse intercropping practices (planting beneficial plant pairs adjacent to each other) or in succession planting of single crops.

∿ A Sampling of Companion Plants ∿

Basil (*Ocimum basilicum*)	controls tomato hornworms
Catnip (*Nepeta cataria*)	deters flea beetles
Dandelion (*Taraxacum officinale*)	attracts lady bugs, lacewings, and other predators; repels Colorado potato beetles
Dill (*Anethum graveolens*)	attracts aphid predators and parasites
Marigold (*Tagetes* spp.)	attracts hover flies; repels root nematodes, Mexican bean beetles, aphids, and Colorado potato beetles
Mustard (*Brassica* spp.)	attracts cabbage worm parasites; repels aphids from Brussels sprouts
Southernwood (*Artemisia abrotanum*)	repels moths and flea beetles on cabbage
Tomato (*Lycopersicon esculentum*)	repels flea beetles on cabbage

∿ The Three Sisters ∿

The interplanting of corn, beans, and squash (the Three Sisters) by North American Natives is an excellent example of the benefits of companion planting. Natives recognized the potential benefits from this grouping of plants by insisting that the three kinds of seeds be planted in one hole because they "wanted to be together." The beans are legumes that fix nitrogen in the soil, providing an important nutrient element for the corn and squash. Corn plants provide support for the climbing bean plants. Squash plants growing as a groundcover on the soil among the corn and bean plants not only serve to lessen erosion, but also to suppress weeds and encourage moisture retention.

This so-called Three Sisters gardening creates a fertile soil that supports strong insect- and disease-resistant plants, and corn, squash, and beans also attract beneficial insects that further contribute to pest control. Finally, this practice of planting the Three Sisters in mounds reduces soil erosion by slowing the flow of water; in contrast, planting crops in rows channels rainwater, thus encouraging soil erosion.

Marigolds, popular companion plants, repel root nematodes from members of the cabbage family. DANA REED

Crop Rotation. Crop rotation is an ancient agricultural practice that has been described in the writings of the Romans, Greeks, and even the Chinese before them. The technique, which advocates planting different crops in a given location every year, helps to prevent nutrient depletion of the soil and the accumulation of soil-borne pests and diseases specific to families of crops. Though crop rotation is most effective when carried out on a large scale, both in terms of space and time available for rotating crops, it is also beneficial for kitchen gardens on the average urban lot. The guidelines developed to help set up rotation schedules are few; however, the more crops you grow, the more complex the scheduling. Don't let this intimidate you. Rather, remember that when it comes to rotating crops, change for change's sake is good, with or without adhering to a rigid and detailed schedule. No matter how much or how little you do, there will be a benefit.

To Improve Nutrition. The first guideline for crop rotation is to rotate plants on the basis of nutritional needs. Some crops are heavy feeders (for example, brassicas), depleting the soil of essential nutrients very rapidly; others are light feeders (for example, root crops), draining very few nutrients from the soil during the course of a growing season. Yet another group of crops are called soil builders; they have the capacity to return essential nutrients to the soil for the benefit of future crops. Legumes, for example, are well known for their ability to build up nitrogen concentrations in the soil. You can maintain a balance of nutrients in your garden soil by rotating heavy feeders, light feeders, and soil builders, in that sequence, through a given location.

To Avoid Diseases and Pests. The second guideline for crop rotation is to rotate plant families, leaving three or more years between the time members of the same plant family grow in a given location. Disease organisms and insects vary in their ability to infect plants. Some attack a single species; others infect a few closely related species or several members of a plant family. They can also remain dormant in the soil for several years. The longer the rotation interval, the greater the likelihood that the disease or pests will disappear completely.

In general, plants within the same plant families are susceptible to the same or similar diseases and pests. If you employ good cultural practices in your garden, you might not even know that a particular crop is ailing in the first year a disease or insect rears its ugly head, especially if it strikes beneath the soil surface. However, if you take the identical crop or one that is closely related and plant it in the same infected location year after year, dependent pests and diseases will increase rapidly, often to serious proportions. It is therefore a good cultural practice to change a crop's location every year. In the absence of the host plants essential to their survival, soil-borne fungi, bacteria, and other diseases will eventually die out through starvation. The same holds true for insects whose eggs and larvae overwinter in the soil at the base of host plants. Resurfacing in the spring with their favourite food no longer handy, they set out in search of the missing delicacies, and with luck starve to death before reaching them.

In reality, some soil-borne diseases and pests residing in very small gardens may be able to negotiate relatively short distances to infect crops that have been rotated to a new position. In addition, some disease-producing organisms called pathogens have the ability to infect across plant family boundaries. When you experience a really serious outbreak of disease in your garden, it is important to make a positive identification of the pathogen and to research what other food crops it infects. If you determine the presence of a pathogen that crosses family lines, crop rotation is not the answer to your predicament; you may have to rely on other control methods to eradicate the problem. Despite these potential shortcomings as a method for controlling pests and diseases, crop rotation is still a sensible practice worthy of implementation by all vegetable gardeners.

To Improve Soil Structure. In addition to keeping down pests and diseases, rotations preserve and improve soil structure. Deep-rooted crops break up the soil layer for the more shallow-rooted, less vigorous growers. They also absorb nutrients from deep soil layers and incorporate them; when the residues of these crops decompose, the nutrients become available to less vigorous, more shallow-rooted crops. By alternating deep- and shallow-rooted crops, a gardener makes good use of the full depth of the soil, deepening the topsoil layer in the process.

To Control Weeds. Crop rotation also aids in weed control. Weeds have a preferred range of uniform growing conditions, just as annuals and perennials do. The constant changes in cultural practice required by different crops as they are rotated through a given location make it difficult for weeds to establish themselves. There are also some crops such as squash and potatoes whose growth habits and cultivation requirements help suppress weeds. It is a good idea to follow these "cleansing" crops with crops that are difficult to weed, such as onions and root crops.

~ Guidelines for Crop Rotation ~

🌷 Beans follow detrimental root crops (they suffer the least from their effect)

🌷 Brassicas (heavy feeders) follow legumes (soil builders)

🌷 Corn and beans are not greatly influenced by what precedes them

🌷 Onions, lettuces, squash, endive, and radicchio are beneficial to crops that follow

🌷 Potatoes and tomatoes, which are related, should be separated as much as possible since they are particularly susceptible to the same diseases

🌷 Potatoes follow corn

🌷 Root crops (carrots, beets) are generally detrimental to crops that follow

🌷 Root crops (difficult to weed) follow squash (suppress weeds)

🌷 Squash (suppress weeds) follow potatoes (suppress weeds) to reduce weed problems for succeeding difficult-to-weed root crops

A Sample Crop Rotation Plan. Before drawing up a schedule, it is helpful to understand how the crop rotation guidelines translate into practical terms. The following generalizations are based on the experiences of farmers and gardeners alike; use them as a starting point for your rotation plan, although the specifics will vary depending on your growing conditions.

When you are ready to draw up a crop rotation schedule, evaluate your space and see how you can use it most effectively. The rotation interval you select will depend on the number of distinct growing areas you can define in your vegetable plot and on the number of crops you are trying to grow. The more growing spaces available, the more influencing factors you can take into account.

A very simple plan would consist of dividing a rectangular vegetable plot into quarters and establishing a four-year rotation schedule as follows: legume and pod crops (soil builders); alliums (light feeders); root and tuberous crops (light feeders); brassicas (heavy feeders).

To develop a more complicated plan for a larger number of growing spaces is much like solving a puzzle. To do this, categorize your crops on index cards and then organize the cards, follow-the-leader fashion, using the established guidelines to come up with the best planting sequence. If one sequence doesn't work, reorganize the cards until you find one that does. Keep careful records of your rotation schedules and how they work; then modify them as necessary, based on your own gardening experience.

Here is an example of a crop rotation schedule for growing six crops

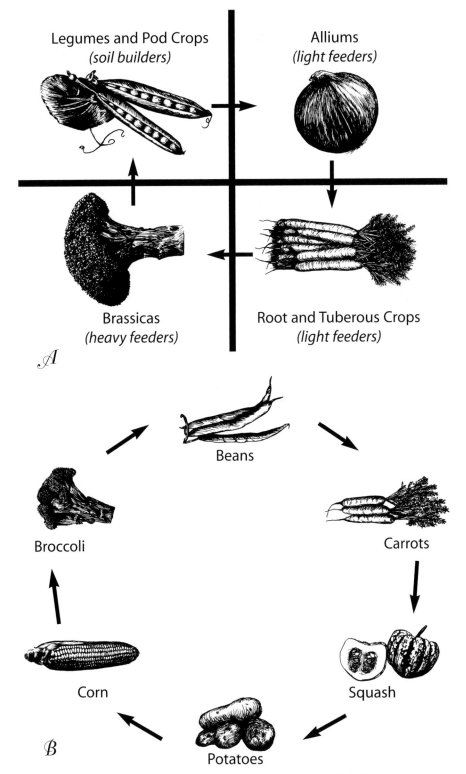

Legumes and Pod Crops
(soil builders)

Alliums
(light feeders)

Brassicas
(heavy feeders)

Root and Tuberous Crops
(light feeders)

𝒜

Beans

Broccoli

Carrots

Corn

Squash

Potatoes

ℬ

(a) A sample four-year rotation schedule. (b) A sample rotation schedule for growing six crops on a six-year rotation schedule. GRACE BUZIK

∿ Plant Families ∿

Refer to this chart when developing a schedule to rotate crops based on plant family.

Cabbage family/brassicas	broccoli, Brussels sprouts, cabbage, cauliflower, kale, radishes, rutabagas, turnips
Daisy family	chicory, dandelions, endive, lettuce
Goosefoot family	beets, spinach, Swiss chard
Grass family	corn
Lily family (alliums)	chives, garlic, leeks, onions, shallots
Nightshade family	eggplant, peppers, potatoes, tomatoes
Parsley/carrot family	carrots, celeriac, celery, parsley, parsnips
Pea/bean family (legumes)	beans, peas
Squash family	cucumbers, gourds, melons, pumpkins, squash

∿ Plant Nutritional Requirements ∿

Refer to this chart when developing a schedule to rotate crops based on nutritional needs.

Heavy feeders	beets, broccoli, Brussels sprouts, cabbage, cauliflower, celery, corn, cucumbers, eggplant, kale, lettuce, parsley, pumpkins, spinach, squash, tomatoes
Light feeders	carrots, garlic, leeks, mustard, onions, parsnips, peppers, potatoes, radishes, rutabagas, shallots, Swiss chard, turnips
Soil builders	broad beans, peas, snap beans.

with a six-year rotation interval; the crops are beans, carrots, squash, potatoes, corn, and broccoli. An ideal schedule can be thought of in terms of a circle, with each vegetable rotating into the position held by the vegetable beside it. Use beans as a starting point since they are not much affected by what precedes them and so can follow carrots, a difficult spot for other crops. Carrots, which are difficult to weed, follow squash to benefit from their ability to control weeds. Squash follow potatoes to continue with weed control. Potatoes follow corn to benefit from the nutrients corn leaves behind. Corn is not much affected by what precedes it, so in this case it follows broccoli, a heavy-feeding brassica, with no detrimental effect. Broccoli, a heavy feeder, follows beans, soil-building legumes that will have prepared the soil for broccoli's demanding nutritional needs.

Xeriscaping

During the 1970s, drought forced many communities in the western United States to deal with the realities of a shrinking water supply and a growing population demanding more of this precious resource. When water became scarce, landscape irrigation was the first water use to be curtailed and plants that required large quantities of water suffered. This led to a re-evaluation of techniques in landscape design, plant selection, and cultural practices, all aimed at developing landscapes that require only the natural precipitation of the area. These techniques and the philosophy underlying them are known as "xeriscaping," which means "water conservation through creative landscaping." The term is

Drought-tolerant plants such as gaillardia, iris, artemisia, veronica, daisies, and mugho pine thrive in this acreage garden where water supplies are limited. Renata Wichmann

derived from combining the Greek word *xeros*, meaning dry, with the Anglo-Saxon word *schap*, denoting a type of view. The value of xeriscaping in many western states has been reinforced through a series of dry years during which water rationing has been the norm rather than the exception. Water conservation is now recognized as an integral part of environmental protection; fresh water is a finite resource not to be squandered unnecessarily.

This would not have been news to the first farmers and gardeners on the Canadian prairies. Water conservation was simply common sense in times of drought, when dugouts shrank to muddy ponds and wells ran dry. In many ways the "new" xeriscaping gardening techniques draw from the old conservation ethic of not wasting a drop of water, for there was no predicting when the rain would come. In fact, many gardeners used xeriscaping principles in the past; it was just sensible gardening practice to make the best use of whatever water was available. While rural gardeners have always been aware of limitations on their water supply, urban gardeners have not needed to give this much thought. Yet there are compelling reasons for all Calgary-area gardeners to adopt a new tradition of water conservation. Calgary is a semi-desert climate, averaging less than 40 cm (16 in.) of precipitation per year. In addition to the lack of precipitation, summer winds and low humidity rob the soil of moisture, and winter Chinooks remove the snow cover most plants need to avoid desiccation.

In the midst of cool summer greenery it is easy to forget that many Calgary gardens thrive only because natural precipitation is supplemented to such a high degree. Over the decades of the city's existence, Calgarians have been fortunate to enjoy an ample water supply, experiencing few water shortages and restrictions on landscape watering. During summer heat waves when water treatment plants reach their peak demand, citizens are asked to refrain voluntarily from using garden sprinklers, the worst culprits for wasting water. However, as the city grows, more water will be needed, and the current water treatment system will be unable to meet the increased demand, resulting in higher costs, which the city will need to pass on to citizens. The necessity for multimillion-dollar upgrades to the city's water treatment facilities can likely be postponed for many years if Calgarians are able to reduce individual water consumption in their homes and gardens. Water meters have become commonplace in many Calgary homes and may be a required fixture in all city homes in the future. These homeowners pay according to the quantity of water they use; therefore, applying xeriscape principles can result in savings on the water bill. Xeriscape gardens can also reduce the stress on the water treatment system, which can only benefit all Calgary taxpayers.

Many people have the mistaken impression that a xeriscape garden must consist of a few cacti, succulents, shrubs, and stones in a gravel bed. While this is one low-maintenance style of xeriscape garden, it is far from the only option. Unless you so choose, a xeriscape garden does not have to look substantially different from any other garden. In fact, most Calgary gardens likely include plants that will survive quite well with little watering if other aspects of the landscape are modified to make efficient use of available water.

There are seven important principles to bear in mind when planning a water-conserving garden. They can be applied rigorously to your entire garden or just to selected areas, so that different zones of the garden can have different irrigation needs. The points to consider are planning and design; soil analysis and amendments; turf reduction; appropriate plant selection; efficient irrigation; mulching; and appropriate and timely maintenance.

Planning and Design. *Topography.* When you begin to plan your garden, take a look at the topography of your site and whether water runs off or is able to soak in to benefit plants. If run-off is a problem, change the grade to direct water to where it is needed. Design driveways and paths to drain onto lawns or planting beds, and terrace slopes to collect run-off. Note the areas where water naturally puddles and the soil stays moist to ensure you plant in appropriate spots.

Plant Grouping. It is extremely important to group plants according to their water requirements, since it is time-consuming to haul out the watering can or hose for the occasional drooping primula amidst the thyme, and wasteful to throw water on an entire flower bed for the sake of two or three thirsty plants. Establish an area for the toughest, most drought-tolerant plants in the garden. It makes sense to locate them on the edges of the property in areas that are least convenient to water and also in places where they will shelter less hardy plants from the prevailing westerlies and cold north winds. It is also wise to use drought-tolerant shrubs and perennials as foundation plantings on the south and west sides of buildings, as these areas are often very dry.

In Calgary, vegetable gardens, annual beds, and containers all require supplemental watering. Locate these close to your house for ease of watering and to better enjoy the tastes and colours they provide. You will also be less likely to forget to water them.

Soil Analysis and Amendments. Before planting your xeriscape garden, analyze the soil in the various zones of the garden. The texture of soil determines its water-holding capacity. Although clay soils, such as those found through much of Calgary, are capable of holding a great deal of water, they can become crusted and compacted when dry. Water cannot soak into this crusted surface and runs off and is wasted. Water can penetrate sandy soils, but they drain too quickly. The addition of organic matter to both soil textures helps to achieve the balance required for most plants to make the most efficient use of available water. Bear in mind, however, that many drought-tolerant plants are prairie species that thrive in lean soil in their natural habitats; they may be grouped in an area with a soil less rich in organic matter than may be required for other plants.

Turf Reduction. Lawn areas often take up a great amount of space and consume a commensurate amount of water. You can plant drought-tolerant grasses, such as crested wheatgrass or Russian wild rye, but since most drought-tolerant grasses are bunch grasses with a coarser and more prickly texture than the Kentucky blue grass mixtures Calgarians are used to, the lawn may be uncomfortable for sitting on or for walking on barefoot. Instead of trying to adapt the lawn, consider eliminating any areas of grass you don't really use and planting alternative groundcovers. If you decide to retain your conventional lawn, save water by allowing the grass to grow longer, as longer blades are better able to shade the roots and thus reduce evaporation.

Appropriate Plant Selection. For areas of your garden you have designated as low-watering zones, you need to select plants that use little water or have a high tolerance for drought. These plants may be prairie natives or come from a similarly dry climate. A large number of xerophytic plants are low growing, an adaptation that keeps them out of drying winds. Xerophytic plants often have small leaves, thus limiting the leaf surface area through which moisture is lost through transpiration; some plants achieve the same effect by rolling up their leaves during a drought. A coating of tiny protective hairs on many xerophytic plants, for instance artemisia and lambs' ears, lends the leaves a silver or grey-green cast; others have a waxy appearance as the protective layer on the surface of leaves is generally thicker in drought-tolerant plants. Some drought-tolerant plants, like lavender, produce aromatic oils to prevent leaves from drying. Succulents such as sedums and hen and chicks have thick, fleshy leaves to store water; other plants draw stored moisture from bulbs and tubers. Despite these adaptive features, even xerophytic plants require water initially to build healthy root systems. Water new trees, shrubs, and perennials regularly until they are established, and give them additional deep waterings during the first year of growth. Trees and shrubs will likely require regular watering in their second year as well.

Efficient Irrigation. An essential component of the xeriscape philosophy—to use water efficiently—involves watering accurately by delivering water only to those plants that need it and in the quantities they need. Water once a week, applying 2.5 cm (1 in.) per watering; you can measure the amount of water you put on with a rain gauge. A well-designed timed automatic watering system is the most efficient and least labour-intensive way to ensure that plants receive enough water, but not too much. Drip systems deliver water to the root zone of plants and because they have low flow rates, you can water many more plants from a single line than with a spray system. Pop-up lawn sprinklers can efficiently irrigate a lawn without sprinkler overspray. If your garden is small or you do not wish to install these systems, there are many other tricks for reducing water use. Consider reducing the rate of flow from traditional spray watering systems while maintaining the same area of coverage, so that surface run-off is reduced and the water has more time to penetrate deeply into the root zone. Do not water in windy weather or in the heat of the day when evaporation rates are high. Rainfall may be harvested by running downspouts into flower beds or rain barrels, which can be equipped with taps for filling watering cans or with a drip-hose/valve combination to irrigate flower beds in the vicinity. If you have a small garden, consider hand watering with a watering can or wand; you can direct the water where needed and avoid the waste caused by overhead sprinklers. Container plantings also allow you to water plants precisely yet adequately, although they also dry out more easily than beds.

Mulching. The best way to prevent water evaporation is to use mulches on the soil of annual, perennial, and shrub beds, and even around trees. A mulch is a protective layer of material, either organic or inorganic, used as insulation and protection. In winter, mulches are most often used on perennial beds, where they help keep the ground frozen, preventing harmful fluctuations in temperature and premature thawing of the ground. Summer mulches serve a different function, preventing the hot sun from sucking moisture out of the soil around shrubs, perennials, and annuals. They should be laid down in late spring, after the soil has warmed. Mulches also help control soil erosion, prevent compaction when soil is walked on, and discourage weeds, and as organic mulches break down, they improve the structure and moisture-holding capacity of soils.

Inorganic Mulches. Inorganic mulches have a decorative or formal appearance. Popular choices in the Calgary area include stone, gravel, shale, and permeable landscape fabric, which is usually used as a base for a further layer of inorganic or organic mulch. Stone, gravel, and shale all radiate stored heat and cause temperature increases in the surrounding area.

Organic Mulches. Organic mulches are more natural looking and are better at keeping the soil surface cool. They are also cheaper than inorganic mulches but need to be applied more frequently, as they decay. Apply organic mulches to a depth of at least 10 cm (4 in.) and replenish them regularly.

There are several types of organic mulches frequently used in Calgary gardens. They include grass clippings from lawns that have not been sprayed with herbicides, compost, and leaves, preferably composted or shredded. Peat moss is not the best choice in this windy climate as it tends to dry up quickly and either wick water out of the soil or blow away. Wood and bark chips may be purchased in varying sizes to suit your plantings; use larger sizes around trees and shrubs, smaller sizes around perennials. Some organic mulches, such as newspaper, hay, and straw, are unsightly for use in ornamental gardens, but may be useful for a vegetable garden tucked in an out-of-the-way corner. However, hay and straw can contain weed seeds and provide a haven for rodents.

The fact that organic mulches decay, adding nutrients to the underlying soil, is beneficial to gardeners. However, during the first year after application of some mulches, the activity of soil-nitrifying bacteria rises dramatically, causing a temporary nitrogen depletion in the soil.

∾ Plants for Xeriscape Gardens ∾

Trees

Amur maple (*Acer ginnala*)

Crabapple (*Malus* spp.)

Dwarf Colorado spruce (*Picea pungens* 'Fat Albert', 'Globe')

Hawthorn (*Crataegus x mordenensis* 'Snowbird', 'Toba')

Russian olive (*Elaeagnus angustifolia*)

Scotch pine (*Pinus sylvestris* 'Nana', 'Viridis Compacta')

Shrubs

Buffaloberry (*Shepherdia argentea*)

Caragana (*Caragana pygmaea*)

Cotoneaster (*Cotoneaster lucidus, C. acutifolia*)

Golden-flowering currant (*Ribes aureum*)

Honeysuckle (*Lonicera* spp.)

Juniper (*Juniperus horizontalis; J. scopulorum*)

Lilac (*Syringa* spp.)

Nanking cherry (*Prunus tomentosa*)

Potentilla (*Potentilla fruticosa*)

Sea buckthorn (*Hippophae rhamnoides*)

Perennials

Artemisia (*Artemisia schmidtiana* 'Silver Mound', *A. ludoviciana* 'Silver King')
Bearded iris (*Iris* x *germanica*)
Blanket flower (*Gaillardia aristata*)
Coral bells (*Heuchera* spp.)
Daylily (*Hemerocallis* spp.)
Hen and chicks (*Sempervivum* spp.)
Iceland poppy (*Papaver nudicaule*)
Maiden pinks (*Dianthus deltoides*)
Peony (*Paeonia* spp.)

Ribbon grass (*Phalaris arundinacea picta*)
Sea holly (*Eryngium* spp.)
Sheep's fescue (*Festuca ovina glauca*)
Sneezewort (*Achillea ptarmica* 'The Pearl')
Speedwell (*Veronica* spp.)
Stonecrop (*Sedum* spp.)
Yarrow (*Achillea* spp.)

Annuals

Ageratum (*Ageratum houstonianum*)
Baby's breath (*Gypsophila elegans*)
Bachelor's button (*Centaurea cyanus*)
Calendula (*Calendula officinalis*)
Cosmos (*Cosmos bipinnatus*)

Dusty miller (*Centaurea cineraria*)
Geranium (*Pelargonium* x *hortorum*)
Nasturtium (*Tropaeolum majus*)
Portulaca (*Portulaca grandiflora*)
Zinnia (*Zinnia* spp.)

Herbs

Borage (*Borago officinalis*)
Chives (*Allium schoenoprasum*)
Dill (*Anethum graveolens*)
Hyssop (*Hyssopus officinalis*)
Parsley (*Petroselinum crispum, P. hortense*)

Rosemary (*Rosmarinus officinalis*)
Sage (*Salvia officinalis*)
Tarragon (*Artemisia dracunculus sativa*)
Thyme (*Thymus vulgaris*)
Winter savory (*Satureja montana*)

After a year or so, the nitrates under these mulches are greatly augmented by dying soil bacteria, which creates an excellent growing medium. The types of mulches most likely to cause nitrogen depletion in the soil are wood based: sawdust, shredded bark, and wood chips. The solution to this problem is a simple one—spread a high-nitrogen fertilizer (high first number) on the soil before applying such a mulch. Also, be aware that using a permeable inorganic landscape fabric under an organic mulch prevents the organic mulch from enriching the soil.

Appropriate and Timely Maintenance. Maintenance tasks in a xeriscape garden are much the same as in any other garden, although several of the tasks are particularly important. Make sure that weeds are not allowed to gain a foothold and compete for water. Renew mulches as necessary, and if you are relying on an automatic sprinkler system, check it regularly to ensure it is providing plants with the right amount of water. If you have replaced water-guzzling turf areas with lower maintenance groundcover, you will find your xeriscape garden will reward you with more leisure time and less time spent mowing and fertilizing.

FIVE

The Resourceful Gardener

Calgary gardeners have always been an adaptive and innovative lot, making the most of what was on hand. In recent years, however, the proliferation of available plant varieties and gardening equipment has reduced the need to make do with limited choices and resources. Many exciting plants are finding their way into Calgary gardens, plants that most gardeners never expected to survive in this difficult climate; helpful tools and gadgets abound to make gardening tasks less onerous; and there are books published on every gardening topic imaginable.

Since gardeners invest a great deal of time and energy into their gardens—and can sink sizable sums of money into this passion—it pays to be resourceful, to make informed choices when purchasing plants and equipment, and to be aware of alternatives. By thinking smartly and spending wisely, you can minimize costs without sacrificing quality and make the most of every dollar you spend. The most important first step is to know your garden and its microclimates so you can determine the possibilities and limitations you face. Knowing this before you buy will help you achieve success, even with borderline plants.

Creating the garden of your dreams doesn't have to be an expensive proposition. In fact, some of the most beautiful gardens in Calgary have evolved on very modest budgets. Just as people can take many different routes to reach a chosen destination, so too gardeners can follow many paths to achieve the perfect outdoor retreat, usually with equally pleasing but refreshingly different results. Careful planning, patience, and, admittedly, a bit of extra effort are the keys to accomplishing more in your garden for less.

Selecting Plants

In spring, the plans and ideas that have been germinating in the imaginations of gardeners all winter long begin to surface, gaining momentum and leading inevitably to many wonderful expeditions to local garden centres and greenhouses. The first visit of the season is particularly inviting for the joy of immersing yourself in the delicious smells of damp soil, fresh foliage, and fragrant blooms, the excitement of revelling in the thousands of annuals, perennials, trees, and shrubs spread before you, and the anticipation of "buying." True, it is sometimes difficult to know how to proceed as you stand there facing aisles full of four-packs, six-packs, small pots, big pots, and flats, but armed with a bit of knowledge on what to look for when choosing plants, you will be able to leave knowing your purchases are good investments.

Whether you are buying from a reputable garden centre or a discount department store, the key to choosing perennials, annuals, trees, or shrubs is to inspect before you buy, making sure your chosen plants are healthy, both above and below the soil line. In a typical display some plants are healthier than others, and you certainly don't want to pay top dollar for an inferior product. This process takes time, so don't be in a hurry—be patient. Always check the labels for important information about plant species and cultivar names, colour, light requirements, and hardiness. Sometimes local retailers bring in perennials, shrubs, and trees that are not hardy here. Many are attractive plants that can be treated as annuals; just don't expect them to survive a Calgary winter. It is risky to purchase an unlabelled plant unless you don't mind the occasional surprise or disappointment.

Finally, a few words about selecting seeds. Most importantly, always buy fresh ones. While some seeds will remain viable for several years when properly stored in a cool and dry place, most start to deteriorate after about one year. It is impossible to know how seeds have been stored in a nursery or garden centre from one year to the next, so it is best to check the date stamps on seed packages before you buy. Seeds packaged in foil envelopes will stay fresh for several years, although once the seal has been broken, they too will start to deteriorate.

Planning for Sun and Shade. If you are planning a new garden or renovating existing flower beds, it is wise to evaluate the amount of sun each planting area receives and at what time of day. Once you have mapped out these areas, you can draw up a wish list of plants based on catalogue descriptions, books, and information provided at local garden centres. Trips to public gardens or to those of fellow plant enthusiasts will undoubtedly flesh out your list. It is much more helpful to see a plant in situ than to read a disembodied description.

Sun. The amount and type of sunlight your garden receives vary, depending on the orientation of the planting areas. East-facing flower beds enjoy the warmth of the morning sun, but escape the afternoon heat. West-facing beds are shaded in the morning, but receive the full force of the sun for the rest of the day until sunset. South-facing flower beds bask in intense sun all day and can become dry. North-facing beds against solid fences or houses may receive little or no direct sunlight and will remain cool and moist.

Plants in south-facing beds will be the first to show signs of growth in the spring and will display the first blooms; however, they will also finish blooming first, and the blooms may be of shorter duration than those of the same plants in slightly cooler locations, such as east-facing beds. Flowers in east-facing beds tend to have more vivid colours than those with a southern or western exposure. Plants that do not receive enough sunlight will be stretched, spindly, and weak, with fewer leaves and flowers; however, you should also watch for plants that receive too much sun and show burned foliage and stunted growth, or even just flag temporarily in the heat.

Calgary's short growing season and cool nights mean many shade-loving plants do quite well in the sun, if well watered. Most fruits and vegetables and many annuals and perennials prefer full sun. This means they require six hours of sun per day, preferably during the peak hours of mid-morning to late afternoon. If they receive this amount of sun, they should not suffer if they are shaded early or late in the day.

Shade. If an area of your garden receives morning sun, but little in the afternoon, or is in direct sun only late in the day, it should be considered partly shaded. Shade gardens can vary dramatically in the amount of light they receive. Dappled or filtered shade is often found under open deciduous trees, the moving leaves producing dancing patterns of sun and shade with the breeze. This is the lightest type of shade, and plants rated for part sun should do well under these conditions.

Areas that receive no direct sunlight, such as the north side of buildings or spaces under a heavy deciduous tree canopy, are classified as full shade. However, if they are open to surrounding sunny areas, under trees with high branches, or receive reflected light from buildings, they will still be bright and hospitable enough for many plants.

The most difficult areas in the garden to plant are deep shade areas, those places with no direct sunlight or reflected light, generally north-facing locations shadowed by structures or large evergreen trees. Few plants succeed under these conditions, and since these areas take up only a small proportion of the average garden, you may wish to devote your planting time and money elsewhere and settle for a natural-looking or ornamental mulch in these problem spots.

∾ Modifying Sun and Shade ∾

You can modify areas of a garden that have too much shade or too much sun for the plants you wish to grow.

Too much shade

🌹 Relocate plants to areas that better suit their preferences

🌹 Selectively thin the canopy of deciduous trees, or even remove trees that should not be pruned, such as spruces, to increase the amount of light reaching your plants

🌹 Paint fences or walls white to increase the amount of reflected light

Too much sun

🌹 Choose suitable trees to plant for future shade where desired

🌹 Create shade with solid fences, lath trellises, or arbours planted with vines

🌹 Use cedar shingles to make an A-frame shelter over newly planted seedlings or transplants, or insert single shingles in the ground positioned to cast a shadow over plants

🌹 Use a 2 x 4 resting on bricks to provide a roof over a row of seedlings; for larger beds, rest a panel of lath trellis on bricks to provide partial shade

Most annuals and many perennials only reach their potential in a sunny location.
RENATA WICHMANN

Nursery Beds. An easy and inexpensive way to collect plants of all types for your garden is to grow them yourself. Construct a nursery bed for this purpose, an out-of-the-way place in the garden devoted to growing annuals, perennials, and even shrubs and trees from seeds, cuttings, and root divisions. Seedlings and other young plants are much easier to care for when they are grouped together rather than randomly located throughout the garden.

Locate your bed in sun or partial shade, close to a water supply, and where you will remember to tend to it on a regular basis. Make sure the soil has a fine texture, is rich in compost, leaf mould, and other organic matter, and is well drained. A steady and generous supply of water is critical for the well-being of seedlings, cuttings, and divisions until they are rooted and established. Use a mist-type sprayer with the garden hose for this purpose. Be prepared to protect seedlings from the full force of the midday sun, wind, and heavy rain. Finally, remember to label your plants to avoid surprises.

∾ Uses for Nursery Beds ∾

Plant the following in a nursery bed until they are ready for transplanting into a permanent site in the main garden.

- 🌷 Seeds for annuals that don't mind being transplanted (calendula, marigolds, alyssum); use them as backup for bare spots in the garden, as replacements for the occasional dead plant, or as additions to container plantings suffering from the mid-summer blues
- 🌷 Seeds for perennials that often take several years to establish themselves before they are ready for the border
- 🌷 Cuttings and divisions of established perennials; these can be much smaller (and therefore more numerous) than would be appropriate for planting directly back into flower borders
- 🌷 Plants doing poorly in the border and needing a time out for some tender loving care before being reintroduced the following season
- 🌷 "Orphaned" plants that land on the bargain tables at garden centres, sometimes available at greatly reduced prices
- 🌷 Hardy spring-flowering bulbs that have finished blooming, to allow the foliage to ripen without being an eyesore in the main flower borders; replant in the border in the fall

Dappled shade is the perfect environment for growing a favourite collection of woodland plants.
LIESBETH LEATHERBARROW

Herbaceous Perennials. When selecting perennials, minimize loss through winterkill by choosing plants known to be hardy in the area. Native plants are particularly good bets as they have evolved under local growing conditions. Plants that are prolific self-sowers, such as columbines and delphiniums, will help fill in the landscape quickly and at no cost.

The best bargains for perennials are donations from friends after they have divided their overgrown plants in the spring or fall. Be wary of accepting plants with invasive growth habits. Learn how to divide perennials yourself for redistribution in your own garden, for trading with a friend, or for sharing at plant exchanges sponsored by local horticultural societies.

No quest for perennials is complete, however, without a trip to the local garden centre. Of course, the temptation to indulge and throw caution to the wind is great on such an outing, but if you make a list of what you need before you go, time your trip to coincide with summer sales, and remember that many garden centres will give you a discount if you buy in quantity, you can nip a potential spending spree in the bud. Plants bought towards the end of the season may be pot-bound; transplant them carefully and baby them for a while to help them develop healthy root systems.

How Perennials Are Sold. Perennials are usually sold as container-grown plants in a variety of pot sizes and prices; the larger the pot, the more mature and more expensive the plant. It may be worthwhile on occasion to buy the larger, more costly version of a plant you covet, just to have the pleasure of instant gratification in the perennial border. However, smaller, less mature perennials establish themselves in the garden more readily than older ones, catching up to the bigger plants in short order. This makes them a better buy, though you may have to wait a year before they bloom in profusion. Some local garden centres are now also selling perennials in four-packs or six-packs, also called cell-packs. By definition, these are relatively small, immature plants, but for the patient gardener, an excellent choice; they are inexpensive and make mass planting a realistic option.

What to Look For. When shopping for perennials, look for plants that are compact, bushy, and multi-stemmed. Avoid tall spindly plants that have likely been grown under poor light conditions or have simply been growing in pots for too long. Next, check the foliage for a deep uniform colour; abnormal or spotty leaf colouring may indicate disease or lack of nutrients. Also take a close look for insect pests. Check carefully beneath the leaves, along the stems, at new growth tips, and on soft buds for aphids, mealy bugs, and other unwelcome visitors. Stickiness, distorted leaves or crowns, blackened areas, mushy spots, holes, or jagged bites taken out of leaves also indicate potential problems. Not only will the plants be weakened by whatever ails them, but you also run the risk of importing the problem to your garden.

Although it is tempting to choose perennials that are in full bloom for instant colour, it is better to get them before their blossoms unfold. They will establish themselves more readily in the perennial border if they haven't already expended large amounts of energy on flower production. Of course, if you are after a particular cultivar or colour and doubt the accuracy of the labelling, choose a plant with an open blossom to confirm your choice; just make sure you pinch back blooms after putting the plant in the border so that its energy can be directed into developing strong roots before the onset of winter. To complete your above-soil inspection, make a quick check for perennial weeds, mosses, and liverworts, which may have been robbing the soil of nutrients essential for healthy plant growth. You definitely don't want to transplant perennial weeds into your flower border as they can be a nuisance to eradicate, and mosses and liverworts are an indication that the soil mix is poorly drained, with a good chance that the plant's roots may have rotted or died back.

Finally, tip the plant out of its pot and inspect the root mass. The roots should be firm and white, and sufficiently developed to retain most of the soil when the plant is removed from the container. If the roots are pot-bound, either packed into a solid mass or tightly coiled, the plant may be slow to adapt to conditions in your garden. Also, coiled roots will not uncoil of their own accord, even if given more room to grow; they just continue spiralling, eventually strangling the central root. Should you bring home such a messy root ball by mistake, make the most of the situation by teasing the roots apart before planting. Better still, don't buy pot-bound plants in the first place.

Perennials are also sometimes available as relatively inexpensive, dormant bare-root plants in the spring; roses, especially, are often sold this way. When buying bare-root plants, make sure they have a healthy root system and the roots aren't dried out, crushed, broken, or damaged in any other way. Should dormancy have been broken, any emerging shoots should appear healthy and unwithered. Keep bare-root plants cool and damp, and get them into the ground as soon as possible in the spring.

Annuals. Annuals—plants that grow from seed each year—can be quite expensive. If you must part with cash for annual bedding plants, don't be in a big hurry to put them out in the spring or you may lose your investment to late frosts.

How Annuals Are Sold. Annuals are generally sold in cell-packs, large flats, or as potted specimen plants. The large flats are the most economical way to buy annuals on a per plant basis, but not necessarily the most practical unless you need large quantities of the same plant. If you don't, and you can't find a friend or two who would like to share a flat of annuals, then cell-packs are the way to go. Although potted annuals give instant results,

❧ Alternatives to Purchasing Perennials ❧

Herbaceous perennials can be expensive to buy, and many Calgary gardeners take advantage of propagation techniques to reproduce herbaceous perennials at minimal cost. Here are some techniques you can try.

- 🌹 Start perennials from seed under a grow light
- 🌹 Set aside a part of your garden as a nursery bed where you can start and nurture slow-growing perennials until they reach a good size for transplanting into your flower borders
- 🌹 Collect seeds from your favourite plants to start under grow lights or in the nursery bed for the following season
- 🌹 Divide and replant existing perennials in the spring
- 🌹 Take stem cuttings of chrysanthemums, dianthus, cotoneaster, caragana, and lilacs in spring or early summer to grow in rooting medium and plant out in late summer
- 🌹 Take root cuttings of oriental poppies, bleeding hearts, and perennial cornflowers in early spring to grow in rooting medium and plant out when stems are 8–10 cm (3–4 in.) tall
- 🌹 For groundcovers, sever growing tips that have established roots from the parent plant to create a new plant, or bend stems over and cover with soil to encourage root formation; new plants can be severed from the parent when they are firmly rooted

Too long in the pot, this plant may have difficulty adapting to growing conditions in a garden; avoid buying pot-bound plants. LIESBETH LEATHERBARROW

Columnar trees such as these Swedish columnar aspens are ideal for the average urban landscape, offering both privacy and visual interest without casting too much shade.
LIESBETH LEATHERBARROW

they don't transplant as well as less mature plants, which will catch up quickly and give you an equally fine show of colour at a fraction of the price, albeit a few days later. Visit garden centres early for the best selection of annuals, but remember that it is not safe to plant them out in the Calgary area until late May (for cold-tolerant ones, such as pansies, snapdragons, and pot marigolds) or early June (for cold-sensitive ones, such as impatiens, zinnias, and nasturtiums) unless you are prepared to give them protection against late frosts.

What to Look For. Sturdy young annual plants with healthy foliage give the best results. They should have well-developed root systems and must not be pot-bound. Although plants growing in a dried-out medium or with discoloured foliage will continue to grow, in general, they will not develop well and will produce fewer flowers. Choose non-blooming plants unless you are after a specific colour or cultivar, keeping in mind that it is preferable for the plants to do their growing and blossoming in your garden, and not in their pots at a garden centre. Be vigilant about bugs and disease to avoid introducing them into your garden.

Bulbs. Hardy bulbs are a relatively inexpensive, long-term investment, requiring little care after the initial planting. Hardy bulbs such as species tulips, crocuses, and Siberian squill provide good value for money spent since they multiply rapidly to carpet the garden floor. You may also wish to grow tender bulbs, which are planted in the spring and lifted for indoor winter storage in the fall.

How Bulbs Are Sold. Bulbs are available by mail order and at your local garden centre. By all means, use the pictures in glossy catalogues to choose them, and place your order if the price is right and the mail-order company has a good reputation. At the same time, remember that local garden centres bring in a great variety of bulbs every year, including many of those displayed in catalogues, and there is a definite advantage to hand picking from the bins—"you sees what you gets."

What to Look For. When choosing bulbs, look for those that are plump, smooth, and firm; free of mould; and heavy for their size. A seemingly light bulb has probably dried out and will not be viable; a soft one is probably suffering from rot. Since bulbs store the energy for growing flowers, it is true that the bigger the bulb, the bigger and more numerous the flowers; plant the biggest bulb

The delicate fronds of the cinnamon fern unfurl rapidly in early spring; many ferns grow in Calgary when given the moist, shady locations they prefer. Liesbeth Leatherbarrow

∽ Alternatives to Purchasing Bedding Plants ∽

Some annuals grow well when seeded directly into the ground in late April or early May; cosmos, calendula, bachelor's buttons, nasturtiums, sweet peas, and marigolds all put on a reliable show of colour when planted this way, at a fraction of the cost of buying them as bedding plants. Many also self-seed for continued pleasure, year after year. Other annuals are easy to grow from seed under grow lights. Still others can be kept alive during the winter, either by taking cuttings and rooting and growing them under artificial light, or by storing the whole plant in a cool, dry place during its dormancy. Geraniums and scented geraniums, two types of tender plants that are expensive to repurchase every year, can be perpetuated this way.

possible for spectacular blooms the first year. However, smaller, less developed (and less expensive!) bulbs are good buys too. They just need a season or so to catch up with bulbs of higher, costlier grades. Avoid sprouted bulbs—no energy should go into producing top growth until the roots have been established. Finally, check all bulbs for signs of disease and insect damage and discard infected ones in the selection process. If you should end up with a diseased bulb, cut away the diseased portion with a sharp knife, dust the cut surface with sulphur or a fungicide, and let the bulb surface dry before planting.

When choosing corms, tubers, and other bulbous plants, the procedure is much the same as for choosing bulbs. They should be firm, plump, unblemished, and pest and disease free.

Trees and Shrubs. Trees and shrubs represent a large investment for gardeners, both in terms of time and money. To play it safe, choose healthy trees and shrubs that are known to be hardy in the Chinook zone. While it is fun to experiment with herbaceous perennials of borderline hardiness, this risk isn't worth taking with trees and shrubs unless you have the resources to replace failed experiments.

As you develop a plan for the trees in your landscape, keep their mature size in mind. For example, mature spruce trees, though lovely to look at, can reach a spread of 7 m (20 ft); this is far too big for the average urban lot. To avoid the cost of cutting down such beauties when they have outgrown their welcome (and to avoid throwing away your initial investment), don't plant them in the first place. Instead, choose dwarf cultivars of evergreens, columnar cultivars of deciduous trees, and smaller ornamental trees such as hawthorns, crabapples, and Japanese tree lilacs to provide accents in the garden. Give each tree enough room to grow to its mature size in your garden plan. Planting them more densely to create a lush look right from the

～ Caring for Newly Purchased Plants ～

Here are some steps to follow once you bring home your new plants.

❀ Open boxes of mail-order plants immediately upon receipt and moisten any dried-out plants.

❀ Harden off annuals, perennials, shrubs, and trees that may not be acclimatized to Calgary conditions. This is done by keeping the plants in a sheltered area away from intense sunlight during the day and then moving them inside or providing shelter from cold or frost at night. Over the course of one to two weeks, gradually increase their exposure to the sun and leave them outside or uncovered if there is no risk of frost.

❀ Bare-root plants should be planted in your garden as soon as possible. You may leave a bare-root plant in a cool place, keeping the roots moist, if you are able to plant within a day or so. If it will be longer than three days, bare-root plants should be "heeled-in" until they can be permanently planted. Dig a shallow trench in a sheltered spot in the garden out of the midday or afternoon sun. Soak the plants in a solution of 30 mL sugar to 23 L water (2 tbsp. sugar to 5 gal. water) for two hours, and then lay the plants in the trench, cover the roots with soil, and keep them moist. Alternatively, plant them in potting soil in large containers with adequate drainage.

❀ Annuals or perennials that are outgrowing their containers and becoming root bound should be moved to larger pots. If the roots have spiralled around in the pot or are in a tightly packed mass, break them up and spread them out in the new container.

❀ Pinch off blooms to save the plant's energy until it is settled in its permanent home.

---

start only results in unhealthy overcrowding and the eventual need to remove them anyway.

How Trees and Shrubs Are Sold. Trees and shrubs are long-term investments, so shop carefully to make sure you are making the best choices possible. Although you can find trees almost everywhere perennials and annuals are sold, it pays to go to a reputable nursery for your tree purchases. The best will have good return policies; just save your receipt and return an ailing plant within the permitted time. Guaranteed trees are slightly more expensive than those with no guarantee, but they are well worth the additional expense if you have to replace a dead one.

The most economical way to buy trees and shrubs is to purchase them in containers in late July or early August when they are on sale. If you plant them immediately and carefully, they will have plenty of time to establish a good root system before frost. The exceptions are junipers, which do not seem to do as well when planted late in the summer. Remember that cedars can be "iffy" here; they are susceptible to winterkill if exposed to the sun and wind, but can be reliable against east- and north-east-facing walls. Be sure to give all newly planted shrubs and trees a good deep watering before freeze-up in late October or early November to help them survive the winter.

Trees and shrubs are usually sold in one of three ways: bare root; in containers; or balled and burlapped. Each option offers advantages and disadvantages.

Bare Root. Bare-root plants are the least expensive but also the most vulnerable to root damage; sometimes the root ball is inadequate to support growth at all. Bare-root purchases must also be planted immediately upon arrival or shortly thereafter.

Containers. Container-grown trees and shrubs usually transplant reasonably well, and they can survive for a time in their pots before being planted if kept shaded, cool, and moist. However, they often come in a soil-less mix that resists watering when dried out, even after planting, which can slow down their growth considerably. Avoid this potential problem by gently shaking the soil-less mix from the root ball before planting directly into the rich loam in your garden. The roots of container-grown trees may also be pot-bound; check for this before you buy.

Balled and Burlapped. Balled-and-burlapped trees and shrubs have usually been locally field grown, dug up, root-pruned, and wrapped in burlap to protect the root ball. They tend to be stronger than the equivalent container-grown plants, not pot-bound, and easy to re-establish in your garden. However, they are also more likely to dry out than container-grown plants because more of the root system is exposed to air. Woody plants that have been allowed to dry out may suffer excessive root damage, which can lead to poor growth, die-back, leaf loss, and even death. Remember to cut away the string from balled-and-burlapped trees before planting. Remove the top third of the burlap to prevent wicking of moisture from the ground; then completely cover the root ball and remaining burlap with soil.

What to Look For. When inspecting a tree or shrub, look for uniform foliage colour. Variations in colour and other abnormalities can indicate root damage from improper fertilizing or watering or from disease. If you are buying a woody plant at the end of the summer, be wary of premature fall colour in the leaves. It is usually an indication of stress and may be the result of poor summer care. It is also important to make sure your tree or shrub is completely pest free.

When selecting a tree, also take its shape into consideration. The branching should be evenly distributed on all sides of the plant, and upright trees such as pine and spruce should have a healthy growing tip, called a leader. It is hard to grow a straight tree without a leader, although you can train a top branch to grow vertically, thereby creating a substitute leader.

If you are looking to purchase a woody plant early in the season while it is still in its leafless, dormant state, you would be well advised to make sure it is, in fact, alive. To do this, scrape a small portion of bark off the branch and inspect the colour of the exposed area. If it is alive, it will look faintly green and moist; if it is dead, the colour will be grey or dull beige. Some woody plants suffer tip kill during the winter, so if your tree appears dead, check another spot to confirm you are not just looking at tip kill.

If you have an opportunity to check the root ball, do so by tipping the container on its side and slipping the plant out part way. When this is not an option, poke your fingers into the soil and try to get a feel for the roots' health. Roots should be light in colour, firm to the touch, have an earthy odour, and branch out into fine feeder roots. If you cannot do a visual inspection, look for other clues about a plant's root ball. For example, the trunk of a container-grown woody plant should be supple but not wobbly, staying firmly rooted in the container when you give it a gentle pull. If wobbling the trunk or stem creates a hole in the soil at the base of the plant, then it is probably not well rooted. Moving the major stem or trunk of a balled-and-burlapped tree should move the entire root ball. If it doesn't, the roots may be in bad shape.

Staking Newly Purchased Trees. Small trees should be staked only if they are planted on windy sites or have been purchased bare root. Large trees that have been moved also require staking because some roots will have been lost in the transplanting process and those remaining may not be adequate to anchor the plant against the force of the wind in the crown.

Trees may be supported with single tall stakes or with guy wires or ropes attached to several shorter stakes. If you use a single stake, it should not reach higher than one-third of the tree's height and should be put in the planting hole first, on the windward side of the tree. Ties that attach the stake to the tree should be made of soft plastic, nylon, or rubber. Use a figure-eight loop in the tie to make sure the tree is not rubbing directly against the stake.

Guy wires attached to stakes will support a tree from several points. The number of stakes and wires needed will depend on the size of the tree and the windiness of the location. Stakes should be short and sunk at least 45 cm (18 in.) into solid ground. Attach guy wires just high enough on the trunk to stabilize the tree, yet still allow the trunk to flex. Run the wires through a loop of cut garden hose to prevent them from cutting into the bark when attached to the tree, or purchase rubberized guying packages at local garden centres.

Whichever method you use, do not stake trees too firmly. If they are allowed to sway slightly in the wind, they will develop strong, tapered trunks. Check trees periodically to ensure they are not secured too tightly.

~ Woody Ornamentals for City Gardens ~

Dwarf evergreens

Black spruce (*Picea mariana* 'Nana')

Colorado spruce (*Picea pungens* 'Cecilia', 'Corbet', 'Fat Albert', 'Globe', 'Hillside', 'Procumbens', 'Mesa Verde', 'Morden Blue', 'Pendula', 'R.H. Montgomery')

Engelmann spruce (*Picea engelmannii* 'Hoodie')

Juniper (*Juniperus scopulorum* 'Cologreen', 'Green Ice', 'Moonglow', 'Skyrocket', 'Tolleson's', 'Wichita Blue')

Mugho pine (*Pinus mugo* 'Compacta', 'Mops Mugo', 'Teeny', 'White Bud Mugo')

Norway spruce (*Picea abies* 'Compacta', 'Gregoryana', 'Nidiformis', 'Pendula', 'Pumila')

Scotch pine (*Pinus sylvestris* 'Nana', 'Viridis Compacta')

Small to medium deciduous trees

American mountain ash (*Sorbus americana*)

Amur maackia (*Maackia amurensis*)

Amur maple (*Acer ginnala* 'Bailey's Compact', 'Embers')

Apple (*Malus* spp.)

Birch (*Betula* 'Trost Dwarf')

Canada plum (*Prunus nigra*)

Caragana (*Caragana arborescens* 'Lorbergii', 'Plume')

European mountain ash (*Sorbus aucuparia* 'Pekenensis', 'Rossica')

Hawthorn (*Crataegus x mordenensis* 'Snowbird', 'Toba')

Japanese tree lilac (*Syringa reticulata* 'Ivory Silk')

Mongolian linden (*Tilia mongolica*)

Nannyberry (*Viburnum lentago*)

Pagoda dogwood (*Cornus alternifolia*)

Pear (*Pyrus* 'David', 'Golden Spice', 'John', 'Michener')

Plum (*Prunus* 'Brookgold', 'Brookred', 'Opata', 'Pembina', 'Tecumseh')

Rosybloom crabapple (*Malus x adstringens* 'Arctic Dawn', 'Kelsey', 'Pygmy', 'Red Splendor', 'Rudolph', 'Selkirk', 'Strathmore', 'Thunderchild')

Russian olive (*Elaeagnus angustifolia*)

Salt tree (*Halimodendron halodendron*)

Sea buckthorn (*Hippophae rhamnoides*)

Showy mountain ash (*Sorbus decora*)

Smooth sumac (*Rhus glabra* 'Laciniata', 'Midi')

Staghorn sumac (*Rhus typhina*)

Ussurian pear (*Pyrus ussuriensis*)

Weeping birch (*Betula pendula* 'Youngii')

Weeping caragana (*Caragana arborescens* 'Pendula')

Western mountain ash (*Sorbus scopulina*)

Columnar trees

Columnar mountain ash (*Sorbus aucuparia* 'Fastigiata')

Columnar Siberian crab (*Malus baccata* 'Columnaris')

European birch (*Betula pendula* 'Fastigiata')

Juniper (*Juniperus scopulorum* 'Gray Gleam', 'McFarland', 'Medora')

Saskatoon (*Amelanchier alnifolia* 'Thiessen')

Scotch pine (*Pinus sylvestris* 'Fastigiata')

Sutherland caragana (*Caragana arborescens* 'Sutherland')

Swedish columnar aspen (*Populus tremula* 'Erecta')

Stakes and wires should be removed after one year, but this may be extended by one year if the tree is in an extremely exposed location. Saw off any stakes positioned close to the tree trunks at ground level, to avoid disturbing the roots.

Pushing the Limits. Every summer, hundreds of Calgarians flock to view the winning gardens of the Calgary Horticultural Society's garden competition. Cameras and notebooks in hand, visitors marvel at the gardeners' skill and imagination and at the diversity of design and plants, from the lushness of shaded green nooks to colourful perennial borders, bountiful vegetable plots, and enchanting rose gardens. For those new to gardening, it can be an eye-opening experience (and possibly a revelation that hybrid tea roses can be grown in Calgary). Even seasoned gardeners find inspiration, new techniques, and fresh planting ideas. Many of the most successful and interesting gardens in Calgary challenge commonly held assumptions about what plants will survive or flourish here. Although there are limitations to what will grow in Calgary, gardeners should not be afraid to experiment; it is well worth giving the limits a gentle nudge or even an aggressive push from time to time.

Gardeners can often be slaves to the hardiness zones printed on the plant markers stuck in the pots of trees, shrubs, and perennials, or listed beside plants in catalogues or on nursery signs. Like Calgary temperatures, these zone ratings often seem to be either too high or too low. Cautious commercial growers will rate as Zone 5 a perennial you have had in your Zone 3A Calgary garden for years, while more enthusiastic catalogues may be overly confident in their ratings. This is why the zone ratings of plants should be checked in reliable books before you purchase, and even these should be viewed as general guidelines, not as gospel truth. Zones do not tell the whole story: the Edmonton area and much of southern Saskatchewan and Manitoba (including Winnipeg) are also Zone 3A, yet Calgarians transplanted from these areas can testify to the very different growing conditions in Chinook country. Many of these differences, such as the amount of precipitation and snow cover, the length of the growing season, and the absence of Chinooks, are significant factors in determining plant hardiness.

Fortunately, plants can't read labels or books and may surprise you by asserting their perennial nature when you were resigned to grow them as annuals. If you have had previous success with borderline plants, the microclimates in certain areas of your garden may well stretch to support herbaceous plants listed by dependable sources as Zone 5. If you wish to start pushing the limits, experiment with one or two plants at first, and do your homework so you can pay careful attention to all their cultural requirements. Make sure they are planted in a spot that is adequately sheltered from drying winter Chinook winds and mulch them well as soon as the ground freezes, piling snow on them whenever possible throughout the winter.

When you set your heart on a new and unusual plant, it is worth doing a bit of research to discover where the object of your desire originated; obviously those who call the jungles of Costa Rica home are not likely candidates, but what about recently introduced immigrants from northern China—or even Siberia? There are many useful plants from remote areas of the northern hemisphere that have already found their way into Calgary gardens, such as the Amur maple, the Amur chokecherry, and the dependable caragana. Seeds

---

∾ Plants for Adventuresome Gardeners ∾

Azalea (Northern Lights series, e.g., *Rhododendron* x 'Northern Lights', which includes 'Golden Lights', 'Orchid Lights', 'Rosy Lights', 'Spicy Lights', 'White Lights') - protected spot, continuous winter snow cover, mulch, acid-loving (amend soil accordingly)

Beardtongue (*Penstemon strictus, P. procerus, P. fruticosus, P. pinifolius*) - good drainage, mulch for winter protection

Chinese Siberian iris (e.g., *Iris forrestii*) - prefers moist soil, will flourish in well-nourished border that does not dry out in the summer

Daphne (*Daphne cneorum*) - winter protection, continuous snow cover

Fairy-foxglove (*Erinus alpinus*) - not long-lived, often self-sows

Ferns (e.g., Japanese painted fern) - shade, protection by trees, moist, well-drained soil high in organic matter

Genista (*Genista lydia, G. pilosa* 'Vancouver Gold') - winter protection, continuous snow cover

Hardy ice plant (*Delosperma nubigenum*) - very good drainage, dislikes winter wet, best on slope or in gravelly rock garden

Hydrangea 'Annabelle' and 'Pee Gee' (*Hydrangea arborescens* 'Annabelle' and *H. paniculata* 'Pee Gee') - eastern exposure, sheltered spot, moist soil, partial shade

Japanese blood grass (*Imperata cylindrica* 'Red Baron') - does not like hot, dry soils or heavy, wet soils

Lavatera (*Lavatera cachemiriana*) - winter protection

Lavender (*Lavandula angustifolia*) - good drainage, winter protection

Lewisia (*Lewisia cotyledon*) - perfect drainage; place almost vertically in rock wall or in scree garden; mulch with gravel around crown to keep high and dry

Mt. Atlas daisy (*Anacyclus depressus*) - dislikes winter wet

Primrose (*Primula alpicola, P. japonica, P. pulverulenta*) - mulch for winter protection; some emerge very late in spring (which is likely what saves them)

Red plantain (*Plantago rubrifolia*) - very impressive red foliage plant; even if parent doesn't survive, usually sets seed

Rhododendron (*Rhododendron* 'PJM') - acidic, peaty soil (amend soil accordingly)

Rock rose (*Helianthemum nummularium* 'Dazzler', 'Fire Dragon', 'Rose Glory', 'Raspberry Ripple') - evergreen plant; winter protection, continuous snow cover

Rodgersia (*Rodgersia*) - dappled shade, waterside or moist woodland areas

Russian sage (*Perovskia atriplicifolia*) - plant in well-drained soil, dislikes winter wet; prune back to 15 cm (6 in.) in late fall or early spring; some woody stem must be left each year for new shoots to develop in spring

Snowy wood rush (*Luzula nivea*) - evergreen; winter protection

---

originating in regions with climates similar to ours stand a much greater chance of survival than those from disparate climates. Undoubtedly, many more plants will come from northern and central Asia that will prove equally well suited to Calgary gardens. Don't be afraid to be among the first to welcome these plants to Calgary.

In addition to plant discoveries from far-off places, Calgary gardeners should not overlook new plants coming on the market that have been bred in Canada specifically for our conditions. Plant breeders are pushing the limits by developing and selecting for hardy, disease-resistant trees, shrubs, and perennials, many with unusual flower forms and colours. Their work has enabled Canadian gardeners to expand their gardening horizons, with little risk involved.

But passionate gardeners always take risks, desire the uncommon, and welcome a challenge to test their abilities. Sharing your triumphs with kindred spirits is part of the joy of gardening. After all, there is great satisfaction in hearing a fellow gardener say, "I didn't think that would grow in Calgary!"

Selecting Tools

Sometimes it seems as if gardeners spend the precious short growing season digging, planting, cultivating, weeding, cleaning up, and moving things from one part of the garden to another. Although some would like more leisure time to relax and enjoy the results of this labour, probably a larger proportion are not truly content unless they are working in the garden. Many find it difficult just to sit and enjoy their gardens without casting a critical eye on a hitherto undetected weed or noticing a delphinium desperately in need of support. The pleasure is found in the gardening process itself, in the smell of the earth and the small but wondrous discoveries that go unnoticed and unappreciated by all except those on their hands and knees in the garden.

Both the gardener seeking to minimize the amount of time spent toiling at garden chores and the one who becomes blissfully absorbed in them for hours on end benefit from quality tools designed for the task at hand. As many gardeners strive to manage without the use of pesticides, herbicides, and chemical fertilizers, old-fashioned good husbandry becomes more and more vital to healthy and productive gardens. Proper tools are an essential part of the effort to replace chemical controls with mechanical means whenever possible. Using the proper tools simplifies the job, minimizes physical strain, and ensures good results.

The average gardener does not need a vast array of expensive gadgets. As you build your basic collection of garden tools, invest in solidly built, old-fashioned implements, starting with the essentials and gradually adding more specialized tools as the need arises. Purchase the best quality tools you can afford; they will last longer than cheap ones, possibly saving you money in the long run, while making your work more enjoyable. If the cost of these tools seems prohibitive, check out what's available at garage sales. You may find some bargains hiding under the dirt and surface rust.

In addition to the basic tools described below, gardeners today can choose from a wide selection of accessories and gadgets designed for comfort and convenience. Stools, kneelers, knee pads, and tote bags for small tools and other garden necessities may all be found in garden centres or mail-order catalogues. Gardening clothing ranges from protective gloves, hats, and clogs, to specially designed pants with built-in knee pads, tool loops, and large pockets. It's up to you to decide which of these will improve the quality and efficiency of your gardening time.

Wheelbarrows. One of the best labour-savers in the garden is a wheelbarrow. A large wheelbarrow saves many trips carrying tools and plants from front to back garden and vice versa. When you are amending your soil, loads of compost, peat moss, or sand can be trundled to where you need them, rather than carried from the pile one shovelful at a time. A wheelbarrow is a gardener's best friend at clean-up time, moving piles of pruning trimmings, leaves, or discarded annuals to beds where they will be used as winter mulch.

The wheelbarrow container, or tray, is usually made of painted steel or a heavy-duty polyethylene. There are advantages and disadvantages to each. Steel is stronger but may eventually rust; plastic is lighter but may crack if left out in freezing temperatures. Steel handles are more durable than those made of wood. When purchasing a wheelbarrow, look for one with a pneumatic tire, which will absorb shocks and handle bumps better than a solid one. Don't buy a wheelbarrow that is too small or flimsy; bigger is better, provided you are strong enough to handle it without dumping the load before you reach your destination.

Many gardeners prefer carts to wheelbarrows as they provide more stability over rough terrain. Garden carts have two wheels, solid or pneumatic, fixed just forward of the box centre. Most are constructed of polyethylene, metal, or plywood, and they can be purchased in various sizes to fit your load requirements or gate and path widths. Some models have removable front panels for easier dumping or for carrying longer loads, such as branches or lumber.

Tools for Digging. The hardest working tools in your collection are spades, shovels, forks, and trowels.

Spades and Shovels. A spade has a flat blade and straight digging edge; a shovel has a concave blade with rounded edges, tapering to a point. Which you choose is often a matter of personal preference, or even tradition. The spade is favoured in Britain, whereas North Americans are more likely to use shovels. However, many gardeners prefer spades for serious digging in heavy Calgary soil and employ shovels for transplanting, for moving piles of soil or compost, or for digging post holes.

Look for spades and shovels with D-grip handles and wooden shafts with a straight grain. The socket into which the shaft fits will be either closed or open at the bottom. If it is open, moisture and dirt may accumulate, possibly rotting the base of the wooden shaft. For this reason, closed sockets are preferable. The blade should be forged, not stamped, and have a tread at the top—that backwardly curved piece of metal your foot pushes on while you dig. This important safety feature prevents cuts to your leg if your foot slips. The strongest blade is of a magnesium-steel alloy, with high carbon steel a close second. Stainless steel is another attractive, durable, and much more expensive option.

Garden Forks. A garden fork is indispensable for loosening or turning over soil, breaking up large clods, and working in stony ground. Use a fork for digging up root crops, dividing perennials, turning compost, or mixing in other soil amendments, such as manure or peat moss. The best forks are constructed of forged steel, which is strong and has some flexibility to prevent the tines from bending.

There are different types of forks for different purposes. A square-tined fork provides the best penetration for loosening and aerating compacted soil without turning it over, for example, in established perennial beds where you wish to avoid damaging roots. A spading fork has flatter, broader tines for lifting and turning soil in newly cultivated areas or when renovating perennial beds. The compost or manure fork is lighter than a digging fork and has curved tines to help lift and turn wood chips, compost, or manure. These last two forks have long handles to provide leverage for lifting. If you mulch with straw, you may wish to invest in an old-fashioned pitchfork, which is lightweight and has only three or four tines.

Trowels. The last essential digging tool every gardener should possess is a good trowel. The trowel helps you perform many garden tasks: weeding, transplanting, filling containers with soil, and dividing small plants. There are probably hundreds of inexpensive, bent trowels in the back of Calgary garden sheds, not up to the task of digging in the city's heavy clay soil, so make sure the one you purchase is sturdy and sharp. A trowel cast in one piece of metal is very durable, although many people prefer the less-slippery feel of a wooden handle. Most trowels are constructed of three pieces: a blade riveted or welded to a shaft, which, in turn, is inserted into a handle. Some better quality trowels have blade and shaft forged out of one piece of metal, thus eliminating one potentially weak spot. In addition to a digging

This attractive toolshed not only makes a wonderful garden focal point, but also protects gardening equipment and makes it easily accessible.

Liesbeth Leatherbarrow

trowel, look for a transplant trowel, which is narrow bladed and useful for planting seedlings or bulbs. Because trowels casually set aside have a habit of disappearing into flower beds or vegetable gardens, it's a good idea to put paint or fluorescent tape on inconspicuously coloured handles.

Tools for Finishing Touches. Once the hard work of digging and planting is done, you need tools to keep the garden tidy and the weeds at bay.

Rakes. A soil rake, to level beds in preparation for planting, has short, straight teeth for picking up stones, roots, or weeds. The most useful type has a flat bar across the top of the head so it may be used upside down to level and smooth the soil. When you buy a rake, make sure the head is firmly attached to the handle; if the wooden handle does come off, push it back on and submerge the joint in water until the wood swells to a tight fit.

Fan-shaped leaf rakes are available in bamboo, plastic, or metal. A bamboo rake is inexpensive and light and does a good job of raking up dry leaves without tearing up the lawn; however, it is less effective for wet leaves or grass and wears out fairly quickly. The plastic (polypropylene) rake is also suited to light tasks only. The most versatile and durable leaf rake is a spring-loaded model with steel tines and a long wooden handle. The spring takes the stress off the shaft, and these rakes are often adjustable for tine spacing and width by means of a sliding ring that locks into place.

Hoes, Cultivators, and Diggers. The ongoing battle against weeds is most efficiently waged with a trio of tools: hoe, cultivator, and long-bladed digger. Hoes come in an astonishing number of variations and sizes, but the most useful is the long-handled garden hoe, which has a sharp squarish or rectangular blade to cut through small weeds and loosen the top of the soil. Stirrup or Dutch hoes require a pushing action to remove weeds.

Cultivators are pronged, claw-like implements used to turn the soil and scratch out shallow-rooted weed seedlings. Some cultivators are short handled; others have longer handles for use between rows or if you need a longer reach. Look for a sturdy model constructed of cold-rolled or forged steel, an aluminum alloy, or lightweight, graphite-reinforced glass fibres. Steel prongs are sharpest.

For removing perennial weeds such as tap-rooted dandelions and thistles, you will need a long-bladed digger, also known as a dandelion or fishtail weeder or asparagus knife or fork. These tools pry out the deep roots of persistent weeds. Make sure you dig out the entire root or the weed will return.

Edgers. If you wish your garden to have a neat, well-groomed appearance, add a half-moon edger to your tool assemblage. This tool has a small curved blade and efficiently cuts turf with a sharp, clean edge, helping to prevent grass from creeping into your flower beds. It is also a lightweight but effective tool for chopping roots, digging out weeds and stones, and loosening crusted soil surfaces. The edger should have a strong blade of carbon or stainless steel or of magnesium steel alloy; a T-shaped handle is useful for applying downward pressure.

Secateurs. The Calgary gardener's arsenal should also include a handheld cutting tool known as secateurs. Depending on the model, these small pruning shears cut branches up to about 2.5 cm (1 in.) in diameter. They are useful for deadheading, cutting back perennials, and light pruning on shrubs, including removing suckers. You can choose from bypass or anviltype secateurs.

The bypass, or hook-and-blade, type has a narrow bill or hook with a sharp inner edge, which is easy to get under branches in crowded spaces, and a sharp upper cutting blade, which bypasses the hook when it completes a cut. Bypass secateurs cut soft-stemmed perennials and annuals cleanly and are effective on woody stems up to about 1.5 cm (½ in.). A bypass blade remains sharp longer than an anvil blade as the cutting edge does not contact metal. Anvil-type secateurs have a flat metal plate against which a sharp blade cuts. This action can crush stems, particularly if the blade is not kept sharp, but anvil secateurs are more efficient than bypass secateurs for woody stems, cutting up to 2.5 cm (1 in.) without too much effort.

Look for steel blades on all secateurs you purchase; the better the quality of steel, the less sharpening you will need to do. The type of secateurs you choose will depend on your hand strength and the size, selection, and number of plants in your garden that need light pruning. Try them before you buy; secateurs should fit comfortably in your hand even when completely open. Ratchet-action anvil pruners are the easiest for those with limited hand strength. Better-quality secateurs may feature replaceable parts, tension adjustment, shock absorbers, and rotating handles to reduce hand fatigue; they will be priced accordingly. If you wish to do more ambitious pruning on larger branches, you will require specialized tools.

Tool Maintenance. Good-quality tools can represent a sizable investment, and it is worth taking the time to maintain them properly. Store your tools in a dry place easily accessible to the garden. When possible, hang them up to save space and make it easy for you to spot the tool you need. Keep tools clean and rust free; any accumulated grime and rust can be removed with a wire brush, steel wool, emery paper, or, if necessary, a commercial rust remover.

Well-maintained and sharpened tools make your gardening tasks easier and more pleasurable. After using tools, plunge them in a bucket of sand mixed with oil to clean them and prevent rust. Dried sap on pruning tools may be cleaned off with mineral spirits. Wooden handles should be cleaned after every use and periodically rubbed with linseed oil to help seal the wood. Most gardeners think "pruners, shears, and knives" when it comes to sharpening, but don't forget the spades, hoes, edgers, and other tools that come into contact with the soil. When these tools are kept sharp, less effort is needed to use them.

To sharpen tools by hand, you will need a 20- or 25-cm (8- or 10-in.) mill file with a bastard cut, a whetstone, or a diamond sharpener. Hold your sharpening tool at a slight angle to the blade to be sharpened and push away from the blade. Check the blade regularly to make sure you don't oversharpen it and create too thin an edge. Spades should have a bevel anywhere from 15 to 35 degrees on the back edge of the blade. Whatever angle you choose, it is important to keep the bevel consistent across the edge, since thinner edges will wear down first. Secateurs should have a 20-degree bevel; knives can use a bevel of 11 degrees on each side of the blade.

∽ In Praise of Push Mowers ∽

The following is based on an article by Judith Doyle that appeared in *Calgary Gardening* (vol. 10, no. 6, 1996).

It is a scenario Calgarians are familiar with every summer weekend. You have just settled yourself on your sunny deck or patio to enjoy the soft morning air with that first cup of coffee when the bird song is lost in the sputter of a gas-powered lawnmower being coaxed up to a full-throated roar. From down the street, the high-pitched whine of an electric mower throttling up adds to a discordant duet. We tolerate the noise of these machines as a necessary part of modern gardening, but is it always necessary?

In complete contrast is the humble push mower: it quickly scissors off the grass with never a chewed blade in sight; it is light enough to be pushed easily, even by small garden helpers; and best of all it is so quiet that its gentle whirr can barely be heard by the neighbours. This "green machine" requires no gas, oil, or electricity, only a little muscle power. The gentle (if the grass is cut frequently) aerobic workout warms the gardener up for heavier tasks.

Unless you have vast expanses of turf, a push mower is all you need. Banish those memories of the cheap push mowers of yesteryear that baulked and bucked until in frustration you consigned them to the darkest corner of the garage and replaced them with the new power mowers of the sixties. There have always been better quality push mowers available, such as the Clemson reel mowers now found at garage sales and flea markets since the demise of the Clemson company (due to the shift to power mowers). But times change; fortunately, various brands of push mowers are again displayed in garden centres and hardware stores.

To complete the shift to old-fashioned lawn mowing, you can use hand-held clippers to trim edges. Gas- or electric-powered string trimmers tear grass blades rather than cut them, and this results in brown edges. If not used with care, these machines can also damage annuals, perennials, trees, or shrubs adjacent to the lawn. If you use clippers, edges can be trimmed close enough that you need not clip every time you mow.

❧ Painless Gardening ❧

In addition to using the right tools for the job, here are some other ideas to take some of the effort out of gardening and help you avoid fatigue and unnecessary aches and pains.

🌺 Avoid lifting heavy objects by pushing or sliding them when possible, or by using wheeled carts or wheelbarrows. If you must lift, practise proper body mechanics to prevent back injury:
  - bend your knees, not your back
  - use large leg muscles to lift
  - lift smoothly without jerking
  - shift your feet when you turn instead of twisting
  - stand straight and keep the weight you are carrying close to your body
  - use the largest muscles and joints rather than smaller, weaker muscles, for example, arms rather than hands

🌺 Avoid too many heavy chores in one day; pace yourself

🌺 Avoid bending more than necessary by sitting down to perform tasks or by using long-handled tools

🌺 Try not to work in one position for too long; changing position and stretching frequently will help avoid stiffness

🌺 Before filling large containers with potting mix, place them on wheeled platform trays for easy moving

🌺 Wear protective gloves when pruning or working around thorny plants

🌺 Dress comfortably, but avoid overly loose clothing that may become caught in gardening equipment

🌺 Take frequent breaks and drink plenty of water or other fluids, particularly if you are doing heavy work or the day is very hot

🌺 Don't forget a hat, sunscreen, and sunglasses

🌺 Make time to appreciate your garden; every now and then, reward yourself with a day off from all but essential garden chores

SIX

The Diligent Gardener

Inspecting Your Garden

In spring, the Calgary gardener delights in daily inspections of sun-warmed flower beds, welcoming each awakening crocus and tulip as a sign that winter will eventually depart, if only for a few short months. These garden tours are the start of a summer-long routine that not only brings great pleasure, but also results in a more beautiful, productive, and well-maintained garden.

A daily walk around the garden is akin to visiting friends, a chance to find out what's new, who has decided to bloom, and who looks a bit off colour. It's also an opportunity to keep up with small tasks that can grow to major chores if left unattended for any length of time; as in so many other endeavours in life, the adage "An ounce of prevention is worth a pound of cure" holds true for gardening.

As you make your daily rounds, pay attention to the general health of the plants in your garden. If any are failing to thrive, take a closer look to discover why. Possibly they are not receiving enough sun or are being elbowed out by an aggressive neighbour. Check the soil to see if it is too dry for the plant, or, less commonly in Calgary, too wet. Abnormal leaf colour, loss of leaves, or spots on leaves in distinctive patterns may be signs of nutrient deficiency and may indicate that fertilizing or soil amendment is required. Disfigured foliage is often an indication of disease or the presence of insect pests; treat the problem or remove and dispose of such foliage right away—in the garbage, not the compost.

Look for tell-tale slug holes in leaves or chewed edges that reveal the presence of caterpillars. If you pick off these destructive creatures immediately, they will not have a chance to multiply and devour everything that is to their taste in the garden. Early intervention also reduces the likelihood of you being tempted to use chemical controls, which may be harmful to beneficial insects and, of course, the environment.

～ A Portable Gardening Kit ～

A good idea early in the gardening season is to assemble a kit to carry with you on your garden beat. A portable kit saves many trips to the garage or shed and removes the temptation to procrastinate because the tool you need is not immediately at hand. A good-sized wicker basket with handles is an excellent container for these essentials, but various styles of tool holders are also available at garden retailers. Your kit should include a small plastic pail for compost material such as flower heads, stalks, and soft prunings, and a plastic vegetable bag saved from grocery shopping for diseased or bug-infested material. Add a plastic bowl with a snap-on lid if you expect to harvest any small fruits or vegetables. Tools to pack include secateurs for tall spent flower stalks or light pruning, a small hand cultivator to dislodge weed seedlings, a dandelion digger for tap-rooted weeds and for impaling slugs if you desire, and a small pair of scissors to snip flowers or slugs. Throw in a roll of twine to tie up sagging flowers, a pair of gardening gloves, and, finally, a notebook and pencil to record jobs to be done and musings on plant combinations, relocations, and gardening in general.

～ Working with Maintenance Companies ～

Garden maintenance companies provide a range of services to lighten the loads of busy gardeners. Power raking, fertilizing, lawn mowing and edging, core aeration, spring and fall clean-ups, tree and shrub pruning, hedge trimming, weed and pest control, even flower bed maintenance and hand weeding can be had for a price. When choosing a company to help you with your gardening chores, look for one that will do the combination of jobs that you require—no more and no less. Don't agree to a package deal that offers services you don't need. Also, make sure that your expectations will be met. For instance, if you like your lawn to be mowed to a height of 8 cm (3 in.), make sure the maintenance company will oblige; if it won't, look for one that will. Finally, ask for references to determine the company's efficiency and reliability.

If you are hiring a garden maintenance company for weed or pest control, make sure it is registered with Alberta Environmental Protection and applications are performed or supervised by a certified applicator. Weed- and insect-control chemicals can be hazardous if not used properly. Don't put yourself or your neighbours at risk by hiring someone who may not be qualified.

In late spring, Calgary gardeners should pay particular attention to delphiniums as they are susceptible to the caterpillars of the delphinium moth. Signs of infestation include leaves that appear tied together and the caterpillars' droppings. Be vigilant in checking for these pests on developing flower buds and the undersides of leaves. Columbines are commonly attacked by leaf miners; check for their light-coloured tracks and dispose of all affected leaves in the garbage. Aphid-prone plants such as lupins should be monitored closely and regularly given a preventive hose down with plain water.

The daily round also gives gardeners a chance to tidy the garden in easy stages. Spent blooms can be deadheaded, stray tendrils of vines tucked into place, and small wayward branches trimmed. Weeds can be detected and pulled out before they become established or go to seed. You can make note of larger jobs to be tackled, such as staking, pruning, transplanting overcrowded plants, or dividing perennials.

If you grow fruit or vegetables, a daily inspection ensures that peas and beans are picked at their peak size, before they become too mature, zucchini will not turn into torpedoes, the spinach won't bolt, and you will find the sweet ripe strawberries before the birds do.

Grooming Flowering Plants

When the ritual burst of spring planting activity draws to a close and annuals and perennials are safely tucked into their new homes, gardeners can step back, catch their breath, and take some time to enjoy the fruits of their labours. The daily tour of inspection and discovery is a good time to carry out the simple and routine tasks of summer garden maintenance; taking a few extra moments on a regular basis to deadhead, pinch back, or shear plants as required transforms already lovely flower beds into magnificence!

Bulb Care. Spring-flowering bulbs such as the large varieties of tulips and daffodils should have their faded blossoms removed and their bloomed-out flower stalks cut back to the base of the plant. If left to go to seed, these plants lose their vigour. Leave bulb foliage in place until it dies naturally; the unsightly leaves manufacture the food that is so important for replenishing the energy stored in bulbs for next year's display of spring colour. Dead bulb foliage is easy to pull by hand when it has ripened and will come away cleanly from the bulb. However, if foliage remains green six weeks after blooming is completed, it may be removed without compromising the vigour of the bulbs.

A hand-made willow basket stores an assortment of gardening essentials and is easily transported on daily garden rounds. Liesbeth Leatherbarrow

Many species tulips and daffodils continue to do well year after year even if you leave the flower heads on and allow them to set seed. They may even re-seed and produce more bulbs. Small bulbs such as crocus and grape hyacinth can also spread by re-seeding.

Pinching. Pinching is a trimming technique that benefits many plants during a growing season. It consists of removing from 2 to 5 cm (1 to 2 in.) from the growing tips of annuals and perennials to encourage the production of new branches from buds lower on the stem. This gives plants a bushier, shorter, more compact look. Plants that branch naturally are good candidates for pinching; those that grow from basal rosettes or from a single, tall flowering stem are not. Still other plants that normally require staking in Calgary might turn out to be self-supporting and less susceptible to wind damage if they have been pinched judiciously early in the season.

Pinching should be done when the plants have reached about one-third of their mature height, and preferably before they have set buds so you don't lose showy blooms and colour later on. For even denser growth, you can pinch them again when they have reached about half of their mature height. Some, like sweet peas, can be pinched when they are seedlings after the third or fourth set of leaves has appeared. To pinch a plant, take the growing tip and the first set of leaves between your thumb and forefinger and break them off just above the second set of leaves so you don't leave a naked stem. Make sure you pinch all stems of a multi-stemmed plant at the same time so they mature at the same rate; a pleasing uniform, symmetric growth habit will be the result.

Pinched plants produce more numerous but smaller flowers than unpinched ones, making this an especially popular treatment for annuals, both in flower borders and in container arrangements. Many herbs will provide a more bountiful harvest of aromatic leaves for seasoning your favourite dishes as a result of being pinched. Even perennials, especially the late-flowering ones, benefit from a pinching session early on, but a word of caution here. Pinching delays flowering by one or two weeks, and with the very real possibility of early frosts in Calgary, care must be taken when deciding which plants to pinch and when. Asters and chrysanthemums, both autumn bloomers that respond beautifully to pinching, can have their growing tips removed until early July without sacrificing bloom potential. If you wait much later than that, you will most certainly risk having your autumn display of colour cut short by killer frosts.

While delayed flowering due to pinching is viewed as a definite disadvantage by some, you may, on occasion, wish to manipulate the bloom times of certain plants so they produce flowers simultaneously with slightly later flowering plants to create a pleasing colour combination. This delay can be achieved by pinching, although it requires some experimentation to get the timing just right. Experiment on just a portion of the plant and record your observations in your journal until you have the details worked out. This will help you remember from year to year how to re-create flower vignettes that would not occur naturally.

Disbudding. Disbudding is the deliberate removal of flower buds. By eliminating all the side buds on a plant, you encourage the formation of single large blossoms at the ends of long stems, which is especially desirable for gardeners interested in producing show-quality roses, chrysanthemums, dahlias, carnations, and peonies. You can also reverse the technique. Instead of removing side buds, you can pinch off the terminal bud, which results in the side shoots producing numerous, though smaller, blossoms over a longer period of time. Some culinary herbs should be disbudded continuously during the summer; basil, oregano, and mint will all have more intensely flavoured leaves as a result.

Deadheading. Deadheading—the task of removing spent flowers from annuals and perennials—not only improves a plant's appearance, but also encourages it to bloom for longer stretches of time. Sometimes diligent deadheading even initiates a second flush of bloom later in the season. When fading blossoms are snipped before seeds are formed, plant energy is directed towards plant growth and increased flower production. No seeds also means no seedlings, a bonus for those gardeners who do not favour the uncontrolled, riotous growth of a cottage garden. Baby's breath, bellflowers, daylilies, delphiniums, pinks, blanket flowers, phlox, lavender, all daisies, and yarrow are just a few of the many perennials that should be deadheaded. Although most annuals benefit from the same treatment, some are "self-cleaning"; most self-cleaning annuals are sterile, hence, no seeds are produced. These plants shed spent flowers of their own accord and on a continuous basis, making them welcome additions to the garden. Impatiens, begonias, and salvias fall into this category.

The best way to deadhead is to make a quick snip with sharp garden scissors, hand clippers, or a garden knife. These tools all make clean cuts, leaving healthy tissue and a quick-healing wound. However, with very soft-stemmed plants, your index finger and thumb serve just as well. Individual cuts should be made back to a leaf, bud, or other stem. Plants with leafless flowering stems should have their spent stems cut close to the ground; bare stem stubs are an eyesore. Do look carefully before deadheading to be sure you are not removing unopened flower buds in the process.

Plants that flower in spikes, such as delphiniums and mullein, are difficult to deadhead because of the small size and close proximity of individual flowers. Their grooming needs are better served by cutting back entire spikes to the foliage when they have finished blooming. This encourages the development of smaller but equally beautiful side spikes. Alternatively, prepare for one magnificent flush of colour by pinching out the smaller side spikes on a regular basis to encourage the formation of fewer but larger showy central spikes.

There are, of course, times when gardeners choose to overlook the task of deadheading their plants. Those striving for the wild abandon of a cottage or wildflower garden welcome the self-seeding qualities of such plants as columbines, daisies, delphiniums, cornflowers, and lady's mantle. In addition, the attractive seed heads of the sedum 'Autumn Joy', bee balm, coneflowers, astilbe, ornamental grasses, and other plants not only add visual interest to winter gardens, but also attract and feed birds during the frigid prairie winter. These should all be deadheaded in early spring before the plants resume active growth.

Shearing. Cutting back, or shearing, refers to the pruning of plants after flowering to a uniform height either to refresh and tidy their appearance or to encourage a new flush of growth and flowering. You will want to do this to all of your stragglers: plants that have grown leggy from too much shade or fertilizer, bloomed-out perennials, rangy herbs and annuals, and low-growing, spring-flowering edging plants. Delphiniums, lupins, hardy geraniums, and columbines can look particularly bedraggled and tatty after they have bloomed, but will rebound once they have been trimmed. Even some biennials such as sweet William and foxglove, with a natural two-year life cycle, might return a third year if cut back immediately after flowering, although you may wish to leave a few stems to encourage seed set. It is not guaranteed that all cut-back plants will re-bloom the same season, but they will at least be able to hold their own in the perennial border as attractive foliage plants.

In general, when cutting back plants after blooming, you should remove from one-third to one-half of the stem length. In the case of disease-prone plants such as bee balm (powdery mildew) and columbine (leaf miners), your treatment can be more radical. If plants show signs of infection, cut them back to ground level and dispose of the infected foliage in the garbage (not the composter). New growth will be healthy and the plants themselves will once again be attractive in the border.

Thinning. Some plants such as bee balm, garden phlox, and delphiniums produce a thick clump of stems that eventually crowd each other sufficiently to reduce air circulation and prevent light from reaching the centre of the plant. This often results in poor bloom production and an increased susceptibility to disease. Solve the problem by thinning these plants; remove half their stems early in the season. The remaining stems will be more vigorous and may produce at least as many blossoms of an even larger size.

Staking. Some perennials grow in an orderly fashion, pushing up flowers on straight, strong stems, bending with the breeze but compliantly

---

∾ Grooming Techniques for Specific Plants ∾

Plants to pinch

You should pinch most annuals, including zinnias (*Zinnia elegans*), petunias (*Petunia* spp.), snapdragons (*Antirrhinum majus*), sweet peas (*Lathyrus odoratus*), and pansies (*Viola* x *wittrockiana*). You should also pinch most herbs, including basil (*Ocimum basilicum*), oregano (*Origanum* spp.), marjoram (*Origanum majorana*), and mint (*Mentha* spp.). Other plants you should pinch include:

Aster (*Aster* spp.)
Bee balm (*Monarda* spp.)
Catmint (*Nepeta* spp.)
Chrysanthemum (*Chrysanthemum* spp.)
Fleabane (*Erigeron* spp.)
Obedient plant (*Physostegia virginiana*)

Phlox (*Phlox* spp.)
Purple coneflower (*Echinacea purpurea*)
Russian sage (*Perovskia atriplicifolia*)
Sage (*Artemisia* spp.)
Tickseed (*Coreopsis* spp.)

Plants not to pinch

Columbine (*Aquilegia* spp.)
Coral bells (*Heuchera* spp.)
Delphinium (*Delphinium* spp.)

Hollyhock (*Alcea rosea*)
Mullein (*Verbascum* spp.)

Plants to shear

Candytuft (*Iberis*)
Catmint (*Nepeta* spp.)
Creeping phlox (*Phlox* spp.)
Dead nettle (*Lamium maculatum*)
Garden pinks (*Dianthus* spp.)
Goutweed (*Aegopodium podagraria*)
Hardy geranium (*Geranium* spp.)

Lobelia (*Lobelia erinus*)
Painted daisy (*Pyrethrum*)
Rock cress (*Aubrieta* spp.)
Rock soapwort (*Saponaria ocymoides*)
Sweet alyssum (*Lobularia maritima*)
Thrift (*Armeria* spp.)

Self-cleaning, easy-care plants

Ageratum (*Ageratum houstonianum*)
Browallia (*Browallia speciosa major*)
Coleus (*Coleus* spp.)
Globe amaranth (*Gomphrena globosa*)
Impatiens (*Impatiens wallerana*)

Periwinkle (*Vinca minor*)
Portulaca (*Portulaca grandiflora*)
Salvia (*Salvia* spp.)
Spider flower (*Cleome spinosa*)
Wax begonia (*Begonia semperflorens*)

Plants to deadhead

Deadhead most annuals and spring-flowering hardy bulbs. Also deadhead:

Baby's breath (*Gypsophila* spp.)
Balloon flower (*Platycodon grandiflorus*)
Bellflower (*Campanula* spp.)
Blanket flower (*Gaillardia* spp.)
Columbine (*Aquilegia* spp.)
Daylily (*Hemerocallis* spp.)
Delphinium (*Delphinium* spp.)
Foxglove (*Digitalis* spp.)

Phlox (*Phlox* spp.)
Sage (*Artemisia* spp.)
Shasta daisy (*Chrysanthemum* x *superbum*)
Thrift (*Armeria* spp.)
Verbena (*Verbena hortensis*)
Veronica (*Veronica* spp.)
Yarrow (*Achillea* spp.)

Plants with attractive seed capsules and spikes

Leave seed heads intact over the winter and deadhead in the spring.

Astilbe (*Astilbe* spp.)
Coneflower (*Rudbeckia* spp.)
Globe thistle (*Echinops ritro*)
Goatsbeard (*Aruncus* spp.)
Goldenrod (*Solidago*)

Lavender (*Lavandula angustifolia*)
Love-in-a-mist (*Nigella damascena*)
Ornamental onion (*Allium* spp.)
Poppy (*Papaver* spp.)
Sedum (*Sedum* 'Autumn Joy')

Plants to disbud

Carnation (*Dianthus* spp.)
Chrysanthemum (*Chrysanthemum* spp.)
Dahlia (*Dahlia* spp.)

Peony (*Paeonia* spp.)
Rose (*Rosa* spp.)

Plants to thin

Bee balm (*Monarda* spp.)
Delphinium (*Delphinium* spp.)

Garden phlox (*Phlox paniculata*)

returning to position in moments of stillness. Unfortunately, these good citizens of the plant world often appear to be in the minority in Calgary gardens. Some of our favourites are the worst culprits: oriental poppies slouch messily; full-blown peony blossoms drag in the dirt; and those splendid, long-awaited delphinium blooms snap and hang sadly in the first summer thunderstorm. Many plants need staking, some to tidy their shape and appearance and others to prevent weather damage to vulnerable hollow flower stems. Staking individual plants improves the appearance of perennial borders by keeping each one distinct and out of the lap of its neighbour. Successful staking gives plants a natural appearance; it is unobtrusive, visible only on close inspection.

The secret to supporting perennials invisibly lies in timing and the selection of appropriate methods. Gardeners are well advised to be vigilant in staking plants early in the season, before they reach half their full size. If staking is left until it is obvious plants are in need of support, the results will likely be unsatisfactory. Most gardeners have had the experience of cramming floppy perennials into too-small wire cages, damaging leaves and flowers in the process. Tall flower stems break easily when you are attempting to straighten them up and tie them to stakes with string. Garden retailers now stock a large number of useful staking devices; durable green plastic-coated metal grids and hoops, link stakes, loop stakes, and stem supports are all good garden investments.

Peony Rings and Tomato Cages. Top-heavy plants and plants that fall open at the centre are best controlled with ring supports. These consist of concentric hoops arranged with the largest on the top and the smallest on the bottom, linked by vertical wires that are inserted into the ground. Some models feature detachable legs. Ring supports are available in different diameters to suit various plants, and there is also a choice of length for the detachable legs. Large rings are often referred to as peony hoops and smaller ones as tomato cages. You can make your own cage supports out of chicken wire or cement reinforcing wire, supported by a wooden stake. As plants grow through the support, it soon disappears in the foliage.

Ring supports are ideal for bushy plants such as peonies, tomatoes, bleeding hearts, Shasta daisies, painted daisies, yarrows, coreopsis, or oriental poppies. They may also be used to hold up the stems of tall vase-shaped plants, such as Maltese cross, solidaster, veronica, and monkshood, or to contain large, sprawling herbs, such as lovage, comfrey, and tarragon. Make sure you purchase ring supports with legs that are sturdy enough not to bend beneath weighty blossoms, and position the rings at a height that will allow the plant a natural-looking spread and shape. Supports that imprison plants too closely give them an unnatural appearance.

A

B

C

D

E

(a) Wire cage; (b) peony ring;
(c) grid ring; (d) link stake; (e) loop stake.
GRACE BUZIK

Stakes. Wide-spreading clumps of plants can be held up by stakes and string. Insert stakes angling away from the plant to allow for growth; additional string may be added farther up the stake as necessary. Whenever possible, choose green stakes and twine to camouflage your handiwork.

Linking stakes are used to support multi-stemmed plants. These L-shaped stakes have a loop at the top of the upright and a hook at the end of the horizontal arm to join to another stake. They are adaptable to individual plant shapes as several can be linked to make irregularly shaped enclosures. They are also the easiest and least-damaging means of emergency support for plants that were not staked early enough in the season.

Calgarians grow many perennials with tall individual flower stems that are susceptible to wind and can become top-heavy after rain. Staking single stems protects the blooms of plants such as delphiniums, hollyhocks, gladiolus, and lilies from weather damage. Loop stakes are uprights to which opening metal loops are added at intervals to embrace tall stems. Other single-stem supports have a ring at the top. Green bamboo or simulated bamboo plastic stakes also work for tying up individual stems. Covered or cushioned plant ties are available that will not cut into stems, or you can cut up old pantyhose for this purpose.

To avoid giving your plants a stiff, upright bearing, insert these stakes in the ground at a slight angle, following the natural line of the stem, and make sure they do not project above the bloom. It is a good idea to insert stakes beside vulnerable stems well before blooming, adding loops or ties as the stem lengthens. If you cross the string or plant ties between the stem and stake in figure-eight loops, the stems will not rub against the stakes. While most perennials can easily tolerate minor root damage caused by inserting stakes, you must take care not to damage fragile lily bulbs by inserting stakes too close to the lily stems.

Strong, straight branches saved from pruning or collected willow branches can be used for stakes with a natural appearance. Insert branching twigs beside small perennials in need of support.

The well-staked perennial garden will have a tidy, but not regimented appearance. Effective, unobtrusive staking requires a considerable effort on the part of the gardener, but if the task is begun early in the growing season, many mid-summer plant disasters can be avoided.

∽ Preparing for Extended Absences ∽

Some Calgarians steadfastly refuse to leave their gardens during the precious and fleeting growing season, finding it difficult to tear themselves away for even a few weeks just when favourite perennials are about to bloom and the burgeoning growth is most in need of careful stewardship. Others welcome a mid-summer break from garden chores or must schedule vacations to suit family circumstances. Whether you leave grudgingly or gladly, the following steps will help prepare your garden for your absence.

- Do a thorough pest and disease patrol before you leave. Remove all harmful insects or diseased plant material and wash down plants. Dig up small weeds; they can grow rapidly and compete with desirable plants.
- Stake any plants that may grow large enough to require support while you are away.
- Deadhead any rampant self-seeders that you wish to keep under control. If you will be gone for more than a few weeks, you may wish to cut flowers from all plants, leaving developing buds to provide bloom on your return.
- Group containers of annuals in partly shaded, sheltered areas.
- Move hanging baskets out of windy or hot locations.
- Apply a layer of mulch, such as wood, bark chips, grass clippings, or compost, to the surface of perennial beds and to the soil in containers to help retain moisture.
- Pinch or shear annuals to encourage bushy growth and blooming later in the summer.
- Fertilize annuals and heavy feeders such as tomatoes.
- Ask a gardening friend or neighbour to cut your lawn and water your plants, remembering that containers and hanging baskets need daily attention during hot weather.
- If you have an automatic watering system, check that it is programmed for plants to receive an adequate amount of water.
- Cut an armful of the biggest and most beautiful flowers from your garden that are appropriate for drying and hang them in small bunches in a warm, dark place. Peonies, roses, delphiniums, larkspur, monkshood, and many others will bring summer memories into your home during the coming winter. If you do not wish to dry these flowers, give a bouquet to a friend or relative who does not have access to a garden or to a hospital or seniors' home.

Pruning Trees and Shrubs

Of all the early horticultural endeavours in Calgary, tree planting was the most significant. Besides being practical, it was also a symbolic and optimistic act; trees denoted permanence and signalled that the new citizens were themselves putting down roots, determined to stay and survive. This hopeful act continues to be repeated by gardeners who appreciate the aesthetic and environmental benefits of a garden graced with mature trees. Trees shade and protect, contributing to the creation of the slightly milder microclimates that are so important to successful gardening in the harsh Calgary climate. Because trees are such valuable garden assets, both in terms of replacement value and the amount of time required for them to reach their mature size, you should not approach tree pruning in a haphazard manner.

The Chinook climate is not kind to non-native trees. In the course of the average year, trees in this region must withstand extreme temperature fluctuations and drying and damaging winds. Drought, leaf-shredding hail, or broken branches caused by heavy snowfall while leaves are on the trees are other potential hazards. In addition, trees need to deal with attacks from insects or disease. Overly severe or improper pruning can leave trees with inadequate resources to combat nature's challenges; they will become unhealthy and may even die. It is particularly important in the Chinook zone to ensure there is a good reason for every pruning cut you make and, if substantial pruning is required, to do it over several seasons. Big pruning jobs can be avoided by choosing trees that fit your planting space and by regular light pruning of young trees to give them a strong framework as they mature.

Trees are pruned for many reasons. Unfortunately, pruning is frequently done too heavily and too late in an attempt to rectify unsuitable tree choices. However, pruning can benefit a tree by removing dead, diseased, damaged, or structurally unsound branches. The gardener prunes to improve the appearance of a tree, to increase fruit production and quality, and to rejuvenate old or neglected trees and shrubs. Pruning techniques and the amount to be removed vary depending on the tree and the purpose of pruning.

When to Prune. Stress to trees can be reduced by pruning at the appropriate stage of a tree's annual cycle. Avoid pruning during the active spring start-up period, that is, from the time the buds swell before breaking in the spring until the time the leaves harden off. Until the leaves have reached a mature size and are photosynthetically active, all of the start-up processes are fuelled by stored energy. Severe pruning, resulting in the loss of many leaves, reduces the tree's internal volume of healthy tissue that can store energy, and so most trees are best pruned either while dormant or in the summer, from mid-June onward. Although in the past it was recommended to wait until July to prune maples and birches, recent observations made by professionals suggest it is safe to prune these trees once new foliage has completely developed. Begin by clipping off small twigs before attempting to cut any larger branches; if the small pruning cuts drip sap, postpone the job for a week or two.

How to Prune. Before pruning, identify the natural shape of the species so you can prune to enhance it. Then, inspect the individual tree or shrub to determine what needs pruning. Finally, make the right kind of cut.

Careful pruning is based on an understanding of how trees respond to injury, and how the branch-trunk interaction zone is structured.[30] Like all living organisms, trees function as closed systems to the outside environment. When trees are wounded by wind damage, trunk impacts, boring insects, self-wounding branch growth, or pruning, there will be a time when the closed system is opened at the injury site. Trees defend themselves by a process called compartmentalization. When trees compartmentalize, they are engaging in a big trade-off, defending themselves against injury at the cost of a reduced interior volume to store energy.

Compartmentalization works by using a series of chemical protection zones that isolate the damaged area and dissociate it from the living tissues of the tree. These zones consist of a concentration of phenols and other chemicals that act like antibiotics to contain the injured area. Such compartmentalized wounds are obvious in longitudinal sections of branches or tree trunks; compartmentalized wood is a darker colour than the living, whiter sapwood. Trees do not heal. Once a cell has been damaged, either by exposure to the outside environment or by the aging process, the cell dies and stays locked in place forever, as long as that tree—or sections of its lumber—exists. The knot in a piece of furniture is a branch core that has been compartmentalized. It grew inside the trunk to the depth of growth rings equal to the age of the branch. Dutch elm disease is a study in compartmentalization because the tree walls off large amounts of tissue to avert the attacking fungus. Eventually the tree has little or no healthy uncompartmentalized tissue and, thus, no room for liquid transport or energy storage, resulting in death.

Before you prune any branch on a tree, take a good look at the point at which the branch is connected to the trunk. A swollen branch collar is visible where the trunk and branch tissues intersect. This collar is where nature intended for the branch to be removed, and where most branches will abscise, or shed, on untouched forest trees. The branch collar is one of the tree's strongest protection areas. Since in nature most lower branches are removed over time through decline, die-back, and shedding, the branch collar is naturally a place where fungus and pathogens can attack the trunk.

Research shows that when a branch is pruned properly, only the branch core will be compartmentalized. When the branch collar is injured and the natural protection zone destroyed, a tremendous amount of invasion can occur into the trunk and a much larger volume of living tissue will be compartmentalized.

When pruning, always stub cut large branches, that is, cut the end off the branch and leave a 5–8 cm (2–3 in.) stub. Next, undercut the bottom of the branch to prevent bark tear-out. Then, look at the branch collar from both sides and project your imaginary pruning cut through the branch base against the collar. When you make the cut, be careful not to turn your saw in towards the trunk or the bottom of your cut will be too deep. If in doubt, cut farther out from the trunk. Trees can more readily deal with stubs than with flush cuts that remove collar protection zones.

Do not cover your pruning cuts with any substance; it does not help the compartmentalization process. Tree tar, used for many years, can promote rot, as it does not allow the cut surface to breathe. Remember to sterilize tools with a fresh 10 percent bleach solution between trees and between cuts on diseased trees to avoid spreading harmful pathogens.

What to Prune. Prune to remove deadwood as this speeds up compartmentalization. When a tree tries to abscise a dead branch, the branch protection zone is extended, which means that dead branches often have collar protection zones that extend outward. Look for the point just outside the original collar where there is a distinct change in the diameter of the branch. Your cut should be just where the smaller-diameter dead section of the branch meets the larger-diameter extended protection zone.

Small branches on trees and shrubs are covered with a series of potential growth buds—one at the end of each branch (terminal buds) and several on the sides of each branch (lateral buds). Always make a pruning cut directly above a lateral (side) bud that points outward, at an upward angle, in the direction you want the branch to grow. This means that the new growth will occur away from the main trunk, opening up the central area to air and light.

Prune to remove disease. Do not remove healthy branches on an affected tree; this would only cause additional stress to the tree. Fungal infections, such as cytospora canker, are usually quite localized and can be dealt with where they originally appear, either by removing them with a knife or spraying them with a systemic fungicide. Bacteria, such as fireblight, move much more freely within the system of the tree and thus pose a greater threat to its life. Cut off the diseased wood and keep a careful eye on the tree for further signs of infection.

Prune to suit your landscaping requirements. Trees will stay healthier if you can do this without destroying their natural shapes and growth tendencies. Although many gardeners have traditionally pruned up to one-third of a tree per year, given the stresses of the Calgary climate, you may prefer to prune more lightly and wait a year to observe the tree's reaction to your work before pruning further.

Never prune the top off a tree. Topping destroys both the health and appearance of a tree. If you need to prune a tree to allow more light into your house or garden, thin out selected branches at their branch collar sites to produce a more open tree instead. This will maintain the tree's natural shape and allow it to properly close off pruning wounds. Cutting off the ends of branches robs the tree of far too many chlorophyll-producing leaves and opens many wounds for the tree to compartmentalize; not only that, the weak, spindly shoots produced by topped trees are unsightly and ruin the tree's appearance.

When to Consult an Arborist. Arborists are specialists in the care and maintenance of trees. They have been trained to prune shrubs and trees of all sizes, to recognize and treat tree diseases and pests, and to move or remove trees when necessary. Tree pruning is a task that should not be taken lightly, both for the continued healthy existence of your trees and for the safety of the person doing the pruning. A well-pruned tree will be robust and have a pleasing, open, natural form; a poorly pruned tree will have an unappealing shape and be susceptible to rot and disease. In general, the well-informed, knowledgeable home-owner can keep up with the mainte-nance and corrective pruning of shrubs and small trees. However, when it comes to large, mature trees, an arborist can save you a lot of time, aggra-vation, and possible injury. Good arborists have the knowledge and equip-ment to do the big jobs safely and efficiently. They are also best consulted by the inexperienced pruner, no matter what the size of shrub or tree.

Similarly, when it comes to disease, the knowledgeable gardener can deal with many circumstances as they arise. However, if a large limb or main trunk of a tree is affected by disease, it is safer to call in an arborist, who will be able to evaluate the problem accurately and let you know if the tree is worth saving. Home remedies under these circumstances might adversely affect a tree's stability, making it susceptible to wind damage—a potential danger for people and buildings in the immediate vicinity—and an open invitation to pests and disease.

Selecting an Arborist. A recommendation from a friend or experienced gardener is the best way to find a good arborist, but if such a recommenda-tion is not forthcoming, take a walk around the neighbourhood to identify well-done jobs. A polite enquiry to the home-owner should elicit the name and phone number of the contractor responsible for the effort. If this still does not land you with a dependable arborist, then you will have to rely on blind phone calls.

First, ask prospective contractors about their credentials, keeping in mind that there are no regulated certification programs in Alberta; although many existing programs are excellent and extensive, some are not. The best way to determine whether contractors are knowledgeable is to read appropriate reference books and then ask questions—lots of them. For example, ask their views on tree-topping, the unceremonious and somewhat indiscriminate lopping of the top branches of overgrown trees. If they indicate that tree-topping is acceptable to them, stay clear; severe tree-topping damages trees, sometimes to the point of death. Clearly indicate your expectations for the job at hand and take careful note of their responses. If you don't like what you hear or if they are adamant about carrying out a procedure that makes you uncomfortable, don't go with them. Beware of so-called tree care specialists who own all the right equipment but have no training in arboriculture; they can cause you and your trees no end of unnecessary problems. If you are having work done on a big tree and there is a potential safety risk to both the worker and to adjacent structures, you might also want to check on the company's safety record and find out whether or not they are insured. Finally, ask for references and do the follow-up: go and see work done by the contractor you wish to hire, just to make sure you will be satisfied with the results.

Tools for Pruning. If you do your own pruning, you need the proper tools. A pair of hedge shears is useful for trimming formal hedges or tidying shrubs with dense foliage; do not use them for other pruning chores. Secateurs may be used to remove small branches; long-handled pruners or

---

∿ Tree Pruning Safety ∿

Pruning trees can present many dangers. The following tips will help you prune safely.

- Recognize your limitations and call a professional if the job is difficult
- Do not prune trees near power lines yourself; this is a job for professionals
- Avoid using chain saws for pruning, as they are extremely dangerous
- Inspect tools and equipment before starting the job and sharpen cutting tools, if necessary
- Wear a long-sleeved garment
- Wear heavy gloves to protect your hands from scratches and to cushion them from pressure
- Wear safety glasses at all times
- Wear a safety belt and a hard hat if you must climb up into a tree
- Tie your ladder onto the tree securely
- If you are working with an assistant on the ground, make sure that person also wears a hard hat

loppers will be effective on branches up to about 5 cm (2 in.) in diameter. For bigger jobs you will need a pruning saw. There are many different sizes and types available; select one suitable for the size of branches you need to cut. A curved-blade tree saw works well in tight spots and is sufficient for most do-it-yourself pruning jobs. Choose a size of saw that you are

A branch should be pruned just outside its collar (a swelling that occurs where the branch intersects the tree trunk). LIESBETH LEATHERBARROW

✌ Tips for Hedge Pruning ✌

The following are tips for successful hedge pruning.

- ❦ Bare-root hedge plants should be pruned to half their size when originally set out; container-grown plants should be pruned back by about one-third
- ❦ A newly planted hedge should be left to grow undisturbed for a year or two (no shearing) until the roots become established
- ❦ From the second year on, a hedge should be trimmed lightly each year to encourage dense growth, as it grows slowly to its desired height
- ❦ If the hedge is small-leaved, shear it whenever it looks ragged from new growth, removing almost all the new growth, leaving only about 0.5 cm (¼ in.); this slow, controlled growth will help avoid bare spots and clusters of cut branches
- ❦ Large-leaved hedges should be sheared one branch at a time with hand shears to avoid cutting leaves in half, which gives a "butchered" look
- ❦ Shape your hedge so it is narrower at the top than at the bottom to permit light to reach all parts of the hedge plants and to avoid bare patches at the bottom of the hedge, where inadequate light causes leaves to drop; if low bare patches do develop, cut the hedge back severely to stimulate new growth at the bottom, and then shape the hedge properly as it grows
- ❦ Tall, floppy hedges have been allowed to grow too fast, but regular pruning will slow the growth rate and encourage a sturdy structure; if a hedge is weak, cut it back to the ground and allow it to grow again, this time at a slower rate
- ❦ A hedge that leans into the neighbour's yard likely means you have been pruning your side of the hedge and the neighbours have not been pruning their's; to solve the problem, reduce the height and width of the hedge and let it grow back with an even structure, remembering to prune both sides
- ❦ Bare spots in a hedge are the result of old age and too-frequent shearing; cut away the dead twigs, branch by branch, and then follow proper shearing techniques, cutting to within about 0.5 cm (¼ in.) of the last cut each time

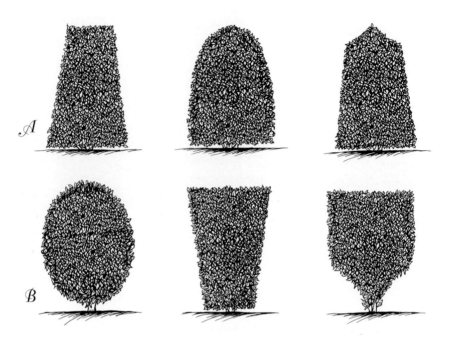

(a) Proper pruning styles for hedges. (b) Improper pruning styles for hedges. GRACE BUZIK

comfortable handling; if the job requires something bigger, call a professional arborist.

Pruning Hedges. The pruning of hedges and other shrubs directs their growth, maintains their health, and can increase their production of flowers and fruit. There are three main techniques for pruning a hedge: thinning, heading-back, and shearing. Choose one of these techniques depending on whether you want an informal or more formal look to your hedge.

Thinning. The pruning technique that results in an informal look is called thinning and consists of removing entire branches back to the main trunk or major branches back to the ground. When thinned, a hedge shrub's energy is used to encourage outward growth of the remaining branches, which results in an open, natural appearance.

Heading-back. To achieve a formal effect, you must either choose hedge plants with a naturally compact and neat growth habit, or you must head back the plants on a regular basis. Heading-back consists of removing only part of a branch, causing multiple branches to grow where there was originally only one. With time, this results in a denser but smaller shrub than one that has been thinned.

Shearing. Shearing is a special form of heading-back that removes the growing points at the ends of branches, using hedge shears or power trimmers, which encourages the dormant growth buds on the sides of branches (lateral buds) to grow, resulting in three or four new growth points where there was previously one. Shearing should be done frequently so that only a small amount of growth is removed each time, with a dense, sculptured plant shape the end result.

Pruning Shrubs to Look Like Small Trees. Many shrubs that have been firmly established in a garden can be selectively pruned to create a pleasing tree shape. To do this, choose a single, vertical stem or small cluster of stems to serve as the trunk of your diminutive tree, and then prune all basal and side growth to the point where you wish the tree canopy to start. At the same time, use proper pruning techniques to encourage strong branching and vigorous, healthy growth above the so-called trunk. As with any pruning job, be sure to remove crossing, weak, diseased, or dead branches and don't eliminate too much live wood in a single season. Rather, view the project as long-term and take several years to complete it; your shrub will be less stressed and will perform much better as the result of your patience.

Shrubs that lend themselves to this pruning technique include lilac, Japanese tree lilac, highbush cranberry, Saskatoon, Nanking cherry, pincherry, double-flowering plum, and Amur maple. The final results work especially well in small-scale gardens, creating the illusion of trees in spaces where it would be impossible to grow the full-sized varieties.

Fertilizing Your Garden

The importance of good plant nutrition in the urban garden cannot be over-stated. Gardeners want to get the most out of limited growing spaces, thus placing a heavy demand on the soil. Many soils can be replenished by the straightforward and continuous addition of organic material (compost or leaf mould) to flower beds and vegetable plots, or by the application of sup-plemental fertilizers, either organic or inorganic. But because gardeners' desires to push the limits also frequently lead them to choose plants whose nutritional needs aren't met by Calgary's alkaline soil, it is often necessary to use supplemental fertilizer and treatments to amend the soil pH. Applying the right kind of fertilizer at the right time is a big responsibility for gardeners. Deciding how to apply it also requires careful thought and knowledge about what is available.

Fertilizers can be "complete" or "incomplete." All-purpose or complete fertilizers are used for general plant nutrition and maintenance. They con-tain the three primary ingredients required by plants—the macro-elements nitrogen (N), phosphorus (P), and potassium (K)—in a number of dif-ferent formulations; they may also contain a few essential micro and trace

Pruning shrubs such as this buffalo-berry to resemble small trees is a simple task. LIESBETH LEATHERBARROW

elements. Some complete fertilizers are even tailor-made for specific plants such as evergreens or roses.

Incomplete fertilizers provide just one or two nutrients. For example, blood meal is an important source of nitrogen; phosphate rock and bone meal are high in phosphorus; and greensand, granite dust, hay, straw, and fruit tree leaves are all rich in potassium. Incomplete fertilizers can correct identifiable nutrient deficiencies in the soil or be used to promote certain plant characteristics over others, such as strong root growth (phosphorus) or healthy green foliage (nitrogen).

Complete fertilizers are available in granular, solid, or liquid form, or you can make your own at home in the form of compost. Incomplete fertilizers come in a variety of packages, depending on the individual chemical involved.

Compost. A complete fertilizer contains the three major elements required by plants—nitrogen, phosphorus, and potassium. Since almost all organic materials used to make compost contain nitrogen, phosphorus, and potassium (and other essential nutrients too), you could say that, by definition, compost is a complete fertilizer. Not as well defined, however, are the ratios and concentrations in which these elements occur. The exact proportion of major nutrients in a batch of compost depends on the original compositions of the raw, organic ingredients used to make it. Also, the greater the variety of organic materials tossed upon the compost heap, the greater the likelihood that all the minor elements necessary for healthy plant growth will be present in the finished product.

Generally, the N-P-K percentages of finished compost are low, but because these elements are released slowly enough for plants to use them efficiently and completely, they are usually present in amounts suitable for gardening use. You may choose to supplement your compost pile with organic materials known to be high in a particular element to alter the ratios of elements. For example, manure or blood meal added to a compost mix are

---

∼ Signs of Nutrient Deficiencies ∼

Nutrient deficiencies can cause a number of problems for plants. Here are some of the common signs that indicate potential problems. Many deficiencies can be corrected by the addition of an appropriate synthetic fertilizer. Natural remedies are indicated in parentheses; use with caution as some may be damaging in large quantities.

Boron: small leaves; heart rot; corkiness (granite dust, borax)

Calcium: foliage abnormally dark green; terminal buds and root tips die; buds and blossoms drop prematurely; stems become thick and woody; leaves develop holes (calcitic limestone, bone meal, wood ashes)

Copper: stunted growth; multiple budding; poor pigmentation in leaves; wilting and die-off at leaf tips; deficiency most often occurs in peaty or mucky soils, so is not generally a problem in Calgary (agricultural frit)

Iron: new leaves turn yellow between veins; veins stay green; older leaves remain green; plants may die if deficiency is severe; common in lime-rich soil such as Calgary's where alkalinity prevents uptake of iron by plants (manure, chelated iron)

Magnesium: late to mature; older/lower leaves turn yellow, then brown, while veins remain green; leaves curl up along edges (dolomitic limestone)

Manganese: mottled chlorosis (yellowing) of leaves from veins outward, veins stay green; stunted growth (manure, compost)

Nitrogen: leaves turn yellow, beginning with oldest; stems become slender and fibrous; growth slow and stunted; new leaves smaller and smaller (blood meal, fish meal, or foliar feed of manure tea)

Phosphorus: leaves turn dull green or grey and are set close together on shorter stems; stems and/or leaves have reddish, purplish tinge; light bloom (bone meal, fish meal, colloidal phosphate, wood ashes)

Potassium: reduced vigour; oldest leaves turn yellow and burn at edges, crinkle or curl, and later become bronzed; shoots die back late in season; plants become lax and susceptible to diseases (greensand, granite dust, wood ashes)

Sulphur: looks like nitrogen deficiency; young leaves turn yellow; plants remain small and spindly and mature late (compost, powdered sulphur)

Zinc: small, yellow leaves that may be deformed or mottled; low yields on fruit trees; deficiency occurs in peaty soils, so not generally a problem in Calgary (manure)

∾ Manure or Compost Tea ∾

Manure or compost tea is made by soaking well-rotted manure or compost in water—just like tea! Place four shovelsful (round-mouth shovel) of manure or compost in a burlap or cheesecloth bag. Tie the "tea bag" at the top and suspend it in a large container of water, such as a large plastic garbage pail, ensuring that the bag is submerged. Locate the container where it will catch the heat of the sun. Cover the container securely and allow the manure or compost to steep for several days. The longer the tea steeps, the stronger it is. Well-rotted sheep manure is the best for manure tea because it is particularly high in nutrients, but steer, cow, horse, pig, and goat manure are also suitable. Use manure or compost tea full strength as a liquid fertilizer or dilute to half strength and use it as a foliar spray to give plants a gentle boost of nutrients every time they are watered.

excellent sources of nitrogen; however, you only need to boost levels of a particular element in your compost pile if there are indications of specific nutrient deficiencies in your plants. Otherwise, finished compost, no matter what its exact composition, will do wonders for the soil in your garden and everything growing in it.

Granular Fertilizers. When you purchase commercial fertilizers, granular fertilizers are the least expensive option per unit weight of nutrients. The nutrients in granular fertilizers become available to plants when the small particles dissolve in rain or water from garden sprinklers. The particles dissolve faster in moist, warm soil than in dry, cool soil. Both quick-release and slow-release (also called controlled-release) varieties are available, and they can be applied in a number of different ways.

Quick-release Fertilizers. Quick-release fertilizers make their nutrients available to plants almost immediately; however, they are depleted rapidly, often requiring replenishment during the course of a growing season. How much replenishment they require varies, depending on the season, climate, and soil. Plants treated with quick-release fertilizers can only absorb 50 percent or less of the available nutrients. Gardeners using quick-release fertilizers must be diligent and apply them only at recommended rates; an overdose of nutrients, especially nitrogen, can cause serious fertilizer burn to a plant.

Slow-release Fertilizers. The granules of slow-release fertilizers are coated with a substance that permits them to deliver nutrients at a slow, measured rate. They require infrequent application and are less likely to burn plants than quick-release fertilizers. The nutrients are delivered so slowly that plants are able to absorb up to 90 percent of them, which means slow-release fertilizers are much less likely to contaminate surface water and groundwater than quick-release ones. Slow-release fertilizers are more expensive than their quick-release counterparts, but they are well worth the extra cost. Some contain sulphur, which helps to reduce the alkalinity of Calgary soil.

Top Dressing. When you plant annuals, perennials, bulbs, shrubs, or trees, you can add fertilizer to individual planting holes or work it into the soil surface around the plants. When top dressing with an inorganic fertilizer, take care to leave a gap, filled in with soil, between the fertilizer and the plant roots; this prevents damage through fertilizer burn to the delicate roots.

Broadcast Spreading. Broadcasting is a good technique for fertilizing large areas, including lawns, vegetable plots, and flower beds. Broadcast fertilizer by hand or with a mechanical spreader. Hand-broadcasting requires some practice to accomplish an even distribution of fertilizer. Place the required amount of fertilizer in a bucket and then, wearing leather or rubber gloves, toss the fertilizer in even bands as you walk slowly forward, using a sweeping, underhand motion. Make sure you overlap each previous pass by a third. Each pass made with a mechanical spreader should also overlap the previous one by a third. Mechanical spreaders have the advantage of producing a consistent, even layer of fertilizer over the ground. If you are fertilizing in an established flower bed, make sure that no granules come to rest on plant foliage as they can cause serious burns. Rake broadcasted fertilizer into the top few centimetres (inches) of soil and then water thoroughly.

Side Dressing. Side dressing is an effective way to deliver supplemental nutrients to plants part way through the growing season, especially to heavy feeders. To do this, apply dry fertilizer in a ring around established plants just outside the root zone (defined by the drip line in larger plants, trees, and shrubs), or in a band next to a row of plants in a flower bed or in the vegetable garden. If you can, work this into the top few centimetres (inch or two) of soil and then water thoroughly. Side dressing encourages root development and precludes the possibility of fertilizer burn because the fertilizer is applied outside the root zone, not directly above it.

Solid Fertilizers. Solid fertilizers come as pellets, tablets, or spikes. Although usually more expensive than granular fertilizers, they are also usually of the slow-release variety, which offsets their cost somewhat. Easy to use, they are preferred by some for this reason. Simply place them beneath the soil surface, either by hammering spikes into the ground with a sharp whack to the top to help initiate the weathering process or by dropping pellets or tablets into pre-drilled holes and covering them with soil. Underground, these compressed fertilizers slowly dissolve, releasing nutrients for a year or more. They are particularly useful for delivering nutrients to container plantings and individual plants, especially trees. Pelletized fertilizers buried at the drip lines of trees deliver phosphorus and potassium directly to the region of active root growth.

Liquid Fertilizers. Liquid fertilizers are sold as concentrates or powders that must be mixed with water. Liquid fertilizers can be applied directly to the soil around the root zones of plants as supplements to dry fertilizers; they will provide short-term nutrients to needy plants, correct nutrient deficiencies, and give transplanted seedlings, trees, and shrubs a good start. They can also be applied to leaves as a foliar spray to provide a quick fix for a specific nutrient deficiency or to bypass the root system when it is too stressed to do its job properly. The main advantage of liquid feeding is the immediate uptake of nutrients by plants. The disadvantages are that liquid fertilizers are more expensive than granular fertilizers, they are not as effective in the long term, and they are rapidly leached into the subsoil.

Applying Liquid Fertilizer. Use a watering can, hose, soaker hose, or drip irrigation system attached to a siphon mixer for applying liquid fertilizer directly to the soil surface, making sure the soil has been wetted thoroughly beforehand to avoid burning delicate roots. A siphon mixer is a hose attachment that allows you to discharge water and fertilizer from the system in the correct proportion. It consists of a threaded brass pipe that fits between the faucet and the hose, and a small black suction or siphon hose. Mix the fertilizer in a bucket of water at high concentration. For example, if the mixer delivers at a rate of 16 parts water to 1 part fertilizer, prepare the fertilizer at 16 times the recommended concentration. Check to see if there is any residue in your fertilizer solution. If there is, you will have to strain it out to prevent your system from becoming clogged. When this is done, drop the siphon hose into the bucket and turn on the faucet. As the water flows through the siphon unit, it draws fertilizer up from the pail and mixes with it, before it goes to the hose end, sprinkler, soaker hose, or drip irrigation line. Caution: Do not drink from a hose or bucket that has been used to apply any type of chemical.

To apply a foliar feed, use a watering can with a perforated sprinkler head (called a rose), a hand sprayer or mister, a hose or overhead sprinkling system fitted with a syphon mixer at the top end, or a hose fitted with a combined reservoir/sprayer for dispensing chemicals at the nozzle end. Any sprayer or mister adjusted to the finest spray setting will work. Never use a sprayer that has been used to apply herbicides; it is virtually impossible to remove all herbicide residue from a spraying system, and even a small amount can seriously damage plants.

Choose a moderately warm, cloudy day for spraying, when there is no rain in the forecast, and remember, liquid fertilizers are absorbed most quickly in the early morning or evening. To avoid burning leaves, make sure

⌘ Guidelines for Applying Fertilizers ⌘

🌹 If you are feeding your soil regularly with compost and keeping it covered with organic mulch, chances are most of your plants won't need supplemental feeding; always think about which plants really need a nutrient boost before applying it.

🌹 Perennials, trees, shrubs, and vines that are growing well will probably continue to do so without any additional nourishment.

🌹 Perennials that have been in place for many years may benefit from a small nutrient boost to replenish the nutrients they have removed from the soil.

🌹 Established trees usually receive enough nutrients from fertilizers applied for other purposes. However, should they need their own fertilizer boost, remember that most of the nutrients and water received by a tree are absorbed in the top 60 cm (24 in.) of the soil. Apply tree fertilizers from a point midway between the trunk and the drip line to a point 60 cm (24 in.) beyond the drip line. You can broadcast a granular fertilizer and water it in; make a series of narrow holes, about 30 cm (12 in.) deep, at 60-cm (24-in.) intervals, fill them with granular fertilizer, and cover them with soil; attach a root feeder containing a fertilizer tablet to a hose and water for five minutes at 1-m (3-ft) spacing to a depth of 45 cm (18 in.); or use fertilizer spikes at the spacing recommended on the package, remembering to give them a firm tap with a hammer to initiate the weathering process.

🌹 Most vegetables are heavy feeders and rapid growers; since the faster plants grow, the more fertilizer they need, vegetables should be given a steady supply of nutrients during the growing season. Salad greens, in particular, require large amounts of nitrogen to promote abundant leaf growth. Tomatoes are heavy feeders that benefit from the application of a high-phosphorus (high middle number) fertilizer.

🌹 Culinary herbs require less fertilizer than vegetables, as nutrient deprivation stresses the plants somewhat and forces them to grow more slowly, which concentrates their essential oils in their leaves and enhances their taste.

🌹 Plants grown in containers rely on frequent feeding to replace nutrients rapidly depleted from the limited amount of soil available. They can be nourished with granular, liquid, or pelletized fertilizers. To prevent root or leaf burn, always dampen the soil before adding fertilizer.

🌹 Regardless of the type of fertilizer or the technique used to apply it, always make sure you are fertilizing at the manufacturer's recommended rate (or even less), which is clearly indicated on the label; exceeding it can lead to severe fertilizer burn. In fact, many people prefer to fertilize routinely at half the recommended rate but twice as often, just to play it safe. Also, if you think "a little bit is good so more is better," when it comes to fertilizing, think again. Plants rarely take up more nutrients than they need and what they don't use stays behind in the soil. The more soluble of these leftover nutrients are potential sources of contamination to local water and groundwater supplies. So, only fertilize when needed, read the labels carefully, and always follow the recommended rates of application.

they are wet before applying the spray; alternatively, apply a more diluted solution. Spray all leaf surfaces until liquid is dripping from the plants. If you wish, use a mild surfactant such as dish detergent 1 mL per 4.5 L (¼ tsp. per 1 gal.) of spray for better leaf coverage; however, be careful, as too much soap can damage the leaves.

Coping with Weather Damage

Every corner of this country has its claim to weather fame and its share of "Do you remember when?" stories. Calgary is no exception. For gardeners in Calgary, a late spring frost or deep freeze, a violent summer hailstorm, or an out-of-season heavy, wet snowfall provides substance for countless conversations and much friendly one-upmanship about ruined flower beds and other evidence of cruel destruction. Weather events have immediate consequences in the garden, handily destroying in a moment what it has sometimes taken years to put together. There is nothing you can do to prevent these catastrophes, but there are ways you can help your garden survive nature's onslaughts.

You will be surprised how resilient trees, shrubs, and perennials can be; gardens that appear to have been totally devastated routinely re-emerge the following growing season almost as good as new. That's not to say that the disappointment of losing a portion of the growing season to weather vagaries isn't justified—the upset of even a portion of a garden's brilliant summer display can leave you with an empty feeling, a sense of missed opportunity and wasted effort. In most cases, however, "waiting until next year" works. What nature takes away with one hand, she usually gives back with the other. All gardeners need is the patience to wait for that to happen.

Hail. Hailstorms are common occurrences during Calgary summers. Small hailstones generally don't cause much damage in a garden, but large ones definitely make their mark. They can strip trees of their leaves, reduce perennials to leafless, flowerless stems, and wipe out annuals completely, leaving a shredded mess of blossoms and foliage carpeting the ground. The first step after a major hailstorm is to sweep the garden floor clean of the detritus and add this to the compost pile, where it will become next year's garden feast. Then, survey the damage.

If any foliage remains on your trees, shrubs, and perennials, leave it there even though it looks tatty and unkempt. Every leaf that continues with its job of photosynthesis, no matter how rough and ragged, will contribute to the plant's future well-being. You might, however, want to remove any surviving seed heads on perennials or fruit on small fruit-bearing trees or shrubs so that no further energy goes into their production and maintenance. A sprinkling of high-phosphorus fertilizer (high middle number) around the base of damaged plants also helps stimulate root growth, an important ingredient for survival.

If the damage to annuals is severe, they will not likely recuperate before the end of the growing season, so remove what remains of them and add them to the compost heap. If the damage is light to moderate, trim them back for tidiness and give them a boost of fertilizer. If they do not revive within a reasonable amount of time, consign them to the compost heap.

Wind. Severe winds come racing across the prairies from time to time to create mayhem for the prairie gardener. Staking herbaceous plants is your best guard against wind damage, but if this task was overlooked, don't despair. Plants that have been savaged by the wind can be cut back to points below stem injuries. This improves their appearance and stimulates new growth, especially if damage occurs early in the season. Although affected plants might not look their best for the remainder of the summer, they will definitely reappear next year, none the worse for wear.

Soft-wooded trees such as poplar, willow, and Siberian elm are the most susceptible to storm winds, with branches often splitting or breaking completely. If a branch breaks cleanly, inspect the area where the break has occurred to determine whether you can tidy it up yourself. Jagged splits, especially in the central trunk area, are best looked at by a dependable arborist, who can recommend whether the tree is worth saving and, if it is, how to do it. An arborist can also assist in the removal of a severely damaged tree that is beyond repair.

Young trees not yet firmly established in the ground are sometimes knocked over and uprooted by strong winds. Replant these at the first available opportunity, water them, and then stake them for a year until they are well anchored.

Thunderstorms. Prairie thunderstorms are often accompanied by torrential downpours that can cause sheet flooding over flower beds and lawns, washing away valuable topsoil or causing more drastic erosion when channels are formed to accommodate the increased water flow. Loss of soil is particularly injurious to shallow-rooted plants. After a heavy rain, inspect your flower beds and replant uprooted annuals and perennials. A shot of high-phosphorus fertilizer (high middle number) helps re-establish roots. Cut back any damaged stems to a point below the injury. The pressure of water from downspouts can cause serious washouts in flower beds; direct them so this doesn't happen.

Heavy Snowfall. Unseasonable heavy, wet snowfalls are an occasional fact of life in Calgary. Whether snow falls in late spring or late summer, annual and perennial plants will definitely be flattened and may be physically damaged; however, the cold temperatures of the snow will not, in most cases, have any lasting adverse effect. Wait for several days after a heavy snowfall has melted to determine how much individual plants will rebound and then cut any injured stems.

Trees and shrubs that have leafed out suffer particularly under the weight of a heavy snow. Shake their branches gently several times during the course of an unexpected snowfall (even if this means getting up during the night!) to relieve them of their burden. If branches do snap under the weight of the snow, check to see what you can do with pruning shears to tidy the break, or call in a dependable arborist for advice.

Frost. Late spring frosts will wipe out any frost-susceptible annuals that have already been planted in the garden and left unprotected. Annuals whose leaves have turned black cannot be saved; the only thing to do is dig them up and replace them. Perennials, however, can tolerate frost, especially if they have been mulched to minimize temperature fluctuations in the soil. True, any leaves already above ground when frost strikes may be damaged or killed, but as long as the roots are healthy, new foliage will continue to emerge; at worst, bloom time may be somewhat delayed.

In Calgary, spring-flowering bulbs planted in beds with a southern exposure surface when the risk of frost is still high. Left unprotected, their foliage will be affected by killer frosts, and in some cases the buds will freeze. Even if bulbs fail to bloom, let the foliage ripen so the bulbs can replenish their nutrient stores to support next season's growth.

New growth on trees and shrubs is sometimes completely destroyed by late frosts, which may also kill blossoms on fruit trees before bees have had a chance to pollinate them. Luckily, most healthy plants can produce new growing points from the base of damaged tissue, which, in turn, initiate a complete regeneration of foliage, although the fruit crop will have to wait for another year.

Chinooks. The extreme temperature fluctuations associated with Chinooks during Calgary winters wreak havoc in the garden, especially among woody plants. The flower buds of flowering shrubs and trees can be damaged when the temperatures plunge after a thaw cycle. They may either drop before blooming or bloom but not set fruit. Flower buds are less hardy than leaf buds, so this can happen even though

This tree trunk has been damaged by sunscald, a common cause of winter tree damage in Calgary.
KATHERINE PEDERSON

the shrub or tree otherwise seems to be in good health. Again, there is no recourse for the gardener in this situation, but if you can at least understand what has happened to your tree, it is easier to be optimistic and look forward to next year's harvest.

Frost Heaving. Wide temperature fluctuations during the winter can lead to extreme frost heaving, especially in newly planted perennial beds. Plants that have been

Snow mould grows in the relatively warm layer between the ground and snow cover. KATHERINE PEDERSON

heaved from the ground during the winter will require some protection for exposed roots and should be kept frozen until you can work the ground in the spring and replant them.

Sunscald. The freeze-and-thaw cycles generated by Chinooks and by sunny days with below-freezing temperatures are responsible for sunscald (also called south-west injury) and bark-splitting on thin- and smooth-barked trees. The bark on the south-west side of the tree first heats up and then freezes when the temperature drops. Thin bark subjected to this cycle eventually dries out and dies, causing a large open wound on the south-west side of the tree. Repeated injuries cause a progressive weakening of the trunk, which may eventually break. Such weakening also makes the tree more susceptible to pests and disease. You cannot undo the effects of sunscald; however, you can keep an eye out for diseases, and treat them appropriately, and be vigilant and take note when an affected tree is too weak to stand up to prairie winds and snows any longer. When a tree has reached this point, it is best to have it taken down before it causes serious injury to an unsuspecting passer-by. White latex paint or tree wrap applied to the trunk of the tree has been found to help reflect sunlight and moderate temperature extremes.

Severe Winters. *Winterburn.* Winterburn is the result of desiccation brought on by a combination of low temperatures and high wind. Conifers are particularly susceptible to winterburn and exhibit the classic symptoms of brown or red foliage, especially in the Chinook belt, where unseasonably high temperatures, strong winds, and frozen ground trigger the effect. Evergreen winterburn can also be caused by the reflection of sunlight from the snow pack; all foliage above the snowline turns brown. Just because a conifer turns brown from winterburn doesn't mean it is dead, although it very well may be. Often, injured trees put out a flush of new growth in the spring and show little further evidence of injury. For this reason, you should give injured trees enough time in the spring to show proof of recovery before deciding that a branch is dead and requires pruning.

Snow Mould. A deep snow pack, usually an indication of a severe winter for the Calgary area, coupled with a slow rate of melting in the spring, can lead to an unsightly infection of snow mould on lawns, organic mulches, and old perennials. Snow mould grows in the relatively warm layer between the organic material and the snow, but is usually kept in check by Chinooks, which periodically melt the snow. Snow mould is partial to Calgary's alkaline soil and water and is encouraged by the use of high-nitrogen fertilizers, which keep lawns green too late in the season. Rake or sweep snow mould from lawns as soon as it is exposed. When you have finished, bleach the broom or rake to kill the mould spores.

Salt. Severe winters lead to an increased use of salt on the main city thoroughfares. The salt melts the snow and ice on the streets, and passing cars cause a fine, salty spray to be deposited on your lawn, at the base of trees, and on the foliage of conifers.

Salt accumulations on lawns cause them to burn and sometimes die. If you notice brown patches on the street side of your lawn in the spring, water the affected area generously and repeatedly to wash away the accumulated salts. Affected trees will show a browning on the side of the plant that faces the road. New growth in the spring will be normal, but stunted growth and possible death will result if salt is allowed to accumulate in the soil. You can't do much about the salt on foliage other than hose it down, but you can try to leach it from the soil by deep and lengthy irrigation.

You can minimize salt damage in your garden by using de-icing products that do not contain salt. Try granular high-nitrogen fertilizers on your paths; in cool winter weather, these should not burn adjacent lawns or plants unless used excessively. The old-fashioned, non-clumping variety of kitty litter scattered over walkways provides grit and traction, without actually melting the ice. Although kitty litter is not harmful to plants, it can have a high clay content, so don't sweep large quantities of it into your flower beds. Granite grit also provides good traction.

Making the Winter Rounds

Gardeners often don't think of making the rounds in winter. Instead, during the long, bleak months of January and February, the horticultural activities of most Calgarians are restricted to indoor gardening, watering house plants, and sitting in a cosy armchair surrounded with favourite catalogues and gardening books, while visions of that perfectly planned perennial border dance in their head. The summer past is but a dim memory and spring seems an eternity away. However, even in winter there are outdoor tasks to attend to, despite the fact that temperatures have plummeted and plants have disappeared under an insulating blanket of snow.

Snow. Snow is one of the best mulches a gardener could wish for to protect plants, shrubs, and vines from harsh winter weather. In the prairies, however, gardeners cannot always count on continuous winter snow cover because in some places arctic winds make large tracts of land virtually snow free for days on end. Elsewhere, the warming effects of Chinook winds can melt a substantial snow cover in just a matter of days, leaving bare, unprotected ground and plants behind. Keeping this in mind, Calgary gardeners must make good use of what snow does fall through harvesting.

In Chinook country, the snow shovelled from walkways, sidewalks, and driveways can be mounded onto flower beds for extended protection during warm spells. Cover, especially, newly planted beds or those located next to house foundations where soil dries out quickly. Also, pay particular attention to keeping evergreen plants such as dianthus and saxifrage heaped with snow throughout the winter. If left exposed, they are susceptible to winterburn and the effects of drying winds. Evergreen shrubs are also good candidates for snow harvesting; branches above the snowline are susceptible to winterkill.

In windy areas, including Chinook country, the wise use of snow fences helps to create snowdrifts where winter protection is desired. Remember that snow accumulates in the lee of barriers (the side sheltered from the wind) and place your snow fences accordingly. If you don't have fencing at your disposal, create a barrier with materials at hand. For example, a good snowdrift will be deposited behind a barricade made of plastic garbage bags filled with leaves collected during autumn clean-up.

Gardeners often worry that heavy snow will snap tree or shrub branches or cause them to bend out of shape. Though this may be the case with heavy, wet snowfalls (which in Calgary most often occur during the late spring when trees have leafed out and so catch more snow), it is not necessarily so with the heavy, dry snowfalls that are characteristic of our winters. In fact, in most cases of mid-winter snowfall, you should leave well enough alone. Subzero temperatures cause tree and shrub branches to be very brittle, and with every attempt you make to free branches of their burden, no matter how gentle, you run the risk of breaking branches yourself. Most winter-hardy woody ornamentals are adapted to carrying the weight of snow on their branches and will rebound, slowly but surely, during the warm days of spring. People who enjoy outdoor lights during the festive season should remember the brittle nature of branches in winter when decorating their trees. It is best to do this task in late fall when the branches are not yet frozen.

Chinooks. Although it is not very pleasant to walk around the garden on a cold winter's day, you should definitely make the effort during a prolonged Chinook. Check for the effects of frost heaving and, if you find any exposed plants, protect them by making sure their roots are kept covered and frozen until you can replant them in the spring. Also monitor the moisture content of beds that tend to dry out quickly. They will be particularly susceptible to drying during windy, warm spells when temperatures are high enough to cause the melting of ice crystals in the soil and in plant roots. If this is the case, water any trees and shrubs that might be affected so they will survive the winter without suffering any more desiccation than necessary. At the same time, care must be taken not to water areas where bulbs or perennials are planted. The combination of water and the elevated temperature associated with a prolonged Chinook might cause them to break dormancy, which can have disastrous consequences once winter returns in full force, as it likely will.

Evaluating the Bare Bones. A winter walk through the garden is an opportunity to examine the bones or the skeleton of your landscape. The placement of trees and shrubs, the shapes of flower beds, and the relationships between soft and hard landscape features can all be easily assessed when perennials are dormant and deciduous trees have shed their leaves. Take advantage of a light covering of snow to try out various shapes for planned beds and modifications to existing ones. Use footsteps in the snow to mark boundaries, which can be erased and redrawn at will, simply by smoothing out the snow and starting over again.

Winter walks also give you the opportunity to assess the pruning needs of trees and shrubs, a relatively simple task when they aren't covered in leaves. When you notice a branch that needs to be pruned, mark it by tightly tying a string or piece of wool around it. If you take the time to identify a few branches for pruning every time you make a quick tour of the garden during the winter, then the actual task will be an easy one. Late winter is also a good time for pruning the marked branches, while trees and shrubs are still dormant.

Renovating Established Gardens

Fortunately for those who love gardening, a garden is never finished and never perfect. Change and renewal are essential to the maturing garden and the maturing gardener. The process of renovation allows you to refine and enhance your existing garden without giving up what you prize the most. Of course, it is possible to renovate one area of your garden at a time, but remember that the domino effect applies to moving trees, shrubs, and perennials, and you will make better use of your existing plants if you reorganize your entire garden at once.

When to Renovate. *Aging.* Most gardens need some renovation as they age. Whereas trees, many shrubs, and some perennials (such as peonies) improve with maturity, increased competition caused by overcrowding may eventually result in some plants failing to thrive. Aging shrubs may need to be pruned to remove a tangle of old wood. Perennial beds, especially, benefit from periodic rejuvenation. This does not mean simply relocating or dividing a few overgrown specimens; you will need to haul most of the perennials out of your flower beds in order to properly dig and recondition the soil before replanting.

Changing Lifestyles. The decision to renovate a garden or to reconsider your garden design can be based on many factors, such as changing family situations or lifestyles. Now that the kids are in high school, why not replace the play structure in that sunny corner of the garden with an apple tree, a bed of hardy shrub roses, or a pond? Do you still need a large expanse of lawn? Do you have more time than before for gardening or less? If more, you can afford to indulge yourself with plants that need a bit of coddling; if less, consider a low-maintenance xeriscape garden, complete with automated watering system. Does your garden need wider paths or raised flower beds to accommodate an older gardener or one with a disability?

New Opportunities. Experience and observation not only teach gardeners to be realistic about what will thrive in Calgary, but also lead to formerly undreamed-of possibilities. Every year brings hardy trees, shrubs, and perennials new to the Calgary gardening market. Although old favourites should not be cast off lightly, it may be time to replace those boring shrubs that just take up space. Find areas in your garden that have not been fully utilized before; convert narrow strips of grass between houses to beds for shrubs or perennials; add spring bulbs under deciduous trees and shrubs; or use more vines to enliven vertical spaces.

Correcting Past Errors. In addition to relieving boredom, garden renovations can correct landscaping errors that become more and more apparent as the years go by. The most common mistake made by beginning gardeners is planting too much, too close together, too near the house. In the urge to create an instant garden, the mature height, spread, and growth habits of trees and shrubs are often overlooked, resulting in eventual overcrowding and inadequate sunlight for many plants that may have thrived in the beginning. Calgary gardens abound with 15-m (50-ft) high poplars and 10-m (30-ft) high spruce trees planted far too close to house foundations, and hedges that encroach over half the width of sidewalks.

Other mistakes, though less monumental, can be just as annoying. Are you still digging around shrubs and perennials trying to remove the goutweed or horseradish you naively planted seven years ago? It may be time to admit that the double-flowering plum will never bloom as long as it lies in the path of drying Chinook and bitter arctic winter winds. Many gardeners live to rue a hastily planted perennial in a completely unsuitable location just because it was the only patch of unoccupied earth available; the intention, of course, was always to move the plant when there was time to create more space. Inheriting someone else's garden mistakes gives you all the more reason to approach garden renovation with gusto and a sense of inspiration and enthusiasm to create something of your own.

How to Renovate. When you redesign your garden, there will likely be plantings and features you wish to retain; after all, not all your past gardening decisions will have been mistakes! There is the comforting sense of pride and permanence you experience when you cut armsful of fragrant blooms from the lilac that was only a twig when you planted it the first year you started gardening. You may be quite happy to work around the mature trees and trade sun-loving perennials for the benefits of the many lovely shade-loving plants that are now more suited to your garden. Decide what you still enjoy about your garden and plan your changes to enhance these desirable aspects.

Trees and Shrubs. Evaluate your existing trees and shrubs to decide which to keep to form the framework of your garden. Most prairie gardeners do not remove trees without considerable soul-searching, but some-

---

∽ Poplar Removal ∾

As the City of Calgary began to sprawl several decades ago, fast-growing 'Northwest' poplars were the trees of choice for new suburbs. Many of these trees are now being removed because of their size, invasive and competitive root system, suckering tendencies, messy flowering habits, and susceptibility to damage in severe weather conditions—a not unusual occurrence in Calgary. If you wish to have a large poplar removed, follow these steps.

- Get estimates for removing the tree and stump and for the clean-up from two or three reputable tree-removal companies
- The best time to remove the tree without a subsequent forest of suckers is just after it has leafed out; the tree's energy stores will be at their lowest point
- Grind or dig out the stump right after the tree is cut down
- If any suckers do appear, mow them down or cut them off as soon as possible; using systemic herbicides is risky as the suckers will be growing from roots that may have grafted to the roots of other poplars, and any chemicals you apply may damage neighbouring trees

times a tree that dominates the yard must be sacrificed for the greater good of the garden. The increased sunlight and reduction in competition from overbearing neighbours will invigorate the remaining trees and shrubs and open up new planting areas. Moving large trees is not recommended, but if you want to try, consult a dependable professional arborist.

If you have space, you may wish to transplant small trees or shrubs to more appropriate areas of the garden. Instead of dotting them here and there, create groupings to show off flowering shrubs to best advantage, as well as to coordinate foliage textures and colour. Plan groupings for year-round interest, such as a combination of double-flowering plum, lilac, mock orange, hardy shrub roses, winged euonymus, and Siberian coral and yellow-twigged dogwoods, together with your favourite dwarf evergreens. Establish a pruning routine to help maintain the natural shape, appearance, and size of shrubs.

Hedges. Old or overgrown hedges may be revitalized by pruning. Thin hedge shrubs by clearing away all weak branches and those that either point inwards or cross other branches; this allows light to reach the hedge interior. Some follow-up thinning may be required in subsequent years to achieve a desirable hedge shape. Revitalization may also be carried out by cutting the hedge back to the ground, an action tolerated by most hedge plants, but not all. If you are not sure how a particular hedge will respond, make a test cut on one branch, heading it back to a leafless stub—if the stub sprouts new growth, it is probably safe to cut the whole hedge back to the ground.

Renewal pruning is a special type of pruning that keeps deciduous hedge shrubs looking young and vital, no matter how old they are. During the first few years, hedge shrubs are pruned to consist of one-third first-year growth, one-third second-year growth, and one-third third-year growth. In subsequent years, only the third-year growth is pruned out, which encourages new shoots to grow and become the new first-year growth. Hedges pruned in this fashion generally produce larger blossoms (should they flower) and are healthier because young, vigorous growth is less susceptible to insects and disease than older growth.

Perennial Beds. Once the "big stuff" has been taken care of, turn your attention to renovating perennial beds. First, look at the size and shape of flower beds; adding half a metre (a foot or so) to the width and giving a bed a gentle curve can make a big improvement. Using a garden hose to lay out the perimeter of the bed allows you to experiment with different lines before you rip up the lawn.

Next, evaluate your perennial collection. Are some insect or disease prone, plants that against your better judgement drive you to chemical warfare? Have some never lived up to your expectations, merely surviving from year to year? Are you harbouring some thugs, plants with a tendency

When planting trees, keep in mind their mature size; at their full potential, some will over-whelm the average city property. LIESBETH LEATHERBARROW

to take over? Don't feel guilty about giving up on them and keeping only those plants that are proven winners. This is also a good time to add a few new perennials you may have admired in the gardens of friends or neigh-bours (checking first to see if they too are renovating and have spare divisions). Draw a plan indicating where each perennial should be planted, taking into consideration desired colour schemes, plant size, blooming time, foliage, and light and moisture requirements.

When your design is ready, it is time to dig up all the perennials in the bed. Although perennial bed renovation may be undertaken in spring when plants are small, many gardeners prefer to do it in late summer. By then many perennials have finished blooming, but there is still time for them to become re-established before the ground freezes. An additional advantage is that many planting faults are still obvious or fresh in the gardener's mind at this time of year, and it is certainly easier to judge the eventual relative height and spread of herbaceous perennials than when they are newly emerged in the spring.

Before digging, lay out a tarp upon which you can set the uprooted perennials, preferably in a shaded area nearby. Using a pointed shovel, dig into the ground approximately 15–20 cm (6–8 in.) from the outer foliage of large perennials, proportionately closer for small plants, and work your shovel down until you can feel the roots loosening from the soil. Try to keep as much of the root mass intact as possible. Place the plants on the tarp with their labels, or make labels for those without one, and keep the roots cool and moist. Once all the plants are removed, you will finally be able to dig out the grass rhizomes or other deep-rooted perennial weeds you have been pursuing unsuccessfully for years. Make sure you do a thorough job of removing all roots; if you don't, the weeds will be back in short order.

After removing all weeds, dig the soil to as great a depth as possible without mixing in the heavy subsoil, which in Calgary is usually a grey-brown clay, noticeably lighter in colour than the topsoil. You should have about 30 cm (12 in.) of topsoil; if not, add extra loam to bring it up to this level. Once you have done this, add a 10-cm (4-in.) layer of organic material, such as compost, well-rotted manure, or peat moss, and incorporate it into the topsoil. The addition of organic matter improves the air and moisture movement in the soil and allows for better root penetration.

Any perennials that are too large or have become woody at the centre should be divided before replanting. As you are doing this, check the roots for any stray grass rhizomes or weeds. Do not feel obligated to provide a home for every single division—give away or compost those that don't fit your plans. Self-discipline exercised at this stage will save you renovating an overcrowded garden again a year later. Replant perennials at the same depth they were previously growing, and water thoroughly with a trans-plant fertilizer solution, such as 10–52–10, which is high in phosphorus for the plant's roots.

Lawns. Most gardeners find that their lawn area decreases with each renovation as perennial borders creep towards the centre of the garden or alternative groundcovers are planted. However, as long as you have grass, don't forget that lawns, like flower beds, benefit from periodic renovation. Lawns may need to be completely replaced if they were originally planted with unsuitable grass or have problems such as dew worms, poor drainage, or poor soil. Some Calgary gardeners who have felled poplar trees find it necessary to strip off their lawns to dig up the trees' large surface roots, which may produce suckers or create bumps in the lawn.

If the lawn is in poor condition because of compaction, weeds, thatch, inadequate soil nutrients, or incorrect pH, you will likely be able to rejuvenate it without taking such drastic steps. A soil test is useful to determine if there is any nutrient deficiency or if the soil is too alkaline and requires the addition of sulphur. If weeds are widespread and persistent, it may be necessary to use a herbicide to get them under control, after which time it is best to control them through proper maintenance practices. It is important to identify the weeds so that the correct herbicide is applied.

Sow grass seed in bare areas and spots where weeds have died. Apply a top dressing of equal parts of compost, soil, and sand to small hollows and uneven areas; however, don't apply more than 1 cm (⅜ in.) at a time or you will smother the lawn. As the grass grows, you can add more top dressing to gradually level the lawn. If you have large dead spots, such as those caused by dog urine, you may prefer to strip out the old sod and patch it with new sod laid level with the rest of the lawn.

❧ Lawn Dethatching and Aeration ❧

Dethatching. Part of rejuvenating an old or neglected lawn is addressing the problems caused by thatch build-up and compaction. Thatch is the layer of grass stems, roots, clippings, and other debris that builds up between the grass blades and the soil. A thin layer of thatch insulates grass roots from temperature extremes; too much can prevent water, air, and fertilizer from reaching the soil.

To determine if your lawn has too much thatch, cut out a small section of grass and examine the depth of the thatch layer; if it is greater than 2 cm (¾ in.), you should remove some of it. Hand raking will not be effective if there is a thick layer of thatch, and you will have to resort to mechanical means. Vertical cutters have a series of revolving vertical blades that slice through the thatch, bringing it to the surface of the lawn. You should then rake it up, remove it, and compost it if it has not been treated with a herbicide. The blades of vertical cutters may be set to penetrate beneath the thatch, slitting and pushing up small amounts of soil. This can open up the soil somewhat to air and water and stimulate root growth as rhizomes are severed from parent plants.

To help prevent excess thatch from accumulating, apply a thin layer of compost, or compost mixed with topsoil; the addition of soil microorganisms will help decompose dead material. Chemical pesticides kill beneficial soil life and should be avoided. Also, avoid using too much high-nitrogen fertilizer, which promotes excessive top growth; do not cut the lawn too short; and water deeply to encourage healthy root systems.

Aeration. Calgary clay soils become compacted easily when walked on, particularly when they are wet. Grass does not grow well in heavily compacted soil, such as in heavy traffic areas of your lawn. This problem may be alleviated by aeration, which opens up the soil to air, water, and fertilizer through the removal of soil cores. If your lawn is small, it is easy to do this yourself with a manual core aerator; if you need to aerate a large area, you may wish to rent a machine or hire someone to do the job for you. For maximum benefit, aerate in the spring when the soil is moist, but not wet. It is not necessary to remove the cores from the surface of the lawn; they will break down and return useful microorganisms to the soil. Soil conditions, lawn use, and maintenance practices vary from garden to garden, but in general a healthy lawn with no heavy traffic areas will not require annual aerating; once every few years should be sufficient.

Collecting Seeds

Saving seeds is a time-honoured tradition, one that keeps many a gardener occupied during the quiet days of mid-summer and beyond. There is often a lull in gardeners' activities during the growing season when plants are settled and growing happily, and weeds and pests are under control. Other than routine maintenance, there are no major tasks that beckon, at least for a while. What better time to indulge in seed collecting, a satisfying activity that boasts many advantages.

Clearly, you can save money by collecting your own seeds instead of buying them. By making intuitive choices about the plants from which to collect seeds (the biggest, the tastiest, the strongest), you initiate a selection process that results in developing plants particularly suited to the growing conditions in your garden and to your own tastes. If the seeds you are collecting come from heirloom varieties of flowers and vegetables, you will also be helping to preserve genetic diversity in plants, an extremely important contribution to the world of horticulture. You can share saved seeds from favourite or hard-to-find plants with fellow gardeners, who will appreciate your generosity. By the same token, you can ask friends or neighbours for seeds from unique or out-of-the-ordinary plants that reside in their gardens. Never collect seeds from a garden, public or private, without first asking permission.

∾ Collecting Seeds from F1 Hybrids ∾

F1 hybrid is the name given to the first generation of plants that result from crossing two distinct parents. F1 hybrids often produce sterile seeds; if viable seeds are produced, the offspring often bear little or no resemblance to the parent plants. If you don't mind taking chances, by all means experiment with collecting and growing seeds from F1 hybrids, but be prepared for possible disappointment.

Planting for Seed Production. If your aim is to collect and grow true-to-type seeds from ornamental and vegetable plant varieties, you must situate parent plants carefully and take some control over pollination.

Self-pollinating plants such as sweet peas, tomatoes, and beans are the easiest to grow for saving true-to-type seed, that is to say, seed that produces offspring with characteristics identical to those of the parent plants. The flowers of self-pollinating plants each have male and female reproductive parts, with pollen from the male organ fertilizing the same or other flowers on the plant. This results in seeds that grow true-to-type.

Vegetables and ornamental plants such as bachelor's buttons, flax, marigolds, squash, cucumbers, and corn have separate male and female flowers and rely on cross-pollination by wind and insects for reproduction. They may or may not produce seed that grows true-to-type, depending on the source of the pollen. If the fertilizing pollen comes from an identical plant variety, then the seeds produced will grow plants with characteristics identical to those of the parents. If the fertilizing pollen comes from a distinct-but-related plant variety, the produced seeds will not grow true-to-type, but will result in offspring that show variations from the parent plants. Even for plants that self-pollinate, cross-pollination occurs up to 5 percent of the time as a result of visits by bumble bees and other flying insects that have collected pollen from either identical or distinct-but-related plant varieties. If you wish to have plants produce seeds that grow true-to-type, you need to prevent random cross-pollination.

You can reduce the risk of cross-pollination in self-pollinating plants in a number of ways. You can separate the plants by distance and by bloom time. By planting distinct-but-related varieties a minimum prescribed distance apart, you can ensure that pollen from one variety of a particular plant does not reach a neighbouring related variety to result in cross-pollination. The minimum distance varies with plant type and should be researched in a quality seed-collecting manual. Cross-pollination can also be prevented by growing distinct-but-related varieties that reach sexual maturity at different times, or by staggering the planting of related varieties with similar maturation rates to ensure they do not flower at the same time.

Another way to avoid cross-pollination in self-pollinating plants is to prevent pollinating insects from visiting the flowers. To do this, cover the seed-bearing flowers with cheesecloth cages or a piece of pantyhose just before blooming occurs, and remove the covers only after seed production has started. Because these plants are self-pollinating, there is no need to hand-pollinate; pollination will occur without human intervention.

To avoid cross-pollination in plants that usually rely on it, collect pollen by hand (using a paint brush) from several male flowers to fertilize female flowers, usually recognized by their swollen bases. Pollen in male flowers matures just after the flowers open; collect pollen at this time and store it in a paper envelope in a cool, dry place until the female reproductive organ (stigma) becomes receptive, usually a few hours to a few days later, depending on the plant. Then isolate the pollinated flower from wind and flying insects by carefully tying a bag around it. Ideally, use a bag that is water resistant but not plastic; it may have to be replaced occasionally if the weather is wet. It is also wise to label the cross, especially if you are pollinating only one or two flowers.

If the prospect of hand-pollinating plants, especially vegetables grown in large quantities, seems overwhelming, try this tidy technique. Cover the group of plants to be pollinated with a floating row cover, well before blooming has started, and trap some insects underneath, before sealing the ends. The trapped insects will pollinate the isolated plants with their own pollen, resulting in seeds that will grow true-to-type. Pollen-bearing insects that have visited neighbours' vegetable crops and might cross-pollinate your plants will have no opportunity to do so.

ᖇ Saving Seeds from Biennial and Perennial Vegetables ᖇ

Saving seeds from biennial vegetables, which include beets, Brussels sprouts, cabbage, carrot, cauliflower, celery, onion, parsley, parsnips, rutabaga, Swiss chard, and turnips, can be tricky. In climates with severe winters such as Calgary's, these crops die if left in the ground to overwinter until their second growing season, which is when they naturally produce seed. To get them to set seed, you must dig them up in the fall, store them inside during the winter, and replant them in the spring so they can flower the second year. Make sure they first have undergone a chilling period of at least 30–60 days, with temperatures no higher than 5–10° C (40–50° F).

Perennial vegetables such as asparagus, potatoes, and rhubarb are usually propagated from cuttings or root divisions to obtain identical plants. Their seed produces plants with unpredictable and varying characteristics.

Selecting Seed to Save. For maximum benefit from a seed-saving program, select the best parent plants possible. Superior parent plants are the most likely to produce seeds that will grow into a new generation of offspring with desirable characteristics. Experts recommend collecting seed from at least two plants of each variety to maintain a broad genetic base in your garden, even if you only need a small number of seeds. The exceptions are self-pollinated plants whose seeds produce little variation in offspring (beans, peas, sweet peas, and snapdragons).

Don't wait until late summer to identify potential parent plants. Start making observations early in the season, taking note of plants with the characteristics you most wish to perpetuate. There are many qualities to look for when choosing plants for saving seeds; the ones you choose will depend on your own tastes and preferences. Desirable traits in both vegetable and ornamental plants include vigour, colour, size, disease and insect resistance, stature, weather and drought tolerance, and fragrance of foliage and blossoms.

Additional traits worth looking for in vegetables include flavour, yield, size, storage life, whether they are early-bearing or late-bolting, texture, tenderness, juiciness, and suitability for purpose. Once you have identified the best parent plants, label them clearly so they are not picked or harvested before the seeds have had a chance to mature or before you have had a chance to collect them.

Collecting Seed. The timing for collecting seeds is critical and varies with individual species. A seed consists of an embryo plant, food to nourish the embryo, and a dry, sometimes hard seed coat. Most seeds require a period of dormancy before germination can take place to prevent the plant from germinating and starting to grow late in the season when its chances of survival are definitely compromised by the arrival of winter. The food supply in the seed must, therefore, be completely developed at the time of picking to ensure the survival of the embryo during dormancy. If seeds are picked too early, there is a chance that the embryo will be immature and that the stored nourishment will not be sufficient to cover its needs during dormancy. This can result in no germination, uneven germination, or inferior seedling quality. If seeds are picked too late, bad weather can adversely affect their quality.

So how do you know when a seed is ready to be picked? Regular inspections of the garden reveal changes in seed pods as they take place. Seeds are usually ready to be picked when the pods are thoroughly dry and break under pressure. In many species, the seed-containing capsules lose their colour, turn brown, shrivel, and dry out as they ripen. The seeds themselves also dry and change colour. The seed capsules of some plants, however, stay green, even as they ripen. Still other seed capsules shatter and disperse their seeds the instant they are ripe, posing a challenge to the seed collector. Try tying a small paper bag punctured with air holes or a piece of pantyhose loosely around the ripening seed head to collect these seeds. It is also useful to remember that seeds of this type of plant (brassicas, lettuce, and onions, for example) ripen one stalk at a time, so if you miss one dispersal, there will still be several others on the same plant.

Collect seeds on a dry, sunny day, making sure they are free of moisture from rain or dew. It does not matter if the seeds have been exposed to frost as long as they are dry when they are collected. If winter comes early, as it sometimes does in Calgary, and the seeds have not finished ripening, cut stems from the plants and place them in water inside to allow the ripening process to finish before collecting the seeds.

If you wish to collect seeds from fruiting vegetables such as cucumbers, tomatoes, or green peppers, you must leave them on the plant until they are slightly overripe: cucumbers will be yellow, tomatoes a deep red and very soft, and peppers will be wrinkly. Make sure that all the pulp is washed

~ Plants to Collect Seed from ~

The following are examples of common vegetable and ornamental plants that lend themselves to seed collecting. Self-pollinated plants are identified with an S, cross-pollinated with a C.

Vegetables

Beans (*Phaseolus* spp.) - when pods are brown, about 6 weeks after reaching full size **S**
Broccoli (*Brassica oleracea*) - when seeds are brown and dry **C**
Corn (*Zea mays* var. *rugosa*) - one month after other ears have been picked for eating, before hard freezes **C**
Cucumber (*Cucumis sativus*) - in fall at time of first frost **C**
Lettuce (*Latuca sativa*) - 12 days after flowering **C**
Peas (*Pisum sativum*) - when pods are brown and dry, and seeds inside rattle **S**
Pepper (*Capiscum annuum*) - when peppers have turned colour and begin to shrivel **S**
Radish (*Raphanus sativus*) - when pods turn brown **C**
Spinach (*Spinacia oleracea*) - when plants turn yellow **C**
Squash (*Cucurbita* spp.) - in fall at time of first frost **C**
Tomato (*Lycopersicon esculentum*) - when fruit is ripe or slightly overripe **S**

Ornamentals

Bachelor's button (*Centaurea cyanus*) - when flowering is done, before seed capsules shatter **C**
Chrysanthemum (*Chrysanthemum* spp.) - when flower heads are dry, before shattering **C**
Flax (*Linum perenne*) - when capsules are dry, before they split open **C**
Nicotiana (*Nicotiana* spp.) - when capsules are dry, before they shatter **C**
Foxglove (*Digitalis purpurea*) - when lower fruit capsules start opening and dropping seeds **C**
Honesty (*Lunaria annua*) - when pods are dry, before they split open **C**
Love-in-a-mist (*Nigella damascena*) - when inflated capsules are dry **C**
Marigold (*Tagetes* spp.) - when flower heads are dry **C**
Nasturtium (*Tropaeolum majus*) - when three-celled fruit has dried **C**
Pansy (*Viola* x *wittrockiana*) - when seed capsules are dry **C**
Sunflower (*Helianthus annuus*) - when seeds are dry, before they drop **C**
Sweet alyssum (*Lobularia maritima*) - when seed capsules turn brown and while they are damp (to avoid seed loss from shattering) **C**
Sweet pea (*Lathyrus odoratus*) - when pods are dry **S**

from these seeds before they are stored; otherwise, they will not be able to "breathe" during dormancy and will die. Don't collect seeds from rotting fruit as the process of decomposition causes the temperature in the fruit to rise, which can damage the seeds.

Once mature, these poppy seed pods will provide an ample quantity of seed for collecting, as will many other annuals and perennials.
MAUREEN IRETON

Preparing Seeds for Storage. Once collected, the seeds need to be cleaned, dried, and stored. Winnowing and screening are two useful techniques for getting rid of unwanted leaves, stems, pods, and insects. To winnow, pour the seeds from one container to another, blowing out the chaff with your breath or a small fan. This method also eliminates the lighter seeds, which usually have a thin seed coat and embryonic deficiencies. To screen, use a piece of screen or a sieve to separate out the coarser, heavier materials from the seeds. The same seeds can be cleaned by placing them in water. The chaff will float to the top; the healthy seeds will sink to the bottom. Tomato seeds benefit from a short period of fermentation to help control the bacterial canker to which they are susceptible. To do this, place tomato seeds and pulp in approximately 55 mL (2 oz) of water and wait until the pulp and worthless seeds float to the top; the healthy seeds will sink to the bottom. Some gardeners ferment cucumber and melon seeds in the same way.

Storing Seed. Cleaned seeds should be dried thoroughly before being stored, as excess moisture lowers the quality of stored seeds, which results in a lower germination rate. To dry seeds, lay them out on newspaper or paper towels in a well-ventilated place for approximately one week, turning them frequently; the bigger the seeds, the longer the drying time required. You can also use gentle heat to dry seeds; just don't let the temperature exceed 32° C (90° F). Seeds that are dried at too high a temperature rapidly lose their vigour and viability (their ability to germinate). Also remember that if seeds are dried too rapidly, they will shrink and crack and then form hard, undesirable seed coats. Some gardeners use silica gel to dry seeds by placing equal amounts of seed and silica gel in a sealed container. Dried seeds should not be left to sit around in the open air as they will reabsorb moisture from the atmosphere. Instead, store them immediately in well-labelled, airtight containers such as plastic film canisters, glass jars, or sealed glassine envelopes (the type used by stamp collectors).

When storing seeds during the winter months, it is essential to keep their metabolic rate as low as possible without letting them die. The viability of seeds can be drastically reduced by poor storage conditions. To ensure successful storage, several potential influences must be controlled: moisture, heat, and pests and diseases.

Store seeds in a dry place. Moisture in a pile of seeds causes warming and an increase in the seeds' metabolic rate, which causes the seeds to use up their food source too quickly.

Store seeds in a cool place. Heat causes early internal activity in the seeds, which uses up the food supply. The ideal storage temperature range for seeds is from 0–5° C (32–40° F). They may also be stored in the freezer to -18° C (0° F), but if you are going to do this, the seeds must be very dry.

Monitor seeds for signs of infection or pests. Seed-borne bacterial and fungal infections are usually not a problem for the home gardener whose diversified plantings don't allow a build-up of serious diseases. Cool, dry storage places help prevent the spread of infections and also help inhibit insect activity.

After storing your seeds for a winter, it is worth testing them to determine their viability or how well they germinate. This will help you decide whether your saved seeds are worth planting in the garden, and, if they are, at what spacing they should be sown to ensure success. To do a germination check, select 10 or 20 seeds of the lot to be planted and spread them on a damp paper towel. Label the paper towel with a pencil, roll it up, moisten it thoroughly, and place it in a sealed plastic bag. Store the bag in a warm place at about 21° C (70° F), and make sure the towel stays damp. You can store several sets of seeds in paper towels in the same bag. When the seeds have sprouted, count the number of sprouted seeds and calculate them as a percentage of the total number of seeds tested. The lower the percentage of germination, the more densely they should be seeded.

SEVEN

The Well-organized Gardener

Calgary gardeners are well advised to make the most of the fleeting growing season by approaching their gardens in an organized fashion. This is best accomplished through various methods of documentation, which will remind you both of successes to be repeated and failures to be avoided. It is worth taking a bit of extra time to ensure plants are accurately labelled and observations recorded in a journal or photographic record. After all, there are many more planning days than growing days in the Calgary gardening season.

Labelling Plants

Accurate plant labelling is an essential part of garden record-keeping. Calgary winters are long and those botanic names that tripped off your tongue last August are almost guaranteed to be swept from memory with the winter Chinooks. Even if plant names are recorded in your journal, it's easy to forget who's who in a closely planted perennial garden, especially before distinguishing blooms appear. As the gardener's appetite for new and uncommon plants increases, so does the necessity for labelling. After all, when your admiring neighbour raves over the deep purple-blue stems and flower spikes of a certain plant, it is not very helpful to respond, "Oh, it's some kind of salvia." A handy marker will quickly identify the blue beauty as *Salvia farinacea* 'Victoria', which must be grown as an annual in Calgary, rather than the perennial *Salvia officinalis*, the common culinary sage.

Markers inserted in the ground beside the resting places of late-emerging herbaceous perennials, such as hostas, will save them from being disturbed

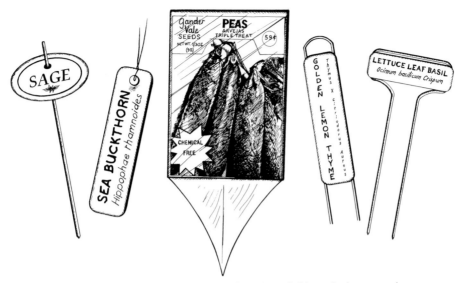

A variety of plant markers suitable for labelling plants is available to the home gardener.
GRACE BUZIK

by the spade of an overeager gardener. It is particularly useful to record the location and varieties of spring-flowering bulbs that will die back to anonymity by mid-summer. When fall arrives, you will be better able to add new bulbs according to height or colour (and avoid digging up the old ones) if you can remember what is already there. Markers gathered up in the fall from containers of annuals or vegetable gardens are insurance against forgetting the names of the best-performing cultivars of annual flowers or the tastiest early-ripening tomatoes.

There are many types of markers and labels, from small, inexpensive plastic or wood stakes, or tie-on metal tags to costly, decorated ceramic or brass name-plates for herbs and flowers. Most gardeners collect an assortment to serve different purposes.

Plastic or Wood Markers. Both plastic and wood markers, which may be written on with an indelible marking pen or a pencil, quickly deteriorate outdoors. Temperature extremes and bright sunlight cause plastic to become brittle, and wood rots in the ground. However, these markers are cheap and useful for identifying trays of seedlings grown indoors. You can also use them for new plants in the garden during their first season; if the plants survive, you may wish to invest in more sturdy markers. Wooden plant markers may be purchased from horticultural suppliers or you can use popsicle sticks available from craft stores. Make sure they are clean and new to avoid adding pathogens to the soil.

Metal Markers. Metal plant markers on wire stakes are more durable and attractive than markers made from plastic or wood. The name-plates of these markers, often made of rust-proof zinc, are angled to make them easier to read. Write on these with a soft pencil or a grease pencil; pencilled names are easily erased should you wish to reuse the marker. Metal markers with impressible aluminum name-plates may be permanently engraved with a ball-point pen. Use slim, hairpin-shaped metal markers if you desire something less conspicuous.

Clear Plastic Holders for Seed Packets. Another recent innovation is a clear plastic holder into which an empty seed packet may be inserted. It is attached to a plastic stake and is probably best suited for vegetable gardens, where you may be growing several different hybrids of a particular vegetable.

Ornate Ceramic or Brass Markers. Ornate ceramic or brass markers are attractive when used sparingly in a herb, vegetable, or flower garden. Since these markers are usually manufactured with only the common name already engraved or embossed on them, they are more ornamental than informative. The keen gardener will likely wish to add an additional, less obvious marker to record important information such as the particular cultivar or hybrid. Avoid ceramic markers mounted on wooden stakes, which will rot and break within a year or two.

Tie-on Labels. Tie-on labels should be used for woody plants, such as trees or shrubs, or may be tied around the bases of plants such as begonias, dahlias, tomatoes, or peppers. Loop plastic labels around branches; metal labels often come with wires for this purpose and should be attached loosely to prevent girdling. Plastic will deteriorate first and the lettering is

---

❧ Botanical Nomenclature ❧

Unlike common plant names, which vary from place to place, botanical names are international and consistent wherever gardeners gather. Botanical nomenclature is based on a series of classifications. A genus is a grouping of closely related species; a species is a specific plant within a genus; and a variety is a further subclassification, indicating a small but significant difference, such as colour. Cultivated varieties, or cultivars, are developed from cuttings or divisions of superior varieties. Hybrids are crosses between species of the same genus, and less commonly between genera, and are indicated with an x, for example, *Salvia* x *superba*.

The plant commonly known as variegated bulbous oat grass has the following botanical nomenclature:

Arrhenatherum	the genus name
Arrhenatherum elatius	the species name
Arrhenatherum elatius bulbosum	the variety name
Arrhenatherum elatius bulbosum 'Variegatum'	the cultivar name

subject to fading; the impressed lettering on copper and aluminum labels is permanent.

Home-made Labels. Enterprising gardeners can create their own labels and markers out of materials readily at hand. If you need a large quantity of markers for seedlings, cut white plastic margarine or dairy product containers into strips and write on them with an indelible marker. These may be washed for reuse if you are growing the same plant varieties in subsequent years. More durable home-made markers for outdoors may be constructed out of sturdy rust-proof wire threaded through holes punched in name-plates cut from scrap aluminum siding. Surveyor's tape cut into lengths makes inexpensive, although rather conspicuous labels, but if they are tied around the plants at soil level, the tape can be camouflaged with a layer of mulch. Less eye-catching labels may be cut out of aluminum pie plates to whatever size you wish. Write on these with a ball-point pen to leave a permanent impression and punch a hole through which you can thread wire or strips of cut-up pantyhose to attach the label to the plant.

Information for Plant Labels. The information you include on your plant labels will depend on the available space, but at the very least, you should note the complete botanic name: genus, species, and any applicable cultivar name. It is often useful to record the bloom colour, the source of the plant, and the date seeded or planted in your garden; this may be recorded in your journal if you run out of room on the marker or label.

Keeping Records

For most gardeners the pastime of gardening revolves around the practical aspects of designing, planting, and maintaining the flower borders and grounds that surround their homes. They usually achieve these goals with a healthy dose of hard work, complete with the filthy fingernails, grass-stained knees, and grime-streaked faces that characterize a gardener. Gardeners are also thinkers, constantly faced with making choices of what plants to buy, where to plant them, how to care for them, and how to make them look better next year. But gardeners as writers of journals? Who has the time and why bother?

Why Keep a Journal? Keeping a journal, no matter how simple or detailed, is actually a very important part of the creative process in gardening, one that is often overlooked by both beginner and accomplished gardeners. Although much gardening knowledge can be gained from friends, guest lecturers, and books, gardeners learn best from personal experiences unique to a particular set of growing conditions and microclimates, and the amount of effort put into their gardens. By recording observations and ideas, you develop a record that helps you remember what you have already done, decide what you would like to do in the future, and predict the likelihood of success, based on previous experience. Another advantage of journal writing is that it gives you a good excuse for taking a break from gardening to "write up the notes."

The Form of the Journal. A garden journal can take many forms: a simple notebook purchased at the corner store; a collection of file cards; a calendar; a computer spreadsheet or database; a photograph album; a series of videotapes or an elaborate annotated garden diary designed specifically for this purpose. How you organize your thoughts and observations in your diary is completely up to you. There is no right or wrong way to keep a journal, and you don't even need to be consistent. In fact, you might start out using a convenient portable notebook for recording facts and observations as they occur to you while working in the garden, and then decide to transfer them to a computer spreadsheet or database at a later time. Or, perhaps a combination of file cards and videotape commentary works best for you. One thing is certain: whatever method you use to keep records, as your gardening experience increases, so too will your desire and need to keep a journal. The more you learn about plants and designing your garden, the more detailed your journal will become and the more you will rely on it.

What to Record in Your Journal. There are many different types of information that you can record in your journal; start out with the scientific facts as they pertain to your garden.

Plant descriptions are an obvious choice. These include botanic and common names and cultivars where applicable, location in the garden, colour, height, spread, bloom time, and a few notes on how the plant fared during the growing season. Don't hesitate to record both successes and failures. All gardeners learn and benefit from their mistakes.

Plot the bloom times on a graph at the end of the growing season to help determine gaps in bloom succession in your flower beds. Then, make notes on how you might fill these gaps the following spring, what needs to be moved where and why, and what additions you foresee making to your plant collection. Planting information is also important. Plant and seed sources, germination and planting dates, and soil amendments are easy to record and will serve as reminders of how to proceed with the same or similar plants in the future.

Don't forget to make a few notes on your maintenance regime, including fertilizing and watering schedules, and weed and pest control efforts. Finally, jot down a few descriptive words about the weather every time you make a journal entry. When you are reviewing how a plant performed in the past, it is useful to know, for example, that the reason plants were late to bloom in a particular year was because of a late frost, or damaging hail, or some other vagary of the prairie climate.

You can also use journals to keep track of other practical details: maps of individual flower beds and what grows in them; photographs taken in your garden; catalogue orders and the expected delivery dates; guarantees and their expiry dates for trees, shrubs, and certain perennials; and landscaping expenses.

If you still feel like writing when all the scientific and practical details have been duly noted, then indulge yourself. Go on at length about perceptions,

---

～ A Personal Approach to Record-keeping ～

Each method of keeping records has its advantages and disadvantages.

🌹 **Notebooks.** Notebooks are a cheap way to record scientific information and can be set up any way you desire. You can keep them with you at all times, whether you are at work in your own garden or admiring someone else's, to jot down notes and ideas instantly, before you forget or start thinking about something else. There is always room to add photographs, pictures cut from catalogues, or articles snipped from the newspaper to supplement your own notes. However, regrouping your collected data into categories for analysis can be tricky; it must be done by hand, which can be a time-consuming task.

🌹 **File Cards.** The same information placed on file cards can be sorted much more quickly into categories of interest.

🌹 **Databases.** If you are technically oriented and like the statistical approach, a computer spreadsheet or database might be a better way to go; the wonders of modern technology make the tasks of sorting and resorting the collected data easy.

🌹 **Photographs.** Photographs taken at regular intervals throughout the growing season are an excellent way to record the evolution of a garden. Whether they are glued into a journal notebook or mounted in a photo album, their value as a planning tool increases significantly when they are accompanied by written notes.

🌹 **Videotapes.** If you are not fond of writing or don't think you will be able to find the time to take notes, then consider using a video camera to film your garden as you make your weekly rounds. Think out loud into the camera microphone as you examine and video your handiwork; identify new plants by name, remark on a pleasing plant arrangement, express your disappointment at something that did not work out as planned, or propose a solution to a particular problem you have identified, all the while filming what you are describing. This method of record-keeping has the advantage of not requiring extra time for its implementation; you will be making regular rounds anyway, and talking into a camcorder is an easy way to collect information.

feelings, flights of fancy, and whatever else is going on in your life at the time. If you come across an appropriate quote, a bit of historical background, some interesting research, or a neat cartoon—include it! Are you artistically inclined? Draw sketches of your landscape, favourite plant associations, or a special plant. If you have a flower press, dry and press a beloved flower and glue it into your journal. Make your diary as personal and as intimate as you want. After all, it is yours and nobody has to see it but you!

Here are a few final words of advice to help you get into the habit of keeping a garden journal. Keep all of your entries as brief as possible and date them. If you have realistic expectations for your journal, then you are more likely to follow through with the project. Also try to make your journal a habit. This doesn't mean you have to spend an hour at it every day, but do try to set aside some small period of time every week for updates. If you do this regularly, writing in your journal likely will become second nature to you. Finally, don't put your journal away after you have made an entry. Instead, keep it close at hand for easy reference, or to jot down new ideas before you forget them.

Photographing Your Garden

Who among us hasn't been drawn to the exquisite full-colour photographs that illuminate gardening books the world over. Whether they convey sweeping landscapes in all their glory, captivating combinations of foliage and blossoms, or enchanting details of individual plant portraits, photographs inspire all who work the soil. Gardens, dynamic as they are, change and evolve on a continuous basis. What looks wonderful one week

Set against the magnificent backdrop of the Rockies, this prairie garden has an impressive vista. RENATA WICHMANN

will look entirely different the next, and different again the next. It makes sense for avid gardeners to devote some time to capturing their horticultural accomplishments on film, to record highlights, progress, and memories.

Photographs are useful not only for chronicling the evolution of your garden, but also for analyzing what you have accomplished so far and determining where there is still room for improvement. In other words, they are useful planning tools. Though images of your garden are strong in your mind during the growing season when you are immersed in its design, development, and maintenance, the details are bound to fade as autumn and winter set in. You will be amazed what a good visual prompt, such as a series of photographs, will do to refresh your memory. Keeping an accurate log of your photographs, especially those taken on trips or as technical experiments, will ensure that no vital information is forgotten. Garden photography is a truly enjoyable pastime, and satisfactory results can be achieved with a bit of knowledge about basic garden photography techniques.

Choice of Camera. Most amateur photographers use one of two types of 35-mm cameras available today: the convenient, compact, fully automatic, and decision-free "point-and-click" variety; or the more complex, single lens reflex (SLR) camera with through-the-lens light metering, variable shutter speeds, and interchangeable lenses. Both types give good results; however, SLR cameras offer users more detailed control with a wider range of options. Some of the newer compact cameras have a manual override, which means that as a photographer you can exert partial control over some variables, but not as much as with an SLR camera.

An Assortment of Lenses. Different lenses accomplish different tasks, and the owner of an SLR camera can take advantage of this to achieve different effects. All SLR cameras come with a standard lens that is useful for shooting garden scenery and groups of plants as close as 50–100 cm (20–40 in.); it has the same angle of view as the human eye, roughly 48 degrees.

Wide-angle. A wide-angle lens has a wider field of view than a standard lens (about 60–180°, depending on the lens). This makes it particularly useful for photographing wide expanses from close range, with the effect of exaggerating the distance between near and far subjects; all parts of the resultant picture are in focus.

This close-up photo captures the delicate beauty of trilliums touched by the morning dew. Maureen Ireton

Telephoto. A telephoto lens has the opposite effect of a wide-angle lens, narrowing your field of vision and bringing subjects closer. With a telephoto lens, you can concentrate on photographing specific subjects; the foreground and background are usually out of focus, which provides a soft framing effect for the principal image.

Macro. A macro lens is ideal for close-ups of plant details in the garden; the actual image recorded on film is at least half life-size. Extension tubes or close-up lenses used in combination with a standard lens achieve results similar to those of a macro lens at a fraction of the cost.

Zoom. A zoom lens is the most versatile of all lenses. By adjusting its position and settings, you can have it do the job of a wide-angle, telephoto, or macro lens as needed, allowing you to focus on a subject and take a range of compositions without having to change your physical position to do so.

Point-and-click cameras come with a much more limited selection of lenses: a single standard lens; a dual-lens system, comprising a standard lens and a telephoto lens; or a single zoom lens, which provides the most versatility for the garden photographer.

Accessories. Telephoto, macro, and zoom lenses are all susceptible to camera shake and are best used in conjunction with a tripod and cable release. Other accessories that can be useful for the amateur photographer include a grey card for taking accurate standardized light readings, a variety of filters to create special effects, an electronic flash and reflector card to supplement natural light under some conditions, and a lens hood to keep out extraneous light. Regardless of what type of equipment you own, film choice, photo composition, exposure, and light conditions will all have a bearing on the outcome of your photographs.

Choice of Film. The choice of whether to take prints or slides depends entirely on what you plan to do with your pictures. Prints are great for photograph albums; slides are better for presentations and reproduction in publications. Also keep in mind that print film is more forgiving of errors in exposure than slide film, so if you are new to the picture-taking game, concentrate on practising techniques using print film until you get the hang of it; then switch to slides.

When it comes to slide film, professional photographers recommend using either Fujichrome, Kodachrome, or Ektachrome; which one you choose will depend in part on your colour needs. Ektachrome and Fujichrome films are excellent at capturing brilliant blues and greens, two colours that figure prominently in landscape photography. In contrast, Kodachrome is better for an accurate rendition of warm reds, yellows, and browns, but its greens are quite muddy, especially in poor light conditions. Differences between colour capabilities for various print films are not so marked since modern processing techniques tend to level the playing field in this regard. If you are interested in learning about the wide variety of specialty films available, visit a quality camera store and ask a knowledgeable staff person to give you the details.

Film Speeds. Films come in a range of light sensitivities, which are recorded in their ISO ratings. Highly sensitive film (also called high-speed film) will have a high ISO number; less sensitive film (also called low-speed film) will have a low ISO number. The lower the light sensitivity of a film, the more accurate the colour reproduction and the sharpness of the image; conversely, the higher the light sensitivity, the more grainy the final result. In general, for normal daytime outdoor light conditions, you want low-speed films ranging from ISO 25 to ISO 100. Yet, high-speed films (ISO 200–3200) definitely have their uses. They work particularly well in poor light conditions without a flash (in the shade or indoors), or when your subject is in rapid motion (plants waving in the breeze, as is often the case in Calgary). You can also use high-speed films if you intentionally want to impart an artistic, grainy quality to your photos. However, a good rule of thumb is to choose the film with the lowest ISO number that is compatible with prevailing conditions.

Controlling Exposure. Manual cameras and automatic cameras with a manual override allow camera owners to exercise control over a photo's exposure, that is, the amount of light allowed to reach the film when a picture is taken. If too much light lands on a film, the picture will be washed out or overexposed; with too little light, a picture will be underexposed. Exposure is determined by two camera settings—shutter speeds and lens apertures, or openings—both of which are a function of the light-meter reading. Shutter speeds are measured in seconds or fractions thereof and control the length of an exposure. Lens apertures, or "f-stops," control the intensity of light that reaches the film by changing the size of the lens opening; they usually range from f2.8 to f22. The smaller the f-stop number,

---

∾ Bracketing ∾

To bracket an exposure, take one picture of the subject at the settings suggested by the light meter, and then take one or two additional pictures with settings above and below that reading. This is especially important for slide films, which are very sensitive to small changes in exposure. To do this, either change the lens aperture or the shutter speed in half- or full-stop increments. Vary the aperture setting if you wish to keep the shutter speed constant, say for freezing motion; vary the shutter speed if maintaining the depth of field is important. By bracketing your exposures in this way, you will always ensure that at least one of your pictures will have been taken with a perfect exposure.

Crimson poppies positively glow when backlit by the morning sun. LIESBETH LEATHERBARROW

the larger the aperture and vice versa. Settings on both shutter-speed and lens-aperture scales are called stops, and every time you choose a higher stop on either scale, you halve the amount of light that reaches the film. Because lens apertures and shutter speeds work in a reciprocal "one stop" relationship, there is a whole range of setting combinations that can be used to achieve correct exposure. For example, an exposure of f8 at $1/30$th of a second is the same as f11 at $1/15$th of a second. Which combination you choose will depend on the effect you are trying to create. Shutter speed compensates for camera and subject movement, while apertures control the depth of field, which is the amount of any picture that is in focus. The smaller the aperture (the higher the f-stop number), the greater the depth of field.

Photo Compositions. Garden photograph compositions can be loosely grouped into three types: vistas that encompass a wide view from a distance; middle-distance images that usually comprise pleasing plant associations and groupings; and close-ups that focus on the intimate details of a single plant. To accurately convey the character and atmosphere of your garden, it is best to take a variety of each type of photo for your collection.

Vistas. Vista shots give an overview of your garden landscape, showing the relationship between plants and other garden features. As such, they provide a context for subsequent photos taken at closer range. Take vistas with a wide-angle lens set to the smallest aperture possible for a sharp image and a focus about one-third of the way into the picture. When possible, identify a focal point in the garden and also use this as a focal point in your photo composition for added interest.

Middle-distance Shots. Think of middle-distance shots of plant associations as group portraits showing flowers in their immediate setting and in relation to neighbouring plants. They are more personal and intimate than photos of vistas, though less dramatic than close-ups. Always avoid placing the subject in the middle of the picture. Instead, keep in mind the Rule of Thirds, which suggests that you mentally divide the picture frame into thirds, both vertically and horizontally, and then place your subject at one of the intersections. Also, try to make the flowers dominant in the frame and downplay the visible background—it should not be distracting. Through the creative use of zoom, telephoto, or macro lenses, you can focus on the subject and at the same time throw the background out of focus, thus minimizing its effect. It is a good idea to shoot from a variety of perspectives to come up with the most interesting image possible. Finally, take a look around the edge of your frame and make sure there are no potential intrusions to detract from the overall picture composition.

Close-ups. Close-ups of plant details are a bit tricky to take but well worth the effort. Not only do close-ups enlarge the subject of the photo dramatically, they also magnify any shortcomings in your photographing technique in an equally dramatic (and disappointing) fashion. When choosing your subject, select the most photogenic specimen, one that is fresh and undamaged, set against a simple background. You will always need a tripod to minimize camera shake for these shots, and the addition of some light from an electronic flash is useful for stopping motion, achieving extreme sharpness, and maximizing the depth of field. Shooting with the smallest aperture possible will also help maximize the depth of field. However, shooting with a small aperture means you are also shooting with a slow shutter speed, so pay particular attention to the effects of breezes if you want sharp pictures.

Making the Most of Natural Light.
To take good garden pictures, photographers must have an understanding of how natural light conditions vary and how to use changing conditions to advantage.

Midday. Although you might guess that the best time for taking garden pictures is midday when the sun is at its most brilliant, this is usually not the case. No film exists that can fully accommodate and accurately record the extreme contrasts generated by such harsh light conditions. Often, pictures taken when the sun is high suffer either from washed-out brights or intensely dark shadows; it is not easy to strike a balance between the two. That is not to say that you can't shoot a great picture at high noon, but you will have to take special measures to achieve satisfaction.

First, choose appropriate subject matter: solid-looking objects such as a building or a tree set against a cloud-studded sky or flowers and foliage with strong colours such as red or orange can be photogenic in intense sunlight. The use of a polarizing filter helps moderate the effects of bright light, reducing haze, distracting glare, and intensifying bright colours. For detailed shots taken at close range in bright light, you would be well advised to use a reflector card, an electronic flash, or a diffusing screen to reduce the contrast between the light and shaded portions of your photo composition.

Early-morning and Late-afternoon Light. Early morning and late afternoon present excellent opportunities for taking photographs; at these times, the angle of the sun is relatively low to the horizon and the light quality is dramatic, warm in colour, and soft in intensity. There is less contrast between highlights and shadows than in midday light, and the shadows that do exist reveal texture, enhancing the three-dimensional quality of your garden. Remember to take advantage of the diffused, relatively uniform light conditions of overcast or misty days to heighten the impact of bright colours and minimize glare, shadows, and hot spots. You can even take dramatic photos during or directly after a light drizzle to capture the charm of delicate, glistening water droplets that sparkle on flowers and foliage. During the long dry spells characteristic of Calgary summers, you can cheat a little to achieve this effect by spritzing a plant with water just before taking its picture.

Directional Lighting. In the same way that time of day and atmospheric conditions create very different light conditions, the direction of the light source can also have a profound impact on the success of a photograph.

Frontal Lighting. Frontal lighting results when the light source is situated behind the camera, illuminating the front of a scene; shadows are cast directly behind the subjects, minimizing the sense of depth and form. This results in a safe, acceptable, but conventional photo with a somewhat two-dimensional feel. When taking this kind of photo, remember to avoid including your own shadow in the image.

Back-lighting. Back-lighting results when the sun shines from behind the subject. Shadows are cast towards the camera, highlighting textures and the third dimension. If the subject is also somewhat translucent, back-lighting creates a halo-like glow that can be breathtakingly beautiful. These shots are not the easiest to take as you are usually faced with a high-contrast situation and must decide whether to concentrate on the lighted or the shadowed parts of the composition. Supplemental light from an electronic flash or a reflector card will reduce the contrast by adding some light to the shaded areas. Also, when photographing into the sun, stray light can cause internal reflections and flare that will blur the final image or produce unwanted spots on the finished photograph. You can eliminate flare by using a lens hood or shadowing the lens with your hand or another part of your body. On some SLR cameras, you can check that you have eliminated all flare by pressing the depth-of-field button for a preview.

Side-lighting. Side-lighting or cross-lighting occurs when the sunlight shines from the right or left side of the camera. It is the best light for emphasizing depth, texture, and a three-dimensional look. As in the case of back-lighting, you have to take into account the high contrast between light and shadow in such compositions when choosing settings for your camera.

Useful Variations. Panoramic Shots. Small disposable cameras that take wide-angle panoramic shots provide colour photographs that can be useful for evaluating garden design or renovation. You can use them to survey your whole landscape at a glance and then analyze its components.

Black-and-white Shots. Colour is by far the most readily apparent design element in a garden, which is why we automatically reach for colour film without even considering the other option—black-and-white. However, for assessing line, shape, form, texture, and pattern in the garden, black-and-white prints are unsurpassed. By eliminating the distraction of colour, the remaining design elements come into sharper focus and are thus much easier to evaluate. Use black-and-white photographs to determine if your garden has pleasing lines, varied shapes and forms, diverse and distinct textures, and repeated patterns of line, shape, and texture to provide unity and continuity.

When you view your garden through this monochromatic filter, potential problem spots become apparent. For example, you might readily notice that plants with similar foliage tend to blend together, that the curve of a bed is not in unison with other lines in the garden, or that a particular plant grouping looks uninspired, with no form or texture to commend it. As part of the process of correcting the balance in problem spots, take potted plants and arrange them in combinations that you think might create greater interest. Photograph each combination in black-and-white and evaluate the results. In this way you will have a good idea of which of your proposed solutions will be the most visually pleasing, before you make the actual effort of executing them.

Afterword

The splendour of Canadian gardens easily rivals the incomparable natural beauty of this country. From the rugged shores of Newfoundland, the emerald green flood plains of the St. Lawrence River, and the fertile valleys of southern Ontario, to the magnificent wide open expanses of prairie and the mystical rain forests of the west coast, the variable and ever-changing landscape has served as a dramatic setting and a source of inspiration for generations of gardeners. Our own Chinook zone has more than its share of resplendent landscapes, both those that have existed since the glaciers scoured the land thousands of years ago and, more recently, those lovingly fashioned and tended by human hands.

That Calgary gardeners have been so successful is a tribute to our perseverance, resilience, and resourcefulness, and to the fact that most of us, sometimes perversely and against the odds, really do love to garden here in our chosen corner of Canada. The reasons for immersing ourselves in the pleasures of gardening in Calgary are as varied and diverse as our backgrounds. Yet as gardeners, we are bound to each other by common threads: the urge to create unique and individual landscapes and the love of a challenge unite us in a strong sense of community, sharing, and satisfaction.

So what makes Calgary such a special place for gardening? The length of the growing season for one thing—although it is short by some people's standards—is just right for most of us. When the threat of frost and snow has all but disappeared from the prairies, gardeners are ready to plunge into the spring ritual of preparing and planting the garden. The pace is fast, furious, and exhilarating for a few hectic weeks, leaving the summer and its long hours of daylight for marvelling at the rapid transformations that take place on a daily basis, refining planting schemes, maintaining the landscape, and enjoying the outcome at a more leisurely pace. Before long, early autumn frosts signal it is time to start thinking about putting the garden to bed, sometimes before we are quite ready to admit that it's over and almost always before we have tired of gardening for the season. This is not a bad thing. Isn't it better to be yearning for a slightly longer gardening season than to regret or resent one that is never-ending?

The long off-season leaves ample time for scheming and dreaming, for reading and researching, all rewarding pastimes in themselves, but even more so when they provide fresh new ideas to apply to the burgeoning garden when spring finally arrives. Winter presents a wonderful opportunity for perusing catalogues and catching up on all those gardening magazines left untouched during the summer. What's more, winter activities can still reflect the pleasures of gardening. Creating unique arrangements with colourful flowers dried the previous summer, building a birdhouse or feeder for feathered friends, or designing trellises for a new-found love of clematis keep images of the gardens alive in our hearts while arctic winds scour the prairies. Most importantly, rest and reflection over the Calgary winter energize us for the meteorological challenges of another season of gardening in the Chinook zone.

Believe it or not, even Calgary weather is not all bad news. The dry climate is a bonus for gardeners; not only does it limit the number of nasty pests waiting to indulge or overindulge on the bounty of our gardens (think of British Columbia's slugs!), but it also affords us an opportunity to develop fairly dense planting schemes without significantly increasing the risk of fungus, rot, or mildew.

The cool temperatures that characterize our northern location and Zone 3A hardiness rating, considered to be a drawback by some, actually have a positive influence on gardening in Calgary. Midsummer burn-out, typical of blooms in hot climates, is rarely a problem here, with most plants maintaining a fresh appearance through-out the summer and well into the fall. Flowers here are brighter and vegetables sweeter than their hotclimate counterparts, thanks to our cool night-time temperatures. And for many, the challenges of overcoming the effects of Chinooks and pushing the limits to include Zone 4 or even Zone 5 plants in the garden are irresistible. Being advised by well-meaning friends, acquaintances,

A feast for the eyes, this exquisite mixed border gently sweeps down to the water's edge. LIESBETH LEATHERBARROW

and even professionals that "that doesn't grow in Calgary" is an invitation to prove that it does, with the joys of unexpected success more than making up for the disappointments of occasional failure. There are surprises in every Calgary growing season, for Chinook-zone gardening is never predictable or boring.

Sharing success stories with fellow gardeners is more important in our erratic climate than in those lush green places where plants actually do what the catalogues and reference books say they'll do. Even small triumphs are significant and worth sharing, for many splendid Calgary gardens are based on an accumulation of such discoveries. Consider how many of your favourite plants were recommendations or donations from friends, and how much of your gardening knowledge consists of gems of wisdom passed on from others. Truly, the most valuable resource available to Calgary gardeners is each other.

William Reader, the most prominent of early Calgary horticulturists, firmly believed in the gardening potential of the Chinook zone. He devoted his entire career to the advancement of horticulture in Calgary, to experimenting with hardy plants from all over the world, and to sharing his extensive knowledge with fellow gardeners. Reader emigrated from England, a land many consider to be gardening heaven, choosing to reside and work in Calgary for the rest of his life. Many of us have made a similar choice and like Reader, who gave us something to strive for, why would we want to garden anywhere else?

Notes

Preface

p. xii\1 "The directors stated as their objectives" Constitution of the Calgary Horticultural Society, 1912.

p. xii\2 "Calgary had developed the reputation of being" *Calgary Daily Herald*, August 27, 1931; September 21, 1935.

p. xii\3 "In 1916, the president reported" Calgary Horticultural Society Prize List: Tenth Annual Exhibition, President's Annual Report, 1917, p. 14.

p. xii\4 "The commemorative spruce was planted" *Calgary Herald*, June 24, 1939.

p. xiii\5 "It was a most appropriate setting for the CHS" CHS Minutes, 1973; *CHS Newsletter*, July 1994, p. 5.

p. xiv\6 "A formal program of workshops" CHS Minutes, 1983.

p. xiv\7 "Although it was issued only intermittently" CHS Minutes, 1983.

p. xiv\8 "Even today the CHS views" CHS Minutes, 1995.

Introduction

p. xx\9 "Around 1914, Reader reported that" Morris Barraclough, "From Prairie to Parks," in *At Your Service, Part I*, Calgary, AB: Century Calgary Publications, 173.

p. xxii\10 "Reader's successor as superintendent" Leslie Sara, "From Sandhill to Mossy Glade," *Gardeners All*, No. 10, C.B.C., C.F.A.C., Calgary, August 11, 1939, Local History Collection, Calgary Public Library, 5.

p. xxii\11 "The home is described as" Ken Liddell, *Calgary Herald*, February 4, 1961.

p. xxiii\12 "Gardeners will find it easy to imagine the sensual pleasures of an early summer stroll" Sara, "From Sandhill to Mossy Glade," 5–6.

p. xxiii\13 "While Alex Munro believed" Liddell, *Calgary Herald*, February 4, 1961.

p. xxiv\14 "He believed plantings should have a natural appearance" William Reader, *The Herbaceous Perennial Garden together with an Annotated Catalogue of Herbaceous Plants Introduced by and Growing in the Garden of W.R. Reader, Parks Superintendent, City of Calgary*, unpublished ms., Glenbow Alberta Institute Library, 2. Another version of this work is in the library at the Brooks Horticultural Research Station. Reader's collection of photographs and lantern slides are housed in the Glenbow Archives.

p. xxiv\15 "Reader also advised that when planting perennials" Reader, *The Herbaceous Perennial Garden*, 3.

p. xxiv\16 "Although Reader planned perennial borders to achieve" Reader, *The Herbaceous Perennial Garden*, 2.

p. xxiv\17 "Reader was eulogized by W. Ingwersen" W. Ingwersen, "An English Tribute to William Reader," *English Gardener's Chronicle*, 1943, reprinted in *Calgary Herald*, May 14, 1943.

p. xxiv\18 "Another tribute from the *Canadian Alpine Journal* noted" "In Memoriam—William Roland Reader, FRHS," *Canadian Alpine Journal*, Vol. XXVII, No. 2 (1942–43), 256.

Chapter One

p. 5\19 "However, with the invention of the lawnmower in 1830" Stevie Daniels, *The Wild Lawn Handbook* (New York, NY: Macmillan, 1995), 4.

p. 5\20 "So influential was he in his promotion of lawns" Allen Lacy, *Gardening with Groundcovers and Vines* (New York, NY: HarperCollins, 1993), 2.

p. 22\21 "The gardens of Princess Augusta at Kew" Ronald King, *The Quest for Paradise* (New York, NY: Mayflower Books, 1979), 195.

p. 22\22 "In the gardens of Count Hoditz in Silesia" King, *Quest for Paradise*, 197.

Chapter Two

p. 36\23 "Pliny the Younger" Ronald King, *The Quest for Paradise* (New York, NY: Mayflower Books, 1979), 35–36.

p. 36\24 "Literary giants Alexander Pope and Joseph Addison" King, *Quest for Paradise*, 174–79.

p. 37\25   "As space was limited" Ogden Tanner, *Living Fences* (Shelburne, VT: Chapters, 1995), 88.

Chapter Three

p. 57\26   "Gardeners should heed the caution" in Deborah Kellaway, ed., *Women Gardeners* (London, Eng.: Virago Press Ltd., 1995), 108.

Chapter Four

p. 88\27   "They also noted the movements of " John Ferguson and Burkhard Mucke, *The Gardener's Year* (New York, NY: Frances Lincoln Ltd., 1991), 6–7.

p. 91\28   "According to Carolyn Jabs" Carolyn Jabs, *The Heirloom Gardener* (San Francisco, CA: Sierra Club Books, 1984), 175.

p. 91\29   "In the case of apple trees" Jabs, *Heirloom Gardener*, 4.

Chapter Six

p. 159\30 "Careful pruning is based" The theories of branch collar function and compartmentalization were pioneered by Dr. Alex Shigo. *See* Alex L. Shigo, *Tree Pruning: A Worldwide Photo Guide* (Durham, NH: Shigo and Trees Associates, 1989).

References

Newspaper Articles

"Hospitality and Beauty at Alberta Home of Prince." *Calgary Herald*, May 15, 1924.

"Ignored by Citizens—Reader Garden Beauty Spot." *The Albertan*, September 21, 1951.

Ingwersen, W. "An English Tribute to William Reader." *English Gardener's Chronicle*, 1943, reprinted in *Calgary Herald*, May 14, 1943.

"Parks Superintendent Retires This Month." *Calgary Herald*, December 11, 1942.

"Reader Rock Garden Inspires Landscapers." *Calgary Herald*, May 13, 1982.

"Rockery Plaque Dedicated." *Calgary Herald*, June 12, 1944.

Sara, Leslie. "Rockery Holds Peace and Charm." *Calgary Daily Herald*, June 9, 1934.

"W.R. Reader Dies While on Way Home." *Calgary Herald*, January 27, 1943.

Books and Articles

Alberta Environmental Centre and Alberta Agriculture. *Weeds of the Prairies*, 1983.

Andrews, Brian. *Northern Balcony Gardening*. Edmonton, AB: Lone Pine Publishing, 1992.

Bales, Suzanne Frutig. *Container Gardening*. New York, NY: Prentice Hall Gardening, 1993.

Barash, Cathy Wilkinson. *Evening Gardens*. Shelburne, VT: Chapters Publishing Ltd., 1993.

Barraclough, Morris. "From Prairie to Parks." *At Your Service, Part I*, Calgary, AB: Century Calgary Publications, 1975.

Beaubaire, Nancy. "A Guide to Fertilizers." *Fine Gardening*, No. 23 (January/February 1992): 34.

The Best of Fine Gardening: Garden Rooms. Newtown, CT: Taunton Press, 1996.

The Best of Fine Gardening: Garden Tools and Equipment. Newtown, CT: Taunton Press, 1995.

Binetti, Marianne. *Shortcuts for Accenting Your Garden.* Pownal, VT: Storey Communications Inc., 1993.

Boisset, Caroline. *Vertical Gardening.* London, Eng.: Mitchell Beazley Publishers, 1988.

Boisset, Caroline, and Greene, Fayal. *The Garden Source Book.* New York, NY: Crown Publishers, Inc., 1993.

Brennan, G. *Fragrant Flowers.* San Francisco, CA: Chronicle Books, 1994.

Brickell, C., ed. *Practical Guide to Gardening in Canada.* Montreal, QC: RD Press, 1993.

Brooklyn Botanic Garden Record. *Garden Photography.* Ephrata, PA: Science Press, 1989.

Burnie, Geoffrey. "Secret Gardens." *Australian Women's Weekly Garden Guides.* Sydney, Australia: ACP Publishing Pty. Ltd., 1994.

Burrell, C. Colston, and McClure, Susan. *Rodale's Successful Organic Gardening: Perennials.* Emmaus, PA: Rodale Press, 1993.

Caduto, Michael, and Bruchac, Joseph. *Native American Gardening.* Golden, CO: Fulcrum Publishing, 1996.

Carney, Nancy. "Buying Bare-root." *Fine Gardening,* No. 42 (March/April 1995): 14.

Carney, Nancy. "How to Shop for Shrubs and Trees." *Fine Gardening,* No. 29 (May/June 1993): 45.

Carr, Anna. *Good Neighbours: Companion Planting for Gardeners.* Emmaus, PA: Rodale Press, 1985.

Carr, Anna, Smith, Miranda, Gilkeson, Linda, Smillie, Joseph, and Wolf, Bill. *Chemical-free Yard and Garden.* Emmaus, PA: Rodale Press, 1991.

Christopher, Thomas. *Water-Wise Gardening: America's Backyard Revolution.* New York, NY: Simon and Schuster, 1994.

Colborn, Nigel. *The Old-Fashioned Gardener.* Vancouver, BC: Raincoast Books, 1993.

Coleman, Eliot. *The New Organic Grower.* Halifax, NS: Nimbus Publishing, 1995.

Cooksley, Rosalie. "You Can Garden on a Budget." *The Calgary Horticultural Society Newsletter,* Vol. 9, No. 3 (1995): 6.

Cox, Jeff. *Creating a Garden for the Senses.* New York, NY: Abbeville Press, 1993.

Cranshaw, Whitney. *Pests of the West.* Golden, CO: Fulcrum Publishing, 1992.

Cullen, Mark. *The Complete Gardener - Furnishings.* Mississauga, ON: Ballantine Books, 1996.

Curless, Chris. "Renovating a Perennial Bed." *Fine Gardening*, No. 37 (May/June 1994): 46–51.

Damrosch, Barbara. *The Garden Primer.* New York, NY: Workman Publishing, 1988.

Daniels, Stevie. *The Wild Lawn Handbook.* New York, NY: Macmillan, 1995.

Doyle, Judith. "The Daily Round." *The Calgary Horticultural Society Newsletter*, Vol. 9, No. 4 (1995): 13.

Doyle, Judith. "In Praise of Push Mowers." *Calgary Gardening*, Vol. 10, No. 6 (1996): 15.

du Toit, Angela. "Staking." *The Calgary Horticultural Society Newsletter*, Vol. 9, No. 5 (1995): 6.

du Toit, Angela. "Trellising Vines." *The Calgary Horticultural Society Newsletter*, Vol. 10, No. 2 (1996): 10.

Duvall, Mel. "Beautiful Gardens on Tour List of Historic Treasures." *Calgary Herald Neighbours*, August 4–10, 1993.

Eddison, Sydney. "Give Your Plants the Support They Need." *Fine Gardening*, No. 43 (May/June 1995): 44–47.

Ellefson, Connie, Stephens, Tom, and Welsh, Doug. *Xeriscape Gardening: Waterscape Conservation for the American Landscape.* New York, NY: Macmillan, 1992.

Erickson, Jonathan. *Gardening for a Greener Planet.* Blue Ridge Summit, PA: Tab Books, 1992.

Eveleigh, Tessa. *The Decorated Garden Room.* New York, NY: Lorenz Books, 1996.

Fell, Derek. *How to Photograph Flowers, Plants and Landscapes.* Tucson, AZ: H. P. Books, 1980.

Ferguson, John, and Mucke, Burkhard. *The Gardener's Year.* New York, NY: Frances Lincoln Ltd., 1991.

Ferguson, Katharine. *Spring Flowers.* Camden East, ON: Camden House Publishing, 1989.

Flint, Mary Louise. "Bt Controls Caterpillars." *Fine Gardening*, No. 37 (May/June 1994): 56–57.

Flowerdew, Bob. *Complete Book of Companion Gardening*. London, Eng.: Kyle Cathie Limited, 1995.

Franck, Gertrude. *Companion Planting*. New York, NY: Thorsons Publishers Inc., 1980.

Franklin, Stuart. *Building a Healthy Lawn: A Safe and Natural Approach*. Pownal, VT: Garden Way Publishing, 1988.

Gardner, Jo Ann. *The Heirloom Garden*. Pownal, VT: Storey Communications Inc., 1992.

Geller, J. "Garden Diaries." *Fine Gardening*, No. 41 (January/February 1995): 40.

Giles, Robert. "Easing the Load." *Canadian Gardening* (June/July 1996): 24.

Giles, Robert. "Gardener's Journal - Four Durable Diggers." *Canadian Gardening* (December 1994/January 1995): 14.

Giles, Robert. "Gardener's Journal - On the Cutting Edge." *Canadian Gardening* (February/March 1995): 12.

Giles, Robert. "10 Essential Garden Tools." *Canadian Gardening* (April 1995): 27.

Giles, Robert. "The Well-Labelled Gardener." *Canadian Gardening* (May 1995): 12.

Gilmer, Maureen. *The Budget Gardener*. New York, NY: The Penguin Group, 1996.

Gouin, Francis R. "Slow Release Fertilizers." *Fine Gardening*, No. 30 (March/April 1993): 58.

Graham, Robert. "Central (Memorial) Park and Reader Rock Garden: The British Landscape Gardening Tradition in Calgary." Paper presented to ICOMOS/IFLA Cultural Landscape Conference, Montreal, May 1996.

Graham, Robert. "Private Citizen's Submission Regarding the Preservation of the Reader Rock Gardens, Union Cemetery, City of Calgary to the Heritage Advisory Board, City of Calgary." September 1989.

Green, Douglas. *Landscape Magic: Tricks and Techniques for Rejuvenating Old Yards and Gardens*. Shelburne, VT: Chapters Publishing Ltd., 1995.

Greenoak, Francesca. *Water Features for Small Gardens*. Vancouver, BC: Cavendish Books Inc., 1996.

Greenwood, Pippa. *The New Gardener*. London, Eng.: Dorling Kindersley Ltd., 1995.

Hallgren, Lee. "The Kinds of Sun and Shade." *Fine Gardening*, No. 31 (May/June 1993): 62.

Harris, Marjorie. *Favorite Garden Tips*. Toronto, ON: HarperCollins Publishers Ltd., 1994.

Hayward, Gordon. *Garden Paths*. Charlotte, VT: Camden House Publishing, 1993.

Hill, Lewis. *Pruning Simplified*. Rev. ed. Pownal, VT: Storey Communications Inc., 1986.

Hillier, Malcolm. *Container Gardening Through the Year*. Toronto, ON: Little, Brown & Company, 1995.

"In Memoriam—William Roland Reader, FRHS." *Canadian Alpine Journal*, Vol. XXVII, No. 2 (1942–43): 256.

"Inventory of Potential Heritage Sites, Site No. 06–232 [Reader Rock Garden]." City of Calgary, Planning and Building Department, October 13, 1993.

Jabs, Carolyn. *The Heirloom Gardener*. San Francisco, CA: Sierra Club Books, 1984.

Johnson, Hugh. *The Principles of Gardening*. New York, NY: Simon and Schuster, Fireside, 1979.

Kam, Barbara. "Enhancing Your Style with Container Gardens." *Calgary Gardening*, Vol. 10, No. 5 (1996): 12.

Keen, Mary. *Colour Your Garden*. London, Eng.: Conran Octopus Ltd., 1994.

Kellaway, Deborah, ed. *The Virago Book of Women Gardeners*. London, Eng.: Virago Press, 1995.

King, Ronald. *The Quest for Paradise*. New York, NY: Mayflower Books, 1979.

Knowles, Hugh. *Woody Ornamentals for the Prairies*. Edmonton, AB; University of Alberta, Faculty of Extension, 1995.

Lacy, Allen. *Gardening with Groundcovers and Vines*. New York, NY: HarperCollins, 1993.

Lawson, Andrew. *The Gardener's Book of Colour*. London, Eng.: Frances Lincoln Ltd., 1996.

Lee, Kevin. "Trees, Spring Growth and Pruning Theory." *Calgary Gardening*, Vol. 10, No. 5 (1996): 14–16.

Loewer, Peter. *Seeds*. New York, NY: Macmillan, 1995.

Martin, Laura. *Grandma's Garden*. Atlanta, GA: Longstreet Press, 1990.

Mather, Jan. *The Prairie Garden Planner.* Red Deer, AB: Red Deer College Press, 1996.

Mathers, Hannah. "The Cold Facts of Winter." *Gardens West*, Vol. 11, No. 1 (1997): 30–33.

Matthews, H. D. "Tendrils of Time Overgrow Rock Garden." *Calgary Herald Neighbours,* October 15, 1988.

McHoy, Peter. *The Garden Floor.* Scarborough, ON: McGraw-Hill Ryerson, 1989.

McNally, Kathleen. "Calgary's Reader Rock Garden." *Landscape Architectural Review* (March 1990): 19–24.

Moore, J. Paul. "Focus Your Camera on Garden Design." *Fine Gardening*, No. 53 (January/February 1997): 50.

Moore, Ken. "Gazing Globes." *Fine Gardening*, No. 23 (January/February 1992): 30.

Nichols, Clive. *Photographing Plants and Gardens* (in association with the Royal Horticultural Society). Newton Abbott, Eng.: David & Charles, 1994.

O'Keefe, John M. *Water-Conserving Gardens and Landscapes.* Pownal, VT: Storey Communications Inc., 1992.

Ortho Books. *All About Bulbs.* San Ramon, CA: Monsanto Company, 1981.

Ortho Books. *All About Lawns.* San Ramon, CA: Ortho Books, Chevron Chemical Company, 1985.

Ortho Books. *All About Pruning.* San Ramon, CA: Ortho Books, Chevron Chemical Company, 1989.

Ortho Books. *The Ortho Book of Gardening Basics.* San Ramon, CA: Ortho Books, Chevron Chemical Company, 1991.

Parks, Joe. "Paths to Beauty." *Garden Design Ideas.* Newtown, CT: The Taunton Press, 1994, p. 50.

Patton, Clancy. "Tea Time with Manure Tea." *The Calgary Horticultural Society Newsletter,* Vol. 9, No. 8 (1995): 11.

Philby, Greg, ed. "By the Light of the Silvery Moon." *Better Homes and Gardens Garden Ideas & Outdoor Living* (Spring 1994): 74.

Philip, Hugh, and Mengersen, Ernest. *Insect Pests of the Prairies.* Edmonton, AB: University of Alberta, Faculty of Extension, 1989.

Pierce, John, and Barnsley, Roland. *Easy Lifelong Gardening.* Toronto, ON: Key Porter, 1993.

Pimentel, David. "Biological Pest Control." *Fine Gardening*, No. 26 (July/August 1992): 48–51.

Pleasant, Barbara. *The Gardener's Bug Book*. Vancouver, BC: Whitecap Books, 1994.

Plumptre, George. *Great Gardens, Great Designers*. London, Eng.: Ward Lock Wellington House, 1996.

Primeau, Liz, ed. *Creating a Garden*. Toronto, ON: Madison Press Books, 1996.

Primeau, Liz, ed. *Great Ideas for the Garden*. Toronto, ON: Madison Press Books, 1996.

Primeau, Liz, and Editors. *Canadian Gardening's Natural Gardens*. Toronto, ON: Madison Press Books, 1996.

Proctor, Rob, and Ondra, Nancy J. *Annuals and Bulbs*. Emmaus, PA: Rodale Press, 1995.

Raymond, Dick. *Down-to-Earth Natural Lawn Care*. Pownal, VT: Storey Communications Inc., 1993.

Reader, William. *Alphabetical List of Plants in Rockery [Reader Rock Garden] as at November 1936*. Local History Collection, Calgary Public Library, Calgary, AB.

Reader, William. *The Herbaceous Perennial Garden together with an Annotated Catalogue of Herbaceous Plants Introduced by and Growing in the Garden of W.R. Reader, Parks Superintendent, City of Calgary*. Unpublished ms., Glenbow Alberta Institute, Calgary, AB.

Reader, William. "A Year's Work in a Calgary Flower Garden." *The Canadian Horticulturalist* (April 1911): 90.

Reddell, R. C., and Gaylean, Robert. *Growing Fragrant Plants*. New York, NY: Harper & Row, Publishers, 1989.

Rees, Yvonne, and Paliser, David. *Container Gardening All Year Round*. Wiltshire, Eng.:The Crowood Press Ltd., 1990.

Rempel, Sharon. *A History of Gardens and Agriculture in Alberta*. Edmonton, AB: University of Alberta Archives, 1996.

Rogers, Marc. *Saving Seeds*. Pownal, VT: Storey Communications Inc., 1990.

Rokach, Allen, and Millman, Anne. *The Field Guide to Photographing Flowers*. New York, NY: Watson-Guptill Publications, 1995.

Roth, Sally. "A Temporary Home for Plants." *Fine Gardening*, No. 53 (January/February 1997): 57.

Roth, Susan. *The Weekend Gardener*. Emmaus, PA: Rodale Press, 1991.

Sara, Leslie. "From Sandhill to Mossy Glade." *Gardeners All,* No. 10, C.B.C., C.F.A.C., Calgary, August 11, 1939. Local History Collection, Calgary Public Library, Calgary, AB.

Shigo, Alex L. *Tree Pruning: A Worldwide Photo Guide.* Durham, NH: Shigo and Trees Associates, 1989.

Squire, David. *The Scented Garden.* Toronto, ON: Doubleday Canada Limited, 1988.

Staal, Ruth. "How Does Your Garden Grow?" *Calgary Gardening,* Vol. 10, No. 5 (1996): 9.

Stevens, Elaine. *The Creative Container Gardener.* Vancouver, BC: Whitecap Books, 1995.

Steward, V. Bruce. "Superior Oil Sprays." *Fine Gardening*, No. 30 (March/April 1993): 68–69.

Tanner, Ogden. *Living Fences.* Shelburne, VT: Chapters Publishing Ltd., 1995.

Taylor, Jane. *Gardening for Fragrance.* London, Eng.: Ward Lock Limited, 1989.

Thorpe, Patricia. *Growing Pains: Time and Change in the Garden.* New York, NY: HarcourtBrace and Company, 1994.

Townsend, Dana. "Council will pick garden's future." *Calgary Herald Neighbours,* July 26–August 1, 1989.

University of Alberta, Department of Extension. *Home Gardening Course.* Edmonton, AB: University of Alberta, Faculty of Extension, 1986.

Williams, Robin. *The Garden Designer.* London, Eng.: Frances Lincoln Limited, 1995.

Williams, Sara. *Creating the Prairie Xeriscape.* Saskatoon, SK: University Extension Press, University of Saskatchewan, 1997.

Wyman, Donald. *Wyman's Gardening Encyclopedia.* New York, NY: The Macmillan Company, 1971.

Yeomans, Kathleen. *The Able Gardener.* Vancouver, BC: Whitecap Books, 1992.

Index

In this index, numbers appearing in bold indicate the main reference to a topic; italic type indicates photographs or illustrations. For your convenience, subjects discussed in both this volume and *The Calgary Gardener* are highlighted with an asterisk.

Campion (*Silene* spp.) 11, 46. *See also* Bladder campion; Rose campion
Canada plum *(Prunus nigra)* 136
Canada thistle *(Cirsium arvense)* 103
Canals (water features) 53
*Canarybird vine *(Tropaeolum peregrinum)* 3, 28, 44
*Candytuft *(Iberis* spp.) 63, 67, 75, 77, 153
*Canterbury bells *(Campanula medium)* 64
Capiscum annuum (pepper) 88, 89, 114, 188, 189, 190
Capsella bursa-pastoris (shepherd's purse) 105
Caragana spp. (caragana) 120, 130, 136, 138. *See also* Sutherland caragana; Weeping caragana
Cardaria spp. (hoary cress) 103
Cardinal flower *(Lobelia cardinalis)* 66
Carduus nutans (nodding thistle) 103
Carnation *(Dianthus caryophyllus)* 63, 75, 77, 151, 154
Carrot rust fly 101
*Carrots 82, 88, 112, 114, 187
Castor bean *(Ricinus communis)* 84
*Catalogues 91, 92, 131
*Caterpillars 99, 100, 101, 107, 147, 148
*Catmint/catnip *(Nepeta* spp.) 61, 85, 107, 109, 153
*Cattail *(Typha latifolia* spp.) 51
*Cauliflower 101, 114, 187
*Cedar *(Thuja* spp.) 16, *38*, 47, 133
Celeriac 114
Celery 114, 187
Celosia spp. (celosia) 63
Centaurea cineraria (dusty miller) 67, 121
Centaurea cyanus (bachelor's button) 63, *82*, 121, 132, 186, 189
Centaurea diffusa (diffuse knapweed) 103
Centaurea maculosa (spotted knapweed) 103
Centaurea repens (Russian knapweed) 103
Centaurea solstitialis (yellow star thistle) 103
Centaurea spp. (cornflower) 85, 103, 130, 152
Cephalaria gigantea (giant scabious) 62
Cerastium tomentosum (snow-in-summer) 14, 62, 67
Chamaemelum spp. (chamomile, Roman chamomile) 80, 83
*Chard, Swiss 114, 187
Cheddar pink *(Dianthus gratianopolitanus* 'Pike's Pink') 61
Chenopodium album (lamb's-quarters) 105
Chervil *(Anthriscus cerefolium)* 81, 83
Chickweed *(Stellaria media)* 105
Chicory 114
*Children's gardens 28, 72, *82*, **82**
*China aster *(Callistephus chinensis)* 63
Chinch bugs 98
Chinese Siberian iris 138
Chinook zone. *See* Zones, gardening
*Chinooks xvi, 22, 174–75, 176, 178
Chionodoxa luciliae (chionodoxa, glory-of-the-snow) 8, 66
*Chives *(Allium schoenoprasum)* 78, 79, 83, 114, 121
Chlidanthus fragrans (perfumed fairy lily) 76, 77
*Chokecherry *(Prunus* spp.) 37, 47, 73, 82, 83

Chrysanthemum spp. (chrysanthemum, daisies, mums, pyrethrum) 10, 44, 58, 62, 67, 72, 73, 78, 79, 85, 99, *115*, 130, 150, 151, 152, 153, 154, 155, 189. *See also* Feverfew; Shasta daisy
Chrysanthemum leucanthemum (oxeye daisy) 103
*Cilantro *(Coriandrum sativum)* 83
Cimicifuga racemosa (bugbane) 62
Cinnamon yam 3
Cinquefoil. *See Potentilla* spp.
Cirsium arvense (Canada thistle) 103
Clarkia amoena (godetia, satin flower) 44
Clarkia unguiculata (clarkia, Rocky Mountain garland flower) 88
Cleaver *(Galium aparine, G. spurium)* 103
Clematis spp. (clematis) 58, 61, 66, 74, 108; uses for 3, 10, 23, 27, 28, 29, 72
Cleome hasslerana (spider flower) 63, 67, 154
*Cliffgreen *(Paxistima canbyi)* 10
*Climate, of Calgary 11, 40, 88, 116, 125, 131, 158, 161, 175, 187, 206–7
*Climbing nightshade *(Solanum dulcamara)* 7
Climbing plants, for trellises 28, 29, *30*. *See also* Clematis; Roses, as climbers; Vines
Cobaea scandens (cup-and-saucer vine) 3, 28
Clovers 107, 108
Codling moths 98
Coleus (coleus) 66, 154
Collecting seeds 185–91
Colorado spruce *(Picea pungens)* 136
*Colour, in garden design 1–2, 7, *43*, 45, **55–63**, *63*, 64–67, 74. *See also* individual colours
Colour theme gardens 56–63; plants for 61–63
*Columbine *(Aquilegia* spp.) 11, 46, 85, 149, 152, 153, 154
Columnar mountain ash *(Sorbus aucuparia* 'Fastigiata') 136
Columnar Siberian crab *(Malus baccata* 'Columnaris') 136
*Comfrey *(Symphytum* spp.) 155
Companion planting 96, **105–9**
Compartmentalization 159, 160, 161
*Compost 96, 104, 127, 165, 166, 167, 168, 171, 183, 184
*Coneflower *(Rudbeckia* spp.) 152, 154. *See also* Prairie coneflower; Purple coneflower
Consolida ambigua (larkspur) 63, 157
Container gardening 2, 3, 40–41, *42*, *43*, 44, 50, 51, 75, 77, 80, 81, 119, 134, 150, 157, 163, 169, 171; plants for 11, 36, 42, **43–45**, 52, 77, 80, 81, 83. *See also* Alpine troughs; Winter containers
*Containers **40–44**, *42*, *43*, 45–48, 51
Convallaria majalis (lily-of-the-valley) 12, 76, 77, 84
Convolvulus arvensis (field bindweed) 103
*Coral bells *(Heuchera* spp.) 61, 121, 153
Coreopsis spp. (coreopsis, tickseed) 66, 153, 155
Coriandrum sativum (cilantro) 83
*Corms 132
*Corn *(Zea mays)* 88, 89, 109, 112, 113, 114, 186, 189
Corn borers and earworms 99, 107
*Cornflower *(Centaurea* spp.) 85, 103, 130, 152

*Turnips 88, 114, 187
Twinflower 7
Typha latifolia (cattail) 51

U

Ulmus spp. (elm) 72
Unity, in garden design 1, 15, 17, 20, 23, 25, 27, 57, 61
Ursinia anthemoides (daisy) 44
Urtica dioica (stinging nettle) 105
Ussurian pear (*Pyrus ussuriensis*) 136

V

Valeriana officinalis (garden heliotrope, valerian) 85
*Variety, defined 194
*Vegetables 29, 187, 193; companion planting 105–9; crop rotation 96, 110–15; fertilizing 107, 157, 169, 171; in garden design 10, 11; perennial 80–81; planting 88, 89; seeds for 186–90
Verbascum spp. (mullein) 62, 151, 152, 153
Verbena hortensis (verbena) 75, 77, 154. *See also* Lemon verbena
Veronica spp. (speedwell, veronica) *6, 10,* 61, 85, 121, 154, 155
Vertical gardens 2, 3, 40, 76
Viburnum spp. (cranberry, nannyberry, wayfaring tree) 47, 82, 83, 84, 136, 165
Vinca minor (periwinkle) 12, 14, 154
*Vines: annual 2, 3, 29, 34, 77, 78; care of 171; perennial 3, 11, 23, 27, 28, 29, 34, *34;* uses for *10,* 11, 23, *25,* 25, 26, 27, 28, 34, 42, 54, 76, 78–79, 84
Viola spp. (Johnny jump-up, viola, violet) 7, 14, *14,* 41, 82, 83, 88
Viola x wittrockiana (pansy) 63, *63,* 83, 88, 131, 153, 189
*Virginia creeper (*Parthenocissus quinquefolia*) xv, 2, 3, 12, 28
Visual impact, in garden planning 55–71

W

Walkways. *See* Pathways
Wall flowers 74
Wall garden 15
Walls 15, 38; decorations for 34, *35. See also* Espalier
Wasp larvae 98
Water conservation. *See* Xeriscaping
*Water features 42, **48–53**, 86, *86;* containers for 48–49
*Water gardens 50–53
Water iris (*Iris versicolor*) 51
*Water lily (*Nymphaea* spp.) 49, 52, **53**
Water plantain (*Alisma plantago-aquatica*) 51
*Watering 104, 178, 196; systems 119, 157, 169; and xeriscaping 115, 117, 118–19
Wax begonia (*Begonia semperflorens*) 42, 151, 154

*Wayfaring tree (*Viburnum lantana*) 37
Web-worms 98
*Weeds: control and prevention of 51, 94, 96, 97, **101–5**, 111, 112–13, 114, 119, 121–22, 129, 148, 182, 183, 196; edible 105; as mulch 108; nuisance 102; restricted and noxious 102, 103
Weeping birch (*Betula pendula* 'Youngii') 136
Weeping caragana (Caragana arborescens 'Pendula') 136
Weevils 101
Western gardens 42
Western mountain ash (*Sorbus scopulina*) 136
Wheelbarrows 140–41, 146
White cockle (*Lychnis alba*) 103
White gardens 56, **59,** *59,* 62, 63, 74–75
White spruce (*Picea glauca*) 47
Whiteflies 98, 100, 107
Wild cucumber vines *34*
Wild ginger 12
Wildflowers. *See* Native plants
*Willow (*Salix* spp.) 16, 88, 101, 173. *See also* Golden willow; Redstem willow; Wolf willow
Wind damage 15, 16, 23, 150, 159, 161, **173**
Winged burning bush (*Euonymus alata*) 47, 181
Winter containers 47–48
Winter damage 174–75, 177
Winter interest, planning for 32, 47–48, 56, 154
Winter savory (*Satureja montana*) 81, 83, 121
Winterburn 175, 177
Wintergreen (*Gaultheria procumbens*) 14, 72, 78, 79
Winterkill 128, 133, 177
*Wolf willow (*Elaeagnus commutata*) 6
*Woodland gardens *6,* **6–7,** 9, 38, 39, *39,* 41
Woody ornamentals 8, 11, **136,** 177
*Woolly yarrow (*Achillea tomentosa*) 58, 62
Wormwood (*Artemisia ludoviciana*) 62, 106

X

*Xeriscaping 114–22; plants for, 120–21

Y

*Yarrow (*Achillea* spp.) 6, 61, 62, 67, 121, 151, 154, 155
*Yellow flag (*Iris pseudacorus*) 51
Yellow gardens 58–59, *58,* 62, 63
Yellow star thistle (*Centaurea solstitialis*) 103
Yew (*Taxus* spp.) 36
Yucca filamentosa spp. (yucca) 72

Z

Zaluzianskya capensis (night phlox) 67
Zea mays (corn) 88, 89, 109, 112, 113, 114, 186, 189
Zinnia spp. (zinnia) 63, 98, 121, 131. *See also* Narrowleaf zinnia
Zones, gardening xvi, 132, **137–39,** 207–8